# THE SPIRIT OF OUR WORK

# THE SPIRIT OF OUR WORK

## BLACK WOMEN TEACHERS (RE)MEMBER

CYNTHIA B. DILLARD

BEACON PRESS ▪ BOSTON

BEACON PRESS
Boston, Massachusetts
www.beacon.org

Beacon Press books
are published under the auspices of
the Unitarian Universalist Association of Congregations.

25  24  23  22      8  7  6  5  4  3  2  1

This book is printed on acid-free paper that meets the uncoated paper
ANSI/NISO specifications for permanence as revised in 1992.

Text design by Nancy Koerner at Wilsted & Taylor Publishing Services

Library of Congress Cataloging-in-Publication Data

Names: Dillard, Cynthia B., author.
Title: The spirit of our work : Black women teachers (re)member /
    Cynthia B. Dillard.
Description: Boston : Beacon Press, 2021. | Includes bibliographical
    references and index.
Identifiers: LCCN 2021026469 | ISBN 9780807013854 (hardcover) |
    ISBN 9780807013878 (ebook)
Subjects: LCSH: African American women teachers. | African American
    teachers and the community. | African Americans—Education. | African
    Americans—Race identity. | Afrocentrism.
Classification: LCC LC2782 .D54 2022 | DDC 370.89/96073—dc23
LC record available at https://lccn.loc.gov/2021026469

*This book is dedicated to Black women, past, present, and future.*
*We are teachers and healers.*
*And the world has so much to learn from us.*

# CONTENTS

# FOREWORD

I vacillated between writing a book foreword and penning a love letter to Dr. Cynthia B. Dillard (Nana Mansa II of Mpeasem, Ghana, West Africa). I will attempt to do both, because to love this book and its contents is to love Dr. Dillard and vice versa. She is indeed an easy person to love; her spirit carries you into her unmatched grace and holds you there long after she has left you. To love her is also to love yourself, your Blackness, your womanness, your Africanness. In her presence, you stand up taller, you speak clearer, and you listen with ears more attuned to the frequency of the sounds of glorious Blackness. Dr. Dillard does not try to change you: you just submit because within her presence you are (re)membering and (re)claiming who you are. Yes, what I am describing is an amazing Black woman. Dr. Dillard is one of our ancestors' wildest dreams. She was made to love us: accepting her love was already written.

In these pages, you will feel Dr. Dillard's spirit speaking to you because this book will place your spirit in a sacred space of Blackness. As you read, you will be transported to a literary hush harbor. Historically, hush harbors were hidden spaces where enslaved Black people would gather in secret to pray, shout, dance, sing, retreat, and rejoice—intentionally creating moments of wholeness, spirituality, Blackness, freedom, and (re)membering. These secluded moments, distinct and removed from whiteness and oppression, were not only precious; they were BLACK.

For Black women, *The Spirit of Our Work: Black Women Teachers (Re)member* is our sacred space of Blackness and Black womanness that makes us whole as educators. As Dr. Dillard writes, "We are Black on purpose for a purpose." I never understood that notion until I traveled to Ghana with Dr. Dillard in 2018. And I have not been the same person since. Reading these pages, I now understand why. It's the whisper. Dr. Dillard writes that our healing as educators "sounds like a whisper not because we are *not* yelling and protesting and singing songs of liberation and freedom: It sounds like a whisper because it is coming from the *inside out.*"

I did not know what the whisper was until that trip, or even the possibilities of the whisper. After returning from Ghana, I could hear my ancestors' whispers so clearly. They now sound like songs to me.

As someone who loves Black people, I wish we all could travel to Ghana (paid for by US reparations, of course). But accompanied by Dr. Dillard, going to Ghana is just part of the journey. The person who guides your experience there is essentially guiding your spirit and connecting you to "flesh, blood, bones, and remains of those who came before us." The work of taking Black people home is the job of a soul that is well and made whole by visions of Blackness on both sides of the water.

Going to Ghana with Dr. Dillard made Black creativity, joy, ingenuity, brilliance, and love real in ways I had never understood before because there my reference was not inhibited, distorted, and interrupted by whiteness. In Ghana, I was Black for the first time in my life. I carry that knowledge and swag with me. I attempt to teach and write with that swag. And more than anything, I learned that Black children in Ghana and in the US are young, gifted, and African. Their identity and connections to Blackness make them limitless. And if we will teach them well, then as teachers, we too must be well. This book is your guide in that journey back to yourself.

I love you, Dr. D! You helped me find a piece of myself I never even knew was missing. You taught me how to "touch my own spirit." *The Spirit of Our Work: Black Women Teachers (Re)member* will help you do the same, Dear Reader. And each time you touch your own spirit, you will heal so that you can teach with the bravery of Harriet, Fannie Lou, Angela, and Cynthia.

Bettina L. Love
Atlanta, GA

# FOR THOSE WHO CHOSE TO SURVIVE

*Our Promise to (Re)member the Ancestors*

> *Where a [wo]man keeps [her] memories*
> *is the place [s]he should call home.*
>
> —Caryl Phillips[1]

> *be easy.*
> *take your time.*
> *you are coming home*
> *to yourself.*
>
> —Nayyirah Waheed[2]

This is a book about (re)membering. It is about what happens when Black women in the Black diaspora (re)turn to the continent of Africa and the ways that such a journey changes our lives from the inside out. It is about how it shifts our bodies, minds, and spirits. It is about how those shifts create what Akasha Hull calls a new spirituality for Black women, one deeply committed to an expanded politics, a spiritual consciousness, and an engaged creativity that both takes us off our center and gives us back our center at the same time.[3] And it is a book about the beauty and wisdom embodied in the spirit of some of the most important people in the lives of any community: Black women who teach.

I recently (re)watched the iconic film by Julie Dash called *Daughters of the Dust*. In this film, Nana Peazant is the matriarch of a family who descended from a great line of enslaved African people on the island of Dawtuh. This rather secluded island is located on the barrier coast of present-day South Carolina and Georgia. Given modernization and a dying indigo industry, moving from the small island to the perceived "greener pastures" of the United States mainland was the dream of her family. Staying behind on the island and faced with the impending separation from her family, Nana has a serious conversation with her great-grandson Eli, a conversation in which he tries to share with her why he needs to leave the island. Her goal is not to persuade him to stay; her goal is to help him *(re)member who he is once he's left*, to (re)member the soul of his people and the wisdom of their memories:

> Nana to Eli: There's a thought . . . a recollection . . . something somebody remembers. We carry these memories inside of we. Do you believe that hundreds and hundreds of Africans brought here on this other side would forget everything they once knew? We don't know where the recollections come from. Sometimes we dream them. But we carry these memories inside we.
>
> Eli to Nana (sarcastically): What we supposed to remember, Nana? How, at one time, we were able to protect those we loved? How, in the African world, we were kings and queens and built great big cities?
>
> Nana to Eli (pleading): Eli . . . I'm tryin to teach you how to touch your own spirit. I'm fightin for my life, Eli, and I'm fightin for yours. Look in my face! I'm tryin to give you somethin to take North with you, along with all your big dreams.[4]

Nana's words made me catch my breath. In her voice are the dilemmas of formerly enslaved Africans living in the diaspora, those dilemmas that we still carry "inside we" today. Dilemmas about who we are, what we have forgotten, what we choose to (re)member and the revolution that (re)membering might create. Here and throughout this book, I posit (re)membering as both the acts of putting back together (as in (re)*membering*) and of (re)*calling* (as in the call or spiritual obligation we answer in becoming a teacher, an auntie, or a mother). (Re)membering is also an act of resistance, given the continuous ways that Black people and our presence in the diaspora are rendered invisible within structures of capitalistic, patriarchal, anti-Black structures of domination. Marshaling the prefix (*re-*) in parentheses is my way of (re)minding all of us that Black people have inherently and always existed as brilliant holders of knowledge, culture, and humanity. Thus, (re)membering is not an initial or original (re)cognition of Blackness: it is used to (re)mind us all of what Black people have *always* known about ourselves in contexts that consistently act otherwise.

Nana Peazant's voice also (re)minds us that touching our own spirits is at the center of (re)membering and being. She teaches that our very spirits and lives are worth fighting for. Most importantly, she teaches that (re)membering is a promise to all of the ancestors: touching our spirits is quite literally a covenant we have made with the ancestors who *chose* to survive so that we might have the awesome opportunity to thrive as Black people today.

Nana's talk with Eli embodies African thought and ways of being. In their conversation, there is an ever-present link between those who have come before, those who are here now, and those who will come in the future. This link undergirds an Akan proverb from Ghana, represented in the well-known symbol of sankofa. This symbol, often rendered as a bird looking back toward its tail feathers, means *to go back and fetch what you need from the past to build what you collectively need in the present and the future.* I am suggesting here that, for Black women who teach, the sankofa is also a covenant between our spirits and the spirits of our ancestors and elders like Nana Peazant. We must (re)member ourselves and our ways of thinking and knowing as Black people in order to teach from that deep well of Black brilliance, Black wisdom, and Black joy.

Our covenant with the ancestors has two parts. First, it is a sacred agreement or promise between two or more parties, especially for the performance of some action. But a covenant is also "the common-law action to recover damages for breach of such a contract."[5] Given this definition, it is important for all of us to ask: As Black women teachers, what are the promises that we need to make to honor the sacrifices of the ancestors? How do we "recover damages" for the breaches of the contracts that have been broken and the greatness of the generations to come?

I am suggesting here that the work Black women teachers do is part of the covenant we've made with those who chose to survive. Some of us have literally answered the call to teach after exhausting what were other more financially lucrative or higher-status professions. Some of us knew from our early years that teaching was our vocation of choice. Others began in different professions and switched when we could not bear to see the violence being done to our babies. Regardless of how and when we entered, many of us have found multiple places of tension and separation (out of necessity, mandate, or because we assumed we had to) between our spiritual and personal lives and our teaching lives. But in moments where we see that spark of brilliance and fire in a Black student, or in our interactions with Black parents about their child, or in drawing on texts and curricula centered in the words and thoughts of Black authors, writers, and theorists, we have engaged a spirituality of (re)membering. We have honored the covenants that we have made with the ancestors, drawing on the lived experiences of Black women and on our knowledges and cultural connections. And our story did not begin as enslaved Black people in these Americas but rather on the continent of Africa. Our ways of knowing and being have traveled throughout the African diaspora and continue to live in Black American culture. Sometimes we are able to understand and acknowledge these links. Sometimes we even choose not, have not, or both. But to understand the long struggles for freedom, Black identity, and education that are worthy of Black people, we must (re)member that we come from those who *chose to survive* the horrors and atrocities from slavery to "freedom" and back again.

That survival was not only about Black bodies and minds: it was about our spirits and our spirituality, too. It was about how we spiritually animated our survival. It was about how the ancestors knew then that we were the future they could already see. To become what Nigerian-American comedian Yvonne Orji calls a *"whole* me," we who live in the Black diaspora must understand that our narrative is informed by Black narratives that (re)member our spiritualities as Black people and our legacies of resistance, persistence, and responsibility.[6] That our existence in the Americas is intimately and inextricably bound up with peoples who are now referred to as Ghanaians, Barbadians, Nigerians, Kenyans, and South Africans, to name just a few. And for diasporic Black women teachers, it is our *responsibility* to (re)member.[7] Because when we (re)member our covenants with the ancestors on whose shoulders we all stand today, it is our living demonstration of the commitment that is *required* to teach Black students in their wholeness—body, mind, and spirit. You may have seen the T-shirt that proclaims boldly in black and white: "We are our ancestors' wildest dreams." In prioritizing our covenants with the ancestors as Black women who teach, not only do we (re)member ourselves: our students then have the chance to (re)member their full humanity, their spirits, and their brilliant dreams, too. As teachers and students, we carry those lessons inside we.

*The Spirit of Our Work: Black Women Teachers (Re)member* is my humble manifestation of that wildest dream. It is a (re)cognition that when Black women teachers (re)member who we are and (re)cognize our relationship to our authentic selves and stories, we are the Black girl magic that our students and others deserve, that the ancestors prayed and died for, and the future for which they survived.

# THE SPIRIT OF OUR WORK

# CHAPTER 1

# MY SPIRIT (RE)MEMBERS ME WHOLE

## The Importance of Black Women's Knowing, Memory, and Spirituality

*We are not a people of yesterday. Do they ask how many single seasons
we have flowed from our beginnings till now? We shall point them to the
proper beginnings of their counting. . . . The air everywhere is poisoned with
the truncated tales of our origins. That is also part of the wreckage of our
people. What has been cast abroad is not a thousandth of our history, even
if the quality were truth. . . . But the haze of this fouled world exists to wipe
out knowledge of our way.*

—Ayi Kwei Armah, *Two Thousand Seasons*[1]

If we are to talk about spirit and spirituality, what is important to
know first and foremost about people we call African Americans
today is this: we are Black on purpose for a purpose. Whether conscious of or willing to name our existence, we are *Africans* first. *Black
people.* Regardless of the names we call ourselves, our existence in the
diaspora has been seducing us to forget the memories of our ways,
"poisoned with the truncated tales of our origins," as Ghanaian author Ayi Kwei Armah says above. Despite these powerful acts of se-
duction, many of us have answered a call that honors a profoundly
different truth, a call to be like Harriet Tubman's light in dark places.
A truth that is about the right to be free. A truth that embraces the
need to push and resist. A call that requires us to agitate and move

toward (re)membering our way and the freedom that brings. We are Black on purpose for a purpose.

Too often in the study of teaching and teacher education, we approach discussions and research about race, gender, and education from a place of presuming Black people *just happened* to be here in the Americas. *Just happened* to be enslaved. *Just happened* to have suffered more than four hundred years of degradation and inequities. We speak and act as if these traumatic conditions occurred *to* an entire race of people (and continue to occur) without regard to the consequences and effects that such a legacy has *on* a people, particularly in relation to teaching, learning, and education. By extension, such narratives imply that it was simply an unfortunate set of circumstances that *just happened* in the United States of America instead of a systematic structure of privileges for some and marginalization for others, conditions that have created the permanence of racism, racial injustice, and racial inequities.[2] We need only look at the recent uprisings in the streets across the US and around the world to be (re)minded of Black people's continued and persistent resistance and revolution in the face of oppression. The insistence of our humanity is in our DNA.

The impacts of racism and racial inequities on Black women continue to be an invisible part of this legacy of oppression, especially in the literature on Black teachers' lives and experiences. This is an invisibility that must be addressed. In my view, there is a different way to think about the presence and work of Black women teachers. We can center the conversation about education on the *spirit* of Black women teachers who have thrived and loved in spite of our unmentionable and multiple oppressions. Black women have always marshaled and (re)membered the legacy of Black people in relation to our spirits, and those (re)memberings have *required* us to lean on the "substance of things unseen"—on our spirituality.[3]

Current conversations about racial and intersectional identities are largely silent about the role of spirituality, spiritual health, and well-being in the lives of Black teachers who are often, by default, also those teachers called both to teach and to provide safe havens from the often detrimental impacts of race, gender, and inequities in education for Black and Brown students.[4] This is made even more insulting because this labor of protecting our children in schools comes in addition to teaching our subject matter or the topics on our syllabi. This is part of the invisible labor and burden that Black women teachers bear every day.[5]

This invisibility is at least partially a result of the separation of church and state that undergirds education in the US. But what scholarship has implicitly told us—and what I have worked over the course of a career to lift up—is that in order to face adversity, oppression, and exclusion and remain steadfast in one's right to exist and be, it is often the *spiritual* life that has supported and affirmed (and continues to support and affirm) culturally relevant and sustaining practices in educational spaces with Black students and their teachers.[6] Throughout this book, I speak of spirituality or a spiritual life in a way that is nuanced by the lived experiences of Black women. Spirituality here is defined as a consciousness of and attention to the order, power, and unity that flows through all of life and that encompasses an energy and responsibility greater than ourselves.[7] But for Black women, spirituality has three additional dimensions that comprise what Akasha Hull describes as the new spirituality of Black women, with "each dimension impacting the others and all of them together generating tremendous power."[8] These dimensions of our spirituality include (1) our politics; (2) our spiritual consciousness; and (3) our creativity. Thus, engaging one's spirituality is also about using it to address, break down, and work to abolish structures and conditions that hamper liberation and freedom for Black people. Such labor requires great creative force and energy. But I believe it also requires Black women teachers to (re)member *who we are*—our history, culture, and contributions—in ways that take into account the long history of Black life, resistance, knowledge, and culture. Our work as Black women teachers has been and continues to be about attending to the spirit of those whom we teach and, at the same time, about "talking back,"[9] resisting and creating the education we wished we had ourselves.[10] But undergirding this labor (and often in hostile climates), we must also (re)member who we are and *whose* we are in order to create more humane conditions in school and university communities. What is important to know for Black women teachers at all levels—from K–12 through higher education—is this: when Black women are able and willing to marshal their spirits in pursuit of teaching and learning, everything we touch can be transformed, including our students.[11]

Despite all that we have been through, Black women have continued to sing our songs and tell our tales as loudly as we are able. But the hunter has always told the story in ways that glorify his conquests, labor, and accomplishment. It is now time for Black women to (re)member and tell our stories in ways that lift up the politics, spiritual consciousness, and creativity that we hold dear and that fuels us. And those stories travel *full circle*: from the continent of Africa, through the diaspora and back again. We have an obligation to make our teaching and living about (re)membering the full circle of *all* of our stories.

So like the voice of Nana in *Daughters of the Dust*, like the wise stories many of us heard as children at the feet of our ancestors in our versions of a village, like those heard from older kids on our block, or at the knees of our mothers as they braided our hair, I begin to tell this collective story of how (re)membering is a central part of the spirit of Black women who teach. My first step in telling this story was to gather texts that have been transformative and life-changing for me as a Black woman teacher and scholar. I (re)viewed them before I wrote a single word of this book. This act was a homage to my ancestors, a literal gathering of their wisdom into the space to support the sense-making that was required from pages of copious notes, interview transcripts, and handwritten journal entries. This process was the precursor to laying hands on the computer keyboard.

One of the first pieces I picked up was a stunning book by Ghanaian author Ayi Kwei Armah published in 2000 and entitled *Two Thousand Seasons*. As I (re)viewed it, I realized yet again that acts of (re)membering are the cultural guidance we need from the ancestors, an inheritance for Black folks that has already been bought and paid for: *we need only put on our crowns.* Knowing who we are and whose we are, knowing that we are enough and walking in that truth, is already deeply embedded inside of us, in our memories as Black people. Even in the problematic realities of the American experience, Black people embody a spiritual knowing, a just knowing, a way of being in relationship with the full circle of life.[12] And who we are is grounded in an energy that is greater than our individual selves alone. Black people, and especially Black women, are the humanizing energy that can lift *all* boats. We have spent too many centuries forgetting our knowings and our ways of being. And it has been long enough. My hope is that, in this reading, you too might be moved to (re)member, to call your very life back to yourself on behalf of the demands of the day, on behalf of Black education, on behalf of the liberation and freedom of Black people everywhere. But to do so, we have to learn to (re)member the things we have learned to forget.[13]

(Re)membering is especially important for those of us who have been chosen by the vocation of teaching. However, Armah cautions that for teachers, our forgetting is not simply about not being able to (re)call in a cognitive sense. Forgetting is akin to what legal scholar Patricia Williams describes as *the murder of the spirit.*[14] The murder of the very essence of who we are and what animates us as spiritual beings having a human experience. It is to forget the wisdom that can both guide us and heal us. Armah states it this way:

> The teachers told us quietly that the way of experts had become a tricky way. They told us it would always be fatal to our arts to misuse the skills we had learned. The skills themselves were mere light shells, needing to be filled out with substance coming from our souls. They warned us never to turn these skills to the service of things separate from the way. . . . Our way, the way, is not a random path. Our way begins from coherent understanding. It is a way that aims at preserving knowledge of who we are, knowledge of the best way we have found to relate each to each, each to all, ourselves to other peoples, all to our surroundings. If our individual lives have a worthwhile aim, that aim

should be a purpose inseparable from the way. . . . Our way is *reciprocity*. [Our] way is wholeness. Our way knows no oppression. . . . Our way is hospitable to guests. . . . Our way produces before it consumes. . . . Our way creates.[15]

So how did we, as Black people—the original people—learn to forget? Why does that forgetting matter? And how do we (re) member? It matters because, from the continent of Africa through her diaspora, *we are one people*. It matters because the strength of a people can be measured in how we take care of the babies and the women and the elders among us. It matters because we are a people who have endured immeasurable suffering and still hung onto each other, and to others, and loved hard.[16] And it matters because the very spirit that animates our being has been inundated with so many lies that our teaching, perspectives, and ways of being demonstrate every day unconscious and learned acts that mirror the widely held beliefs that we are a people with nothing. Granted, it has not helped that structures of dominance around us—embodied in governmental legislation, systems of schooling, and detrimental and inequitable policing policies to name just a few—have presumed these same lies about Black people and acted in line with those distorted views of us (and of themselves). And given that the schooling experiences of Black women teachers featured in this book have often taken place in a post-integration context, what we were even *able* to know deeply about ourselves as Black women and what our babies are still receiving from school systems is still drenched in whiteness and white supremacy. Unfortunately, given this "education," we too, have often acted dysconsciously as Joyce King teaches, without conscious regard to how these inequitable and cruel structures of white supremacy, patriarchy, and formations of gender have shaped us.[17] Most unfortunate for us, we have acted accordingly, acted in the way that Carter G. Woodson made visible in *The Mis-Education of the Negro*: "When you control a [wo]man's thinking you do not have to worry about [her] actions. You do not have to tell [her] to stand here or go yonder. [S]he will find [her] 'proper place' and will stay in it. You do not need to send [her] to the back door. [S]he will go without being told. In fact, if there is no back door, [s]he will cut one for [her] benefit. [Her] education makes it necessary."[18] This is what interlocking systems of oppression do to Black people who do not (re)member their longer history while on these shores. It traps us exactly where we are, where others want us to be, in the place of knowing only what others want us to know. It ensures that Black people are doomed to repeat the cycles of destruction and pain that have been rained upon us.

But what I know for sure? Even if we might have been asleep to our inheritance as Black people, the ancestors have always been awake. They continue to whisper sweetly to our hearts. In our quieter moments, as Tom Feelings suggests, we can "[feel] the truth of our humanity way down deep *inside*," so deep that no one can take it away.[19] But sometimes it feels like you are digging a hole and someone is standing right behind you shoveling the same dirt back into the hole. There's seemingly no way to find your treasure even as the effort is endless. And the loss to our spirits is tremendous.

While Black people have definitely experienced that deep sense of loss, we are not *lost*. As we (re)member our way, we have the opportunity to move into the greatness of our being on our terms. This is the (re)cognition that must find its way to the center of education for Black people on these shores, as teachers and as students. It is the kind of (re)membering that expands us, that moves us to become more fully human in the face of inhumanity, in places that still see and treat dark people as less than human.[20] That is our work and must be our walk as Black people in the African diaspora. But it must also be the work and walk of those who love us to create space that is a "circle that [draws us] in and never needed to keep some out."[21]

And change *is* coming. It is that revolution that Tracy Chapman sang about years ago but with a difference: It sounds like a whisper not because we are *not* yelling and protesting and singing songs of liberation and freedom. It sounds like a whisper because it is coming from the *inside out*. Weary from the trials of being Black in the US, growing numbers of us are digging deep inside ourselves to learn again the joy that we *really* are. "You are enough," the ancestors say. *"You have always been."* In the foreword to Laurent Chevalier's beautiful photographic book of Black American life entitled *Enough*, Cyrus Aaron echoes this moment: "There is a transformative shift taking place in our communities. We are clearing the room in order to make room for ourselves and isn't it about time for such an arrival, for such a gathering. We have traveled unsettling circumstances from a borrowed beginning, but that beginning is not our beginning and the ending to come is far more our decision than any American ideal or system."[22]

Such (re)membering pushes us to answer the question that the phenomenal writer Toni Cade Bambara asked us years ago and to truly hear her response about the meanings of our road to wholeness as a people: "Are you sure, sweetheart, that you want to be well? . . . I like to caution folks, that's all. . . . A lot of weight when you're well. . . . Just so's you're sure, sweetheart, and ready to be healed, cause wholeness is no trifling matter. A lot of weight when you're well."[23]

Through Bambara's voice, questions of being well in our spirit and seeking our wholeness are made more important to consider as we teach Black students. *A lot of weight when you are well.* For Black teachers in the African diaspora, in responding affirmatively to her question, we make wellness and wholeness both priority and possibility.[24] It also means that we say yes to (re)membering the wisdom, history, and culture of Black people that we may not have even known we needed, particularly given that many of our own educational journeys were post-integration and, as such, were never really intended to center Black lives and stories in the first place. It means we must stand firmly in our wisdom, in what we know to be truth, even as the world may tell us otherwise. It means we must honor the covenants we have with the ancestors as well as with our traditions and stories that did not begin on these shores but have continued through us. While not easy, such acts of (re)membering are critical to enlivening the spirit of Black people because they are (re)minders to us that we are enough *as we are.* And believing that we are enough is about understanding our value, our purpose, and our importance as Black people, wherever we find ourselves on the planet and against whatever odds. (Re)membering is what takes us there and that journey begins with our spirits. And needs of the spirit have to be addressed if we are to be whole human beings.

Thinking about spirit, spirituality, and wholeness is nothing short of radical in education, especially in the education of teachers. Frankly, Black wellness, wholeness, and freedom are the only goals of an education that is worthy of Black people. Bambara's call to wellness implies the need for us to be in good spiritual health, without sickness of the spirit. It even gestures toward being joyful and balanced in spirit, body, and mind, given her use of "weight" to describe the consequences and beauty of wellness. While this definition of wellness is key in thinking about the inner lives of Black women who teach, it needs a gentle nudge. What the teachers in this book (re)minded me is that when we (re)member the politics, creativity, and spiritual consciousness of our work as Black women teachers, the goal we seek is *wholeness*. Wholeness is knowing that being well is simply the complementary side of the coin of being sick, out of order, unbalanced. Both are necessary, both are the realities of being human and require balance and (re)cognition. For example, at some point in our lives, we have felt under the weather, maybe with a cold or the flu. This is part of the human condition. However, when our bodies are not well is exactly when we value and even (re)member what it was like to feel healthy. We can't wish away the sickness, but we can sit with it, care for our body, mind, and spirits with nurturing foods, maybe a good movie or quiet time simply being and knowing that, with these acts, we will probably come back to wellness. The point here is that we can understand wellness as a complement of sickness, a given that is not to be avoided but embraced as a part of what it means to be human, something unavoidable but which is nonetheless something to learn from and to be with. To be whole is to know that challenges will come for us to grow through, moving us to the times that we call "good," a (re)turn to the joy and love that we are. (Re)membering serves to honor the complexity of that wholeness in the long history of Black life, a history that moves us to be more fully human through both the joy and the tragedies of our existence as a people, and to learn from all of it. We cannot wait any longer for others to see us, to miraculously feel and understand the depths of the joy and the depths of the sorrow that we have felt for millennia on these shores. "We are the ones we have been waiting for," as Alice Walker's 2006 book by the same title tells us. We must go back and fetch what we need and bring it to this moment in order to move forward and (re)member who we've been, what we've been through, who we are and can become. That is the way to the wholeness that Bambara nudges us toward. And while her call has everything to do with an arrival over four hundred years ago when the first enslaved African people were brought to Port Comfort, Virginia, our spirits and our stories as Black people began long before that moment. They began in villages and homeplaces in Africa. And our way to wholeness in diaspora begins by turning those slave ships around and (re)turning to where we began.

## MY JOURNEY TO SPIRIT: ENDARKENING MY OWN FEMINISMS

I think the desire to know Africa has always lived in me. It's been that constant desire to know the stories and connections to Black people on the African continent about which W. E. B. Du Bois said, "We can feel better than we can explain."[25] Like countless other Black American women, my ambitions and desires have meant that I have continually run headfirst into the walls of white supremacy in both blatant and subtle ways. Growing up surrounded by Black women mothers, aunties, and othermothers, I listened intently to their conversations about the joys, challenges, and burdens of being Black women. But their conversations (usually over a bottle of Ernest and Julio that somebody brought to the house in a brown paper bag) were also filled with a kind of joy and laughter that was both captivating and instructive to me. The Black women who surrounded me had all migrated from the global South to the Pacific Northwest with their husbands, in search of a better life and increased opportunities for their children, particularly in education. They were seeking a life away from the blatant racism of places like West Virginia, the

Carolinas, and the Caribbean, and toward what they perceived as a sort of freedom for themselves and their families unavailable in the places of their birth.

But their conversations were also steeped in dreams deferred as Black women: in careers they could not or did not pursue, in education they were denied, in fears of traveling as Black women too far from home (and certainly not to other places in the world). But like generations of Black women before me, my mothers and other-mothers used their time, energy, and the desires of their spirits in making sure that their children were raised deep in the arms of the family of the church and its religious doctrine. I am grateful for the lessons of Christianity, learned in our predominately Black Presbyterian church that still guide me today. These include the purposeful and powerful act of prayer and many of the moral and spiritual lessons in the stories of the Bible. Those were my conscious beginnings of what animated and has kept urging me toward the meanings of those practices and lessons specifically for African or Black American women. While I cannot pinpoint when those urges became a call so deafening that I could not ignore it, I think wondering *about* spirit and spirituality was matched with the wonderings of my own spirit. It was there as a child when I stared, in picture book after picture book, at happy white faces with curly blond hair and wondered why those pages didn't include people who looked like me or my family. It was there in the fact that I had only one Black teacher in my entire twenty-five years in public schools *and* universities. But the fondness of my memories and (re)membering of my Black woman kindergarten teacher, Mrs. Jones! While her face has dimmed all these years later, her stunning presence and her lessons and example of Black excellence I still (re)member as if it were yesterday. And I strive each day to be like Mrs. Jones, who fed me a steady stream of Black genius. She fed my urge to know myself and my stories more deeply. But, even as that urge to know Black women's stories was nurtured in my six-year-old self by Mrs. Jones, that possibility waned with every year of schooling after that one. But my wondering about spirit and spirituality was still there. It was there when I was told by my

eighth-grade white-woman teacher that Malcolm X was not "an appropriate role model for a young Negro girl" (so I asked about Harriet Tubman, who also turned out to be "inappropriate." Go figure.).
My wondering about my spirit was still there when the Ku Klux
Klan marched in protest of my employment outside the little rural
JCPenney store where I worked as an undergraduate student. That
urge to know my spirit as a Black woman was still there as a master's
and doctoral student in graduate school. It was still there when I
was finally able to have the time, space, and choice to formally study
Black people and our origin stories. I studied where Black people
lived in larger numbers than Seattle, Washington, and began to understand all the places we'd been flung around the globe. I marshaled
languages, discourses, and genre that had always embodied the creative spirit of Blackness (yes, Phillis Wheatley, Maya Angelou, and
Lucille Clifton)! Within my doctoral studies, this desire to know
echoes writer Colleen McElroy's voice when she articulates the *human* need to know "the place that holds my people to this earth."[26]
This was deepened by my (re)search on the importance of naming
in Black/endarkened feminist thought.[27] Amidst my study, with so
many instances of oppressions, rejections, and marginalizations for
Black women in this experiment of a society built on the inequities of capitalism, the heavy hand of patriarchy, and broken promises
called America, I began to wonder what was "American" about me
as a Black woman. But my search wasn't just about coming to know
Black stories, culture, and people or our ways of knowing and being
in America. This deeper thinking and study about identity and the
names by which Black women were called in the US also made me
want to answer an existential question: What was *African* about me?
How was I an *African* (American) woman? By our very existence and
that of the brutal capitalism that brought us here, Black people in the
US have lived in precarious relationship with America. It is a relationship that is sometimes far removed from our souls, from a sense
of belonging or home, way down in "the me of me."[28] The feeling of
not belonging for the Black person in diaspora is challenging as we
attempt to pinpoint—or know with any certainty—our connections

to Africa and the ways that our connected heritage matters to the Black people we have become. Reflecting on decades of (re)turns to Ghana both informally as a traveler and more formally as a leader of study programs with students and others, one thing is true: despite the stories Black American people have been told, we carry Africa in our hearts and in our spirits, in our being and in our ways of being in community. However, according to Joy James, even in centuries of being on these shores, Black community is not bound by temporal or physical limits. So wherever we are as Black people, we belong to the African community. This is true even when not residing in a predominately African or Black community: "Belonging is not determined by physical proximity. . . . You may move out of the state or the old neighborhood to 'escape' your family or people, but you carry that family, the neighborhood, inside yourself. They remain your family. . . . You determine not whether you belong *but the nature of the relationship and the meaning of the belonging.*"[29]

I am suggesting here that Black women teachers who understand the deeper meanings of belonging to the larger African family are teachers who can draw on what Oyèrónké Oyěwùmí calls our *world sense*: a consciousness of who we are in our bodies, minds, and spirits, with and through all of our senses.[30] That is a part of the spirituality I speak of, our ways of always attending to something larger than ourselves in pursuit of wholeness and in pursuit of freedom for Black people.

I went to Ghana for the first time in 1995, with a group of Black educators from New York. Designed as an intensive introduction to a wide variety of schools and schooling in Ghana, it was little more than a quick visit to a plethora of different kinds of school settings: Traditional government primary, junior high, and high schools. Schools for children with disabilities. Private schools and others. While I learned so much about the inherent brilliance of lots of different types of children and those who taught them, I knew I needed to spend much more time in those spaces—and in the cultural milieu of Ghana—to even begin to understand what was really happening there. But the longer I was in Ghana (including on those long bus rides all across the middle and coastal part of the country), there was a beauty and a spirit of wisdom that I could feel way down deep that was not only important to me as an educator but that moved every part of my spirit and being. These experiences were birthing something new in me, giving me ways of being and seeing and knowing that felt nothing short of an anointing. This anointing went far beyond my religious upbringing in our Presbyterian church in Seattle, Washington. As I continue to (re)turn to Ghana every year, sometimes twice a year for nearly three decades, being there has produced in me a new spirituality that is beyond religious precepts and doctrine, beyond church walls and scriptures. What I have come to know by (re)membering Africa is that, as a subjugated people in diaspora, keeping my spirit strong and keeping covenant with my ancestors from Africa to America and back again provides the foundation that my Christian upbringing can both stand *with* and stand *upon*. It is the basis upon which generations of Black people have stood together, addressed, and fought for our rights and freedoms, and through which we continue to rise. And as I kept traveling to Ghana, and through the critical studying that Joyce King suggests is required for (re)membering, I learned that Black life in diaspora has created profound and dynamic spaces of cultural and spiritual production for Black women like me.[31] We are and always have been the freedom dreamers that Robin D. G. Kelley describes, standing on the gifts of our ancestors and the generations of Africans who were born on western shores and have learned to live within and amongst peoples from around the globe.[32]

These powerful voices of Black women's understandings and theorizings continued, through deep dives into Black feminism, theories, and constructs that added nuance and language to things I just knew and felt. As I (re)membered memories of Black women's spirits and culture and lived in Ghana when I could, I also realized that our diasporic knowings needed to be placed against a Black backdrop rather than against the backdrop of white supremacy, patriarchy, capitalism, homophobia, and the continued brutality that we live in diaspora. And as I began to more systematically study the depth and breadth of Black women and feminisms in graduate school, I found there was not a Black feminism in education that both explicitly included spirituality and was informed by knowings from Africa. So I had to write the book that I wished I could have read when I was a student.[33]

It was Black women's brilliance that led me to develop the concept of an endarkened feminist epistemology, which I fully articulated in a publication over two decades ago.[34] In this article, I put attention on Black feminist epistemology because I believed the field of Black feminism needed language that could help to free us from mental, spiritual, and intellectual colonization of the very nature of *how* we know what we know as Black women. Through transforming the very language we use to describe our production of knowledge, I sought to expand and push the very foundations of our knowledge through expanding and pushing the language we used to describe our knowledge. So, in contrast to the common use of the term "enlightened" as a way of expressing the having of new and important feminist insights (arising historically from the well-established canon of white feminist thought), I marshaled the term "endarkened" feminist epistemology (EFE) to articulate how reality is known when based in the historical roots of global Black feminist thought. This embodied a distinguishable difference in cultural standpoint based in our intersectional socializations of race, gender, and other identities and the historical and contemporary contexts of oppressions and resistance for African American women, including the oppressions and dismissal of our spiritual knowings as theoretical and epistemological tools for us to think with.[35]

Here's what all of these inner and outer journeys to Africa have taught me: that as Black women, our spiritual knowings *matter*, that Black women are absolutely and always what Beyoncé called "the answer to generations of prayers."[36] And like generations of brilliant Black women of the spirit, I knew then as I know now that we each have an army of angels watching over us as we attempt to figure out, especially in our work as teachers, how to be *whole* Black women. Joy personified.

After all these decades of living and being in Ghana, what so many Black women in diaspora have asked me is this: How do *we* get there? How do we render clear the ways that we are constructing Africa over and over again, based on memories that are both known and sometimes unknown to us, seen and sometimes unseen to us? One thing I learned even more deeply over these decades is that whatever inner healing I had experienced in my life and work in Ghana needed to be shared. That I can't be free until other people are free. So in the spirit of Harriet Tubman, I started taking friends, family, and eventually students and colleagues with me across the waters to Ghana, our version of the underground railroad that (re)turned us to our heritage homeplace. Group after group have "run away" from North America (by plane, of course), landing in Ghana and then (re)turning to the US and sometimes even bringing others back across those waters themselves.

This book is about sharing these journeys that have led us back to ourselves, to that place where we were first known and first loved, "where the arms that held us hold us still."[37] These trips to Ghana for others have mirrored my memories and journeys. Bearing witness to my sister educators has been as transformational for me as the experience has been for them. However, the most profound truth that runs through every word of this book like the thread of a kente cloth that ties us together as Black women is this: *when our collective story as Black people begins on the continent where our ancestors were born, a profound healing begins there for us too.* We find space to reject the lies and untruths that we have been told and that have been taught to us for centuries about who we are. We "lay those burdens" (of racism, sexism, etc.) down and name our pain and suffering as well as our joys and triumphs. We are able to embrace our selves and our memories as Black women. We replace what's in our minds and hearts about who we are by affirming our humanity and our spirits against a backdrop where, as Audre Lorde teaches, "I feel therefore I can be free."[38] Like our African ancestors, we can begin to create ourselves as Black women who know that we are their wildest dream for our lives. And our healing begins in gathering together to (re)member.

## AFRICA NEVER LEFT US

(Re)membering is a catalyst for healing and creation. Stuart Hall writes prophetically about the ways that our roots in Africa ground Black people so strongly (wherever we find ourselves) that we quite literally "produce 'Africa' again—in the diaspora . . . *[and]* . . . *ourselves anew,* as new kinds of subjects."[39] As Hall's new kinds of subjects, diasporic Black folks draw our strength from memory and acts of (re)membering to construct what it means to stand anew, whether through forced movement like the transatlantic trade in humans or in migrations of other kinds. In his words: "The legacies of Empire everywhere may force people to migrate, bringing about the scattering—the dispersal. But each dissemination carries with it the promise of redemptive (re)turn."[40] While Hall specifically speaks here of peoples of the Caribbean, we too, as diasporic Black people in the US, experience and interpret being in the African diaspora as a kind of becoming or identity in formation. Hall describes this as "a newly constructed collective sense of self and deeply written in as the subtext in nationalist histories."[41] For Black people who have been assigned a racialized category, our identities and becoming can also involve a kind of circling back, a full circle move to embrace its origins, as Hall states, "healing all ruptures, repairing every violent breech through this return. It is by any standards a great vision. Its power even in the modern world to move mountains can never be underestimated." Viewed in this way, our identities as diasporic Black people are always already in touch with the timeless spirit of Africa in a way that binds the past to the present and future. It is a circle that is influenced by its encounters, but it remains unbroken. This spirit is embodied in traditions and ways of being that are changed but that are *of* the origins. Whether we regard them as Truth, truth, or no truth at all, the spirit of Black people according to Hall is what "shapes our imaginaries, influences our actions, gives meaning to our lives, and make sense of our history." But this spirit "works" in that it points to what *will* happen by our understandings and descriptions of what has *already* happened, what it was like in the beginning.

But there are spiritual and material dilemmas for we who exist in the hyphenated spaces that are diaspora, who live in the contradictions that empire created. Because our identities are marked at least in part by the traditions and spirit of Africa (historical realities) and we live outside that physical geography, we have had to continually construct ourselves anew, in societies made of many people of many origins. Not singular but multiple. And the land we live on is not innocent: it has been stolen, violated, emptied, and entire nations of Indigenous peoples slain and disrupted. In the US, everyone around us today used to be somewhere else. As Black people, our relation to modern history is truncated and disrupted by the most violent, abrupt, horrible break from home, created by the transatlantic trade in African people. While Africa might have been the origins of our original route through this horrific trade, we can now trace the routes of our cultural identities across the world and back. And just like the acts that created our diasporic lives, we are not pure. While our beginnings as diasporic Black people arose in various tribes and ethnic groups on the continent of Africa, our common point of origin as Black Americans is in the nexus of the transatlantic trade in Black people and our generations of complex interactions and influences with people from across the globe, especially in the US. We cannot easily pull our new being apart into what is "authentic" and what is not. But what we can (re)member is that we in diaspora were created in the cauldrons of colonial societies. We speak from those spaces, always in a conversation that rings with our struggles and attempts to explain our existence.

These are the whispers of Africa, those trace elements that are parts of the origin that are still with us, as diasporic Black people. These elements have been uniquely combined and woven and configured based in and on the place of our encounters with others, what we can think of as our differences. And in those encounters, we still find Africa. We see African orishas such as Yemaya become the Virgen de Regla in Cuba and the Caribbean. We see names (and thus, personalities) like Kofi and Abena given to Black children in the Americas. We see Du Bois's notion of double consciousness (that is, the way that

Black people consciously exist within the enduring tension of loving Blackness in a world that so often hates it and us) in the paintings and sculptures of Elizabeth Catlett, who was deeply influenced by Henry Moore and Diego Rivera. We see the beats of highlife from Ghana and Nigeria in the beats of Earth, Wind & Fire and Beyoncé. Everywhere, hybridity and difference abound for diasporic Black people.

These acts of (re)membering Blackness in diaspora rest squarely on tenets of Black or endarkened feminism. Not resting on binaries of culture and identity or forced to choose one or the other (in this case, whether we are African or American), we embrace the complexities and expansiveness that our differences as Black women in diaspora *require*. Within the Black feminist concept of *both/and*, we refuse notions of the other within ourselves. As Black women, we (re)cognize that our multiple identities are inextricably woven together: we exist as *both* Black people and as women *together*. Rejecting the notion of binaries, we can better understand that the spirit of Black women teachers requires an embrace of being both Black and women as well as both our inner and outer lives, made even more complex and multiple by our other social identities, socioeconomic positions, geographies, and relations. So the process of (re)membering is not some sort of anthropological project for Black women: it is a humanist, racial, cultural, and spiritual (re)membering, based deeply in a diasporic aesthetic. As Black women living in the US, our fundamental spiritual striving is to exist and breathe deeply within the both/and, in the space of something else between. In our attempts to (re)member, we are seeking our family resemblances across the [world] as a whole, a vision that our nation often obscures. According to Stuart Hall, it is not so much about the fact of a singular African river that has flowed unchanged through our veins and our spirits. It is about how we continue to (re)produce, (re)interpret, and (re)-create "Africa" again and again in our work, in this case as Black women teachers. It is about the way "Africa" provides a foundation for our survival and our thriving today. It is the about the way that "Africa" provides alternative bodies of thought and counter-stories to those imposed by the nation-state. (Re)membering is about how our spirits are animated by the (re)turn of "Africa" to ourselves. It is about what Africa means to us now, after our dispersal to lands we now occupy, which is its own problematic politic that we must also engage. And it is about the way "Africa" was appropriated into and transformed by plantation systems of the New World, of which we are also ascendants:

> The reason is that "Africa" is the signifier, the metaphor for that dimension of our society and history that has been massively suppressed, systematically dishonoured and endlessly disavowed, and that, despite all that has happened, remains so. This dimension is what Frantz Fanon called "the fact of blackness." Race remains . . . the guilty secret, the hidden code, the unspeakable trauma. . . . It is "Africa" that has made it "speakable," as a social and cultural condition of our experience.[42]

For me, the healing is most often next to the wound. Thus, when any person is flung into diaspora and consciously transgresses the violent ruptures that national boundaries represent, healing is possible. For Black people, one way to do this is to (re)turn to the place of the wound, whether through critical study or travel or both. That is where we can critically (re)member more of the whole story and the story we need to be more whole.

### DEEP DOWN, WE *ALREADY* KNOW: THE PROCESSES OF (RE)MEMBERING

When I finished my second book, *Learning to (Re)member the Things We've Learned to Forget*, my editor commented: "I know what your next book should be." Interested, I stopped to listen. She said: "It's about *how* to (re)member, the process of (re)membering." In hindsight, she was right. These pages are all about theorizing, narrating, and articulating the power and processes of (re)membering for Black women's identities and teaching and how (re)membering matters to our work. And as teachers, our work is to teach so that our students learn how to (re)member too.

I set out to understand how we (re)membered, and the Ghana Study Abroad in Education program (GSAE) was the perfect site for that study. While GSAE was technically a study abroad program for students and faculty in education and related fields, it was an incredibly rich space for inquiry. While the actual program syllabus is described in more detail in chapter 2, a little context is necessary here too.

The Ghana Study Abroad in Education program was designed to unsettle dominant and dominating educational experiences for participant teachers and other educational professionals. Two overarching questions guided the study:

1. What happens when undergraduate and graduate students (and, later, faculty) from the US have encounters, dialogues, and interactions with African heritage knowledge, culture, and peoples in West Africa (Ghana)?
2. What does Ghana have to teach us about African American education and personhood?

Data were collected from seventy-five students and faculty over seven cohorts from 2013 to 2020. From in-depth analysis of hundreds of pages of information from observations, interviews, course assignments, and fieldnotes, a theory of (re)membering emerged. With the help of various graduate research assistants, this theory of (re)membering was elaborated to include five related processes that helped us better understand how and why people both came to know and to be differently as a result of their experiences while in GSAE and in the afterlife of those experiences in their teaching and lives. While participants of various ethnic and racial heritages and social identities enacted these (re)membering processes differently based on their personhood, all participants engaged in (re)membering as they attempted to make connections between Africa and the US and back together again. While not necessarily a linear process, (re)membering as endarkened feminist praxis is made up of five related processes:

**(Re)searching.** (Re)searching involves seeking, looking, and searching for something about Black heritage and/or culture that we believe will teach us something new. In this search, we are also open to the possibility that we might be changed in this process by looking again, by our (re)search. Whatever we are searching for within Black identity and culture, what we find also helps us see ourselves more clearly as teachers and as humans.

**(Re)visioning.** (Re)visioning involves an expansion of our current worldview of Black people, culture, and knowledge beyond solely what we can *see* (i.e., people, places, things) to engaging our *world sense*.[43] This involves attention not only to what we see but to what we hear, touch, feel, and intuit, to the "evidence of things unseen."

**(Re)cognizing.** (Re)cognizing involves the work of changing our thinking and our minds about who Black people are, what Black people have accomplished, and the cultural and social brilliance of Black people from the African continent to the diaspora and sometimes back again. While (re)cognizing is often manifest as a change in our minds, it also includes shifts in our heart or feelings.

**(Re)presenting.** (Re)presenting involves placing our understandings of notions of Black womanhood, Black identities and culture into the world in new and fuller ways. This includes how we present the length and breadth of Black culture and heritage in the world through our bodies, minds, and spirits. These acts of (re)presenting can be understood as a kind of truth-telling or a reckoning to right historical wrongs.

**(Re)claiming.** (Re)claiming involves going back (and forward) to lay claim to the legacy of Black/African people and to take your place within or in relation to this legacy.

## TO (RE)MEMBER IS TO GET FREE

These pages address the absence of the stories of Black women educators. These stories were deeply inspired by Paule Marshall's 1983 novel, *Praisesong for the Widow*. The main character of the book is a Black woman named Avey who quite literally (re)members herself and her work through a series of experiences that literally transform her life as she (re)searches, (re)visions, (re)cognizes, (re)presents, and (re)claims her origin stories and legacy as a Black woman. While Marshall's book is considered a piece of fiction, I have continued to be overwhelmed by the ways that Avey's experiences mirrored my own experiences and those of other Black women teachers who have traveled to Ghana with me. Regardless of racial or ethnic identity, for a scant few, the GSAE trip simply added to the stamps in their well-used passports. For some, our trip was the first time they had even held a passport or, in a couple of cases, flown in an airplane. While we all agreed that traveling opened us to new vistas and culture, there was something absolutely transformational when, as Black women educators, we touched down in Ghana. It was something about the way it felt like home and not home at the same time that we immediately sensed, connections that we did not expect. Seeing our own auntie's or uncle's face in Ghanaians walking down the street. Tasting familiar gumbo in the okra stew we ate there. Sisters in their Sunday best, slaying as they engaged their version of a church strut that mirrored our own. As Tom Feelings wrote in his powerful children's book *I Saw Your Face*, there was something about the influence and impact of accurately (re)membering pieces of yourself that transformed our bodies, minds, and spirits.[44] As one participant described: "It literally shifted the molecules in me." As you will read in the chapters that follow, experiences within Ghana served as powerful opportunities for being in the molecule-shifting space that Ghana was for Black American women teachers. Being on the continent of Africa opened space and time for Black American women teachers to know and embrace their spirituality as the common life-affirming thread that is central to all facets of Black identity, that runs through our bodies, minds, and spirits. We found in Ghana a place to situate ourselves as Black women teachers at the origins and to follow the routes and twists of the version of African people we are in the US and beyond. We reveled in the ways our bodies, minds, and spirits just felt lighter in the fact that there was a place in the world where we could breathe deeply. This lightness of being, this little bit of freedom from the weight of racism that we carry heavy in the US, felt like our balm in Gilead. (Re)membering the beauty and power of Ghana quite literally transformed our visions of ourselves and our work as Black women educators into clearer versions of ourselves and clearer visions of our work. Being in Ghana helped each of us to actually feel and find something that the late Ntozake Shange suggested is at the very core of a spiritual life, regardless of the name you call spirit: "I found God in myself and I loved her. I loved her fiercely."[45]

The power of our everyday occurrences as Black women in Ghana emerged from meditative moments the likes of which are often difficult to find in our fast-paced, demanding, sometimes overwhelming lives as Black educators in the United States. But it was through sitting quietly on the shores of Ghana that we could hear how fast our minds raced, where we could (re)cognize garbage that we needed to throw away, old worn-out habits that no longer served us, that we needed to let go of. At a distance from the US and living in the contrast that Ghana herself can also be, we learned about our Americanness through the paradoxes we experienced on Ghanaian soil. We learned to feel and trust our African rhythms, the cultural memories buried deep in our DNA. In the sometimes overwhelming presence of poverty, we wrestled with how worldwide systems of white supremacy, patriarchy, and economic domination manifest in ways similar and different in Africa and in America but are always inextricably connected to the places of our birth in the West. We stood witness to the horrors experienced by our ancestors as they traversed the African continent in shackles, were held in dungeons, died, and survived in ways that forever changed the circumstances for African people on both sides of the water and that, quite literally, created us as African or Black *Americans*. Walking softly and meditatively in Ghana connected us with still waters that allowed us to see our reflections more clearly.

This was not an easy walk. It was not an uncomplicated walk. We struggled with the lies and shame of the stories we had been told and the lies and shame that we had internalized as Black women. We were overwhelmed by perpetual waves of mourning our familial relations and our ancestors that mirrored the ocean waves of this coastal country, the watery graves for so many of the ancestors that had come before us. And we experienced and learned, through ways small and large, the ecstatic joy and amazing grace as we met and talked and experienced what Ghana was to us and what we were to Ghana. We were not alone on our journey because we could *feel* our legacies and lineages. We took every step with the Creator and all of the ancestors who had walked before us, with those in human form who walk with us on our earthly journey, and with those spirits who will walk after us. We (re)membered. And when Black women teachers (re)member, *everything* is possible.

# CHAPTER 2

# "I WAS MISSING SOMETHING, SOMETHING SO IMPORTANT"

## (Re)searching

*Can't you imagine what it must feel like to have a true home? I don't mean heaven. I mean a real earthly home . . . your own home, where if you go past your great-great-grandparents, past theirs, and theirs, past the whole Western history, past the beginning to organized knowledge, past pyramids and poisoned arrows, on back to when rain was new, before plants forgot they could sing and birds thought they were fish, back when God said Good! Good!—there, right there where you know your own people were born and lived and died. . . . That place.*

—Toni Morrison, *Paradise*[1]

*That* place. Morrison's voice above speaks to the everyday realities that many of us live in the African diaspora. She articulates and echoes the disconnections, dislocations, and sustained erasure of memories of Africa for Black people that we often cannot or feel we dare not (re)member. But these are also our memories of home, of places where we, in all of our complexity and beauty, just make sense. And as Black women who live in diaspora, those memories are the essence of something that is missing, the "something so important" that Ntozake Shange reminds us in her epic choreopoem *For Colored Girls Who Have Considered Suicide/When the Rainbow Is Enuf.* I grew up on this choreopoem, performing a number of pieces from it when I was a graduate student and even in my first faculty position at

Washington State University (WSU). We were a small community of Black women at WSU, isolated in this large rural university from the cultural connections that affirmed us as Black women. Performing the work of Black women writers and poets was our way of (re)remembering the essence of who we were as Black women on *our* terms. While our numbers at this rural white university made up less than 5 percent of the enrollment when I was there in the 1980s, we would boldly embody the voices and verses of legendary Black women's poetry every year for the Black Mom's Weekend festivities. This was *our* celebration for Black grandmothers, mothers, sisters, aunties, and those who loved us. And during that one weekend a year, Black women's wisdom and culture ruled the stage, the runway, the parties, and the day. We (re)membered the truth of our spirits and, if only for that weekend, we found *that* place.

Searching for places that affirm us body, mind, and spirit is the existential reality and real labor of Black people in diaspora, and has been since our dispersal from the African continent. Where is *that* place where we create our lives *our* way? Where is *that* place where we govern ourselves, as Ghana's first president, Dr. Kwame Nkrumah, called us to do? Where are those schools and teachers who embody a reflection of us, a reflection that, since our arrival on these shores, we've been trying to find? I know as a child that I searched for that reflection in the textbooks and in my teachers' faces and I did not find them. As a former high school teacher, I searched in the curriculum standards, teaching methodologies, and materials for stories of Black people, Black knowledges and representations, and examples of Black excellence: they were not there. As a new scholar, I searched for theories, concepts, and paradigms that could help me feel and explain the resilient lives of Black people and the beautiful brilliance of Black women specifically to no avail. Many of us had to build these theories ourselves. This has been a treacherous and often painful search that continues today as a teacher educator. The truth? I have found such joy and love in the work of teaching, leading, and learning as a Black woman, but I've had to (re)search to find myself and my people within the walls of my education. (Re)membering the rest of our long story as Africans in diaspora who have shaped the world, loved deeply, and sought justice so fervently continues to chart my path toward creating a world that is less painful and more affirming for Black women than our collective journey of millennia. It is a search *again* that begins to provide the solace of *that* place, the place of our spirits.

Please know that this is not solely a call to return to the continent of Africa as a way to assuage or "cure" whatever is inside of us that diaspora has wrought. But this is about the absolute necessity for Black people to affirm who we are as *Black* people, grounded in our knowledges, our cultures, and who we really are wherever we find ourselves on the planet. Ultimately, it is an inside search to *that* place where we are love personified *and* where we are loved.

In my first book, *On Spiritual Strivings*, I shared how important and necessary it is to engage a counter-search for that place that Morrison speaks of as *that* place:

> You see, it's not that, as a Black scholar, I can't locate my self/scholarship in the Big Four paradigms. I can, given that I was "trained" and socialized in the same institutions as many of my white scholar colleagues. But it's like buying a new pair of shoes. I usually wear a size 12. Now, I can squeeze my big feet into a size 11: I can actually "fit" inside the boundaries of the shoe. But it is very painful, terribly uncomfortable, and it is fundamentally too darn small! Should I continue to wear such a shoe, replete with the pain that would be the result for my whole body? And, at the place where many African-centered scholars have arrived today, we believe the smarter thing for us to do is to take the shoes back to the store and get some that fit, that we can wear comfortably. It's not that we don't find the knowledge that's been constructed into reified paradigms by other scholars as useful or important: We often do. Many of us just don't worship the Big Four or find any sort of solace within them. My solace is found in embracing a paradigm that arises from a world view that is personal and cultural, a unique combination of what it means to be alive, as an African American woman scholar who is deeply attuned to the spiritual nature of my life and work.[2]

So (re)membering begins with a different kind of search, not for someone else's purposes but for our own. It begins with the process of (re)searching or searching again in our own minds, bodies, and spirits. It is the process of a deeper (re)membering that follows the trajectory of Morrison's call to the place where our people were born, loved, and died. It is about (re)membering the legacy of your people, understanding the spirit that animates thought and action past, present, and future. In these pages, it is about the process of Black women teachers seeking, looking, and searching for something about Black and African heritage and culture that we believed would teach us something necessary, something needed, something new, something so important. It was about placing ourselves against our historical backdrop before enslavement and before Africa was carved into fragments called countries by the Europeans. (Re)searching is the healing process where Black women teachers were open to the possibility that we might actually be *changed* as we searched for nuanced ways of looking at race, culture, ethnicity, social identities, and ourselves with a focus on our spirits. Black women engage in a (re)search unceasingly, especially when we know we are brilliant, bold, and beautiful and are continuously told (in ways subtle and overt) that we are not "legitimate" members of the spaces we occupy in diaspora. And in the contexts of our lives being constantly in harm's way given the violence of racism, capitalism, patriarchy, and all the phobias that are the fabric of the US, Black women must courageously *choose* to search again, despite not knowing the outcome of our search. We do so because we know in our spirits that we are not what we are being told we are. However, as we search for the pieces that we *are* within global Black identity and culture, we know in our spirits that our (re)search will help us see ourselves and our work more clearly—as teachers, as women, as humans. Our (re)search is a spiritual desire to (re)member and know who we are and *whose* we are without the stereotypical controlling images and characterizations that have been the burden of Black women, very particularly in the US.[3]

As Black women in diaspora, we have been searching all of our lives for our lives. Our spiritual desire to know deeply who we are and whose we are was the motivation for the Black women teachers whose stories are gathered here. This is our declaration and choice to engage in the critical study with and in Ghana in hopes that such study might teach us about ourselves and about education. For us, that desire was the reason we even chose to participate in the GSAE program. Regardless of our prior schooling experiences, where we grew up in the US, the level of our university degrees, and the place where those experiences took place, these Black women teachers very consciously *chose* to travel to Ghana, to seek a deeper knowing within themselves that books, scholarship, and even travel to other places had not been able to and could not fill. And as Black women, we specifically sought the histories that we had been told and the herstories that we needed. We sought escape from the specter of white womanhood against which we had been constantly measured in subtle and not so subtle ways. We wanted to embrace the blessings of affirmation, critique, and collective Black womanhood that we had too rarely found in our formal educational experience, a blessing that echoed the way we gathered around our kitchen tables and in other Black women's spaces. We yearned for *that* place where we could simply revel in the power and beauty that we "be" and learn about our Black women selves together at school and in our workplaces. As a group of Black women whose work as teachers had been largely carried out in predominately white spaces, we all had cultivated what bell hooks refers to as homeplaces. In her brilliant book *Talking Back: Thinking Feminist, Thinking Black*, she speaks of the necessity of homeplaces for Black women, those places where we find solace and care amongst other Black women (and those who love us) that allow us to survive and even thrive through white supremacy, racism, sexism, homophobia, etc.

Ghana was *that* place at our origins, a call to our spirits to which we surrendered, often to great negative consternation by family, friends, and society who demanded answers as to why we had chosen "Africa," given the negative portrayals and forced distance from shameful stories that we had been told about that place or "those" Black people. But something inside still called us to make this choice.

I think it's because when the African family calls, some of us hear it and answer. Why wouldn't we? Living in the US amidst the pervasive and damaging violence of white supremacy was a major impetus to search for that alternative that affirms who we are. For Black women who teach, our (re)search is often inextricably linked to our personhood and to our vocation. In other words, we (re)search or look again in order to be better not just for ourselves: we also know that being better in our knowing will help us create more affirming and loving spaces of education and personhood for our students, especially our Black and Brown students. Why do we make this choice to be better? We make it because *we* were those same students in our own lives and schooling experiences in the US. We know they deserve better, and so do we. In the voices of the Black women teachers shared in the following chapters, you will hear and maybe even echo our choices to get free enough to create spaces of freedom for our students too.

### JACQUELINE: STUDYING IN GHANA WOULD MEAN THE WORLD TO ME

When I met Jacqueline, she was a twenty-one-year-old African American female student. She was a quiet, introspective, and soft-spoken young woman with a keen sense of observation. Her quiet nature mirrored her modest, humble Christian upbringing, one in which a young person speaks only when spoken to or lowers their eyes in the presence of elders. Her curly brown hair was often straightened or pulled back in a rolled style. Dark tortoise-rimmed glasses framed her skin, the color of butterscotch. Often dressed in university-branded apparel, she came to the university with some community college experience. At the time of the GSAE, Jacqueline was a junior-level undergraduate studying to be an elementary educator. Because of her interest in the social nature of people (and her sharp tenacity and determination), she had also earned a minor in sociology.

A self-described military brat, Jacqueline had traveled widely. She had resided in Germany, visited many parts of Europe, and lived in diverse places in the United States, including Hawaii, Georgia, Colorado, and Pennsylvania. Though her parents were divorced (and her dad was deployed to the Middle East during the time of her experiences in

Ghana), both parents were very involved in her life. However, funding for her university education was a real struggle for Jacqueline and her family. As an undergraduate student, she received some financial help from her family, state-funded scholarships, and federal Pell grants. She also held a part-time job during school years and over the summers. While an undergraduate student, Jacqueline lived with her grandmother and other relatives in a house near the university. This was one of the major ways she had been able to support herself through school. Jacqueline served as an after-school tutor at a local center that served a largely Latinx and Black population. She was also a general member of Kappa Delta Epsilon, an education fraternity.

"*Studying abroad in Ghana would mean the world to me.*" These words were the first I'd heard Jacqueline speak, at a meeting in my office that she had requested to brainstorm how she might raise the funds for her trip to Ghana. Her words seemed animated by a feeling very deep inside of her, a yearning that Jacqueline had been carrying for a lifetime. I was intrigued by her choice of words, as they seemed to be in contradiction with someone who had lived so many places in the world. But this experience at this time with and in Ghana mattered so deeply to Jacqueline that it did not seem accidental to me. It seemed to be a *spiritual* longing, a desire to understand what it meant to really know herself as a *Black* woman. As she spoke, it was clear that she had always known that she was Black: what she seemed to desire was to know and embrace deeper meanings of being a Black woman in her spirit, to explore what animated her life and work. Jacqueline herself often described her desire to participate in GSAE as a spiritual calling: "I don't know. When Dr. Dillard came into my EDEC class discussing the Ghana study abroad trip, *something told me that I needed to be on that trip to Ghana*. As the only African American girl in the class I knew that I would have a deeper connection to Africa than my Caucasian classmates" (emphasis mine).

Like many universities, the University of Georgia offers a plethora of study abroad opportunities for undergraduate and graduate students. Echoing all of the Black women whose stories are gathered here, Jacqueline's (re)search began with the deliberate search for and selection of the Ghana Study Abroad in Education program. Like others, she was specifically seeking an opportunity that would help her to see herself differently and to see "what difference differences make," related to her understanding of Black identity and culture.[4] When asked why she wanted to participate in the GSAE program, Jacqueline enthusiastically replied that she "loves to learn about new cultures." It seems reasonable to expect that she would be comfortable with differences, given that she was a child of military parents and had literally lived all over the world. But her choice to study abroad in Ghana seemed to embody a different motivation, something deeper, something more important and meaningful to her. When I asked further about her choice of GSAE, she leaned forward in her chair. It was clear that she'd given some thought to the deeper motivations of her (re)search as she answered. "I call them my passions," she said, catching my eye. I leaned in as well. "I want to learn about us, about Black people."

One of the passions Jacqueline shared was a desire to explore for herself what she felt were often negative perceptions and portrayals of Africa. Her own admitted lack of understanding was a catalyst for her (re)search and participation, a way to broaden and deepen her own perceptions of Africa generally and Ghana more particularly. Her intentions and emotions were clear:

> When one hears the word *Africa*, there are only a few things that come to mind. With the despairing infomercials, *Invisible Children*, Kony 2012–2013, the AIDS and HIV epidemics, and the history of slavery in general, it is safe to say that Africa as a whole is portrayed negatively. Often times when one speaks of Africa, people forget that Africa is the second largest continent in the world and is comprised of fifty-four countries. With all of that said, I realized that there is so little I know about Africa, Ghana in particular.

And Jacqueline was not the only one who knew little about Africa. In preparing for our time in Ghana (and as part of the GSAE course requirements), we hold five or six study sessions on campus, learning about Ghana through readings, articles, presentations, lectures, and discussions. In the first session of our GSAE class (after we each briefly introduce ourselves), I give each participant a sheet of paper and ask them to make a list of things they know about Africa. While I know that Africa is a continent and that our focus in the course was on Ghana, I ask this broad question on purpose for a purpose. Year after year, group after group, I have watched as most students (and faculty) struggle to make that list, even about the entire African continent! Within the very sparse lists they can create, answers are often limited to three to five basic points including the capital of Ghana (Accra), the name of the former president of South Africa (Nelson Mandela), or noting that there is a lot of (take your pick) poverty, war, genocide, corruption, or disease. Occasionally there is a teacher in the group who was an African studies major or who had clearly engaged in extensive critical studying of the African continent. While I have always been thrilled to engage their expertise, such a teacher was not only very rare: she was always white as well.

## (RE)SEARCHING BLACK IDENTITY IN A POST-INTEGRATION WORLD

What does it mean to be a Black woman teacher who has been denied the opportunity to think deeply about the origins and manifestations of what Frantz Fanon calls "the fact of blackness"?[5] Who hasn't considered how that fact matters beyond its challenges to deeper considerations of who we are today as Black people and to the spirit of our pedagogy and practice? Existence within these absences as Black American teachers has profoundly shaped and continues to shape our lives and practices as teachers. For the GSAE educators (and frankly for so many Black educators in the US), there is a longing to know the deeper meanings of African heritage and Blackness, both collectively and individually. And it is not simply that we have arrived in universities and suddenly felt that desire. To a person, for these Black women teachers, that yearning often began in our own early schooling experiences and continued into our university studies. But unless and until we also began to make conscious decisions to (re)search and explore Black identity and our proper beginnings as free Black people, that knowledge eluded us. White supremacy as a worldwide project purposefully created distortions and omissions of the stories of our exploitation, including the characterization of Black people as less than human that began in Africa and continues in the African diaspora.[6] In light of this worldwide project, Jacqueline's description of her educational experience highlighted a common thread amongst many of the Black teachers in GSAE, especially as Black people who grew up after the racial integration of schools in the US:

> As a military brat, I went to the best schools everywhere. But I was isolated as a Black child. From elementary to high school, the most information I have learned about my culture was that we were slaves. My mom would buy my brothers and I books and magazines so we can learn a little, but the nice gesture did not abate the damage of omitting our history.

As Black women teachers in the US, our group had experienced various educational contexts for our schooling. Some had educational experiences in urban contexts, often surrounded by majority Black and Brown students and teachers. Some grew up and experienced their education in rural contexts, in both the southern and northern parts of the US. Regardless of location, the majority of Black teachers in our GSAE cohorts experienced their formal education in predominately white settings in suburban and small city schools. This was the case not only for our K–12 schooling experiences but for our undergraduate and graduate education as Black women as well. Having had the majority of our education in settings steeped in whiteness (within national and international contexts), the persistent and consistent isolation and disconnection from Black culture, heritage, and information were damaging to our bodies, minds, and spirits. This was also true (albeit to a slightly lesser extent) for those who attended urban schools in predominately Black and Brown communities: they also bore witness to the gaps in their racial and cultural knowledge of Black identities and stories in their formal education as well.

If Black women teachers are expected to be able to center

education in the legacy of Black people, there is a space inside that we must fill in order to do so. We have to (re)search our own racial, cultural, and heritage knowledge, pedagogies, and practices.[7] As teachers who were trained to be teachers in post-integration educational settings, we did not experience an education that grounded us to sufficiently teach the depth and breadth of our legacy and stories and those of other marginalized peoples to our students. This is true of most of our teachers, regardless of their racial identities. But for Black women, it is always a (re)search not just for ourselves: it is rooted in a deep desire to learn about *ourselves* as Black women in diaspora. It is our search again in order to provide the education that would not only benefit our students but that is worthy of them and of ourselves. The GSAE was seen as a way to begin for some, a way to deepen knowing for others. But we understood that it was always about something bigger than us.

## FOR MY STUDENTS AND FOR ME

Even when we may not know the term "cosmology" or "epistemology," Black women teachers have always known in our spirits what orders our lives, how we know something, what is right and wrong, fair and unfair, what smells good and what stinks. We have always known, but some of us have forgotten. As Black women teachers in GSAE, we undertook this search with and in Ghana for ourselves because we believed learning the long lessons of our stories against a Black backdrop would help us (re)member our calling and the traditions upon which it was built. We knew, even if it was way down deep inside of us, that such knowing would help us to teach in ways that nourished and honored our students, regardless of the contexts where we teach them.

While education steeped in Blackness was not a prevalent part of the educational journey for most of these Black women teachers, our (re)search was about learning to (re)member the legacy of Black people and to honor our promises to the ancestors on behalf of ourselves and our students. Choosing to engage with Ghana and Africa provided that opportunity to (re)member and learn an important part of the length and breadth of the struggles that are the legacy of Black women that we live within today. We committed to this (re)search because we were also committed to our students having greater knowledge of global Black presence and our cultural memories that continue to make a strong demand on our present conditions and lives.

In her role as a future teacher, Jacqueline saw the GSAE as beneficial not just to her own understandings of her personhood, but to her future students' understandings of their own as well. She specifically calls to the experiences of Black students as being critical to her own passion and (re)search through the program, a call that is echoed across all of the Black women teachers and, very particularly, for those with responsibilities to teach in K–12 settings:

> This trip is an opportunity not just for myself but for my future students. No matter where I teach, what the demographics of my school are, I will be able to bring Ghana to my students. I will try to diminish the negative perspective so many [have] of Africa as a whole . . . and for my African American students, I will be able to connect with them about a part of history that is not in our history or social studies textbooks.

## BUT CAN I FIND A BLACK WOMAN TEACHER?

You may (re)member my own story of having had only one Black teacher in my entire educational experiences from kindergarten through doctoral studies. I always assumed that was because I grew up in Washington State, where Black people are only about 4 percent of the total population. But what I learned in the GSAE program over the years is that my experience was not only common but also persistent, given that I began my formal education in the early 1960s and my career as a teacher educator over four decades ago. So as it was with my own schooling experiences, it mattered deeply that a Black woman was leading the GSAE program and served as the lead professor. This was also a major reason that Black students selected this particular program, as Jacqueline shares: "Travel to Ghana will guarantee that I will finally have an African American teacher (professor), a role model to look up to that looks like me, especially since there are so few."

There are so few Black women role models and educators for Black women who are studying to be teachers and teacher educators. Hence, there is an urgent need for conversations and explorations of Black women's embodied understandings of the social, emotional, and physical toll that white supremacy has taken on the bodies, minds, and spirits of Black women who are and will be those models. Because ultimately, whether as students in our teacher preparation programs or in leading teacher preparation programs, Black women are always going to protect our students and disrupt racialized harm, harm that we also know intimately as Black women ourselves.[8] And our absence leaves Black and Brown children particularly vulnerable, given the ways that white supremacy is enacted and weaponized against Black and Brown children both in schools and society.[9] Black women educators in each cohort recounted story after story of how having Black teachers generally and Black women teachers specifically mattered to the success of Black students' educational trajectories and imaginaries. And for some of the participants like Jacqueline, I was the first Black woman teacher in their schooling experience. While research tells us that Black students perform better academically when they have Black teachers and that Black teachers are essential to their academic achievement and well-being, what does it mean when Black women teachers have had few Black women teachers from which to draw on as mentors, othermothers, and important role models?[10] How do we learn to not simply survive these systems built on racism and sexism but to thrive as Black women teachers who are able to bring our Black women bodies, minds, and spirits together as a unified, integrated whole? A strong thread in these teachers' desires to search again for an experience of Black education was also their desire to broaden and deepen their personal understanding and knowledge of Black heritage, Black womanhood, Black stories, and Black culture. This included having the opportunity to experience the joy, brilliance, and camaraderie that is always already present when Black women gather! But this (re)search with and in Ghana was also about understanding the power in knowing ourselves as *Black* women. This was critical. In Jacqueline's words, travel to Ghana would "guarantee that I would finally have an African American teacher (professor), a role model to look up to that looks like me, especially since there are so few."

Jacqueline's voice as a future Black woman teacher and her reference to the power of learning from Black women teachers tells us that it is only natural that Black women educators are searching for the company of other Black women educators, specifically as models, mentors, and guides. This is akin to the lessons shared by Beverly Daniel Tatum in her groundbreaking work *Why Are All the Black Kids Sitting Together in the Cafeteria? And Other Conversations About Race*. Quite simply? Black women *need* one another and our children need us. Ours is a spiritual calling as Black women teachers, a call to and for the collective laying on of hands, whether literally or figuratively. It is one thing for systems of education to hear this call with their ears; it is quite another to hold space for Black women's learning and growth as sacred and worthy of reverence. But if we value the learning and professional development of Black women, we must design and plan for the education of Black women's bodies, minds, and spirits. And that means that we hold space and explicitly provide for the experiences and learning that have been absent or missing in the long history of racist, white supremacist spaces called our education system. And as a free Black woman teacher educator, one who sees the value of Black women sitting together at the table they have built, that experience needed to start at the root of Black life: in Africa.

### WHEN HARRIET'S CHILDREN (RE)TURN, THEY (RE)MEMBER: UNEARTHING THE GHANA STUDY ABROAD IN EDUCATION PROGRAM (GSAE)

Like many Black women teachers before us, some of us have had abolition and freedom for Black lives on our minds and in our hearts from the moment we chose the vocation of teaching. What that inherently means is that these same Black women teachers have always and will continue to transgress boundaries and rules, even at great risk to our bodies, minds, and spirits.[11] The Ghana Study Abroad in Education program was designed to provide an explicit example of teaching to transgress, of education as the practice of freedom. It was designed to unsettle dominant and dominating lessons about Black women that have been learned and been taught for centuries in diaspora. These lessons have also been bereft of the *spirit* of Black people. Bereft of our spiritualities. Bereft of our ways of being and knowing. Bereft of the length and breadth of Black stories, culture, and traditions that began in Africa and *not* as enslaved people on the shores of the Americas and other places that are our diaspora. The GSAE program was designed as an experience where Black knowledges, pedagogies and practices, and traditions were privileged and placed at the center of teacher education, professional preparation, and cultural development experiences. Black heritage knowledge and ways of being were the "norm," the healing excellence and brilliance that we all learned from. And while we focused on endarkening the curriculum and our experience, what we also knew is that a rising tide floats *all* boats: to learn through those knowledges and from those who have been most marginalized lifts us all. As such, we drew a very diverse pool of participants to GSAE: undergraduate pre-service teachers, in-service teachers, master's- and doctoral-level education majors, school leaders, those from fields outside education, and educational professionals in counseling, higher education, and educational leadership. Racially, the program has included Black, white, and Asian participants, representing multiple genders, sexualities, socioeconomic statuses, and social identity groups. Over the seven years of the program (2013–2019), more than 70 percent of the participants were Black, including eight Black education faculty members who also participated in the GSAE program. This is in stark contrast to the national representation of Black students in study abroad, who make up approximately 13 percent of postsecondary students who study abroad.[12] So the overrepresentation of Black presence in our GSAE study abroad is an anomaly among study abroad experiences nationally. And what that says to me is something twofold. First, being able to (re)search the length and breadth of Black lives was also at the forefront of Black teachers' lives and thus their choice of a Black-led, Black-centered program. Second, it says that the content of this program appealed to teachers more generally and at all levels because they desired to know better and do better for their students, very particularly for their Black students. That the GSAE also had a strong Black faculty presence from across the entire education college suggests that faculty also felt they had room to professionally develop even more deeply toward their awesome responsibility of preparing the next generation of teachers and education professionals.

The GSAE was also attuned to a growing body of scholarship on the ways that traveling and studying abroad often center poverty as a commodity, in the pursuit of global justice and equity. For example, many education study-abroad programs include visiting schools to "teach" in communities that are dealing with global economic inequities, or bringing supplies and/or money to "happy" (read: grateful) children. These are common tropes embodied in itineraries for studying abroad. But, as a Black feminist educator, it was so very clear to me that underneath the very epistemology of these programs, poverty itself is the main attraction of both the destination and the discourses that constitute what critical scholars refer to as a slum tourism experience.[13] At institution after institution, studying abroad arises from the institution's desire to conjure sympathy for a benevolent donor or to assuage guilty consciences for the generations of omissions and exclusions, as projects of white supremacy always do.

In designing the GSAE, I resonated with Fabian Frenzel, that it was possible for study abroad experiences to be framed in a different way: "While some work on how tourists shape industry, rarely do we ask *how research looks at tourists' engagements in volunteering and philanthropy beyond leaving money.* . . . When poverty is a social/political question, the study of tourist and host engagements could also examine not only philanthropy but solidarity, alliances, and the formulation of shared demands."[14] So the ethos of the GSAE was guided by a question raised by the Reverend Dr. Martin Luther King Jr. as he reflected on Ghana's independence from British rule in 1957 and Ghana's connections to the civil rights struggles for Black liberation in the United States. The question was not what we could bring to or "teach" Ghana. The question was: *What lessons could an independent Ghana teach us?*

So our GSAE course was boldly framed and explicitly centered in African gender studies, Black feminist theories, endarkened feminist epistemologies, and critical and culturally based pedagogies. The stories and texts that we studied represented multiple genres including film, poetry, fiction, and biography, as well as speeches from across the globe. "Texts" also explicated and highlighted Black women and centered our gaze toward various versions of Black thought, culture, and education. I curated these texts to do the important work of (re)membering Africa with her diaspora, centered mostly on the US. In other words, the work of the texts and our study of them was to explore and "put back together" our disconnections and disruptions in what Christina Sharpe describes as the wake of the transatlantic trade of African people. In her monumental book *In the Wake: Blackness and Being*, Sharpe examines the Africa that was, is, and has been created in diaspora and on the African continent, "always swept up in the wake produced and determined, though not absolutely, by the afterlives of slavery."[15] The United States and Ghana, West Africa, were our sites of embarkation, debarkation, and all things in between—the contexts designed to engage us at the level of our personhood and our spirits, our lived counter-narratives versus the abstraction of our histories unknown. What do I know now? We can begin to heal education in the wake of white supremacy, patriarchy, and racism that has constituted the education of Black teachers and others by attending to the knowledge and wisdom of Black women particularly and Black people more generally. And we do that by critically studying Black life in complex and in-depth ways so that we might begin to heal everybody's stories and everybody's education. As Bettina Love cautions us in *We Want to Do More Than Survive: Abolitionist Teaching and the Pursuit of Educational Freedom*: "Education will not save us. We have to save education."[16]

During GSAE study sessions in the US and while in Ghana, we studied together in all our differences, explicitly unpacking the ways

that race, gender, and other social identities structured our relationships, created the privileges and burdens we carried, and constructed
the struggles within our contemporary moment in education and
society. Unlike other courses where the trauma of racism and other
structural oppressions are too often deemed scary or irrelevant
(and thus not discussed), such fragility had no place in our course.
Neither did the management of white discomfort. Our efforts and
learning were focused on (re)searching and understanding what
the Black nation called Ghana had to teach us, focused on what we
(re)membered. Maybe most importantly, we did this in a way that
constantly affirmed the humanity of Black people instead of further-
ing the absences and pathologies that as Black students and teachers we had too often experienced in our schooling. By doing so, we
also interrogated the very systems of education we had both learned
in and now worked in as teachers and educational professionals. We
studied the diversity of our educational experiences and the painful
as well as joyful experiences arising from our various subject positions. We could then see that our work as educators was about abolishing what does not work and building anew. And when things got
tough (and they often did), we *all* waded in those waters of angry,
bitter, painful tears knowing that, as educators for humanity and justice, we were cutting to heal and not to bleed. These practices of (re)-
searching also helped to build the deeper spiritual reservoirs that we
needed to answer a fundamental question: What did Africa (in this
case, Ghana) have to teach us about the spirit of teaching, learning,
and leading? And how could (re)membering Ghana help us to see
ourselves and our students in more truthful and accurate ways? How
could we (re)member connections to Africa in today's terms, not the
mythological tales of Black people in diaspora being solely the descendants of kings and queens but extraordinarily everyday people
as well? What might those connections be for diasporic Black people
like us in Ghana?

Aside from our critical studying of texts, and along with our ongoing dialogues, each participant was required to select a topic or
question into which they would (re)search and inquire deeply before,

during, and after their experiences in Ghana.[17] As might be expected in a program focused on teaching education, topics selected usually represented either a deeply personal interest or something related to classroom culture, teaching, and pedagogical practice. Interestingly, these choices represented that and far more for the Black women participants, who often had a desire to know more deeply what tied their identities as Black American women to women in Ghana and in history. This Ghana-centered study abroad program literally arose from having had too few spaces to gather and study Black women and the length of African legacy in my own education. And the topics that Black women educators wanted to delve into represented a similar existential struggle related to being Black women teachers. These struggles needed answers in our spirits and lives. And a sampling of titles from the individual inquiries conducted by Black women in the GSAE program provide valuable insight into the need and desire to know ourselves and our spirits as Black women teachers more deeply: "The Story of a Lion, the Birth of a Queen: Blogging on the Complex History of Race and Education for Africans on Both Sides of the Water"; "A Sense of Ghana, a Sense of Belonging: Self-Esteem, Given Roles, and Loving Blackness"; and "The Route of the Roots: A Journey and Exploration of Myself." Some of these women's inquiries were very explicitly tied to their roles as teachers and teacher educators, including "Teacher Education for Sites of Racial Trauma"; "'The Ocean Can't Separate What's in the Bloodline': The Educational Impact of Cadence, Creative Expression, and Community"; and "Crafting Black Transnational Identities: James Baldwin and Beyond." As the culminating experience of every cohort, all participants proudly (and often very emotionally) presented the findings from their studies at a college-wide colloquium, sharing the lessons that Ghana taught them about their teaching and their lives.

While the experiences of each of the processes of (re)membering are told in much more detail in the following chapters, three things mattered deeply to the work of this (re)searching for Black women educators. First, the structure of the program and course was all about them and was all about love.[18] Second, it mattered that a Black woman, with deep roots and experiences in Ghana, was teaching the course and leading the program. Third, all aspects of the GSAE were experienced in and as the long traditions of Black excellence and integrity that they were. As such the course was experienced as a space of (re)search that Black women teachers of today have been rarely afforded but desperately need. What I am also saying is that if such courses do not exist, it is our responsibility as a profession to create them. The GSAE was the course I wished I could have had as a Black woman during my own teacher education and professional development. It was the culturally and spiritually sustaining education that I didn't have but wanted to provide for my undergraduate and graduate students and that they wanted to enact in their lives and work as current and future teachers and educational professionals. Studying through Black women's theories and knowings gave us frameworks and language to consider what we were experiencing. Throughout GSAE, opportunities existed in abundance to express, share, create, and be informed by diverse people, places, and things. And in the afterlife of the GSAE experience, engaging in (re)membering in such depth and breadth of Black life continued to transform Black women teachers' personhood and practice.

## SOMETIMES WE NEED MERCIFUL DISTANCE: (RE)SEARCHING AS A STATE OF GRACE

For Black women, letting go of the lies our teachers have told us is often the first step in (re)searching who we are, both individually and collectively. It's what we have to do so that what we know about ourselves (our inner lives) can manifest in our outer lives and work as teachers who can truly educate and influence the next generation and beyond about Black lives. But being a Black woman in America may be the greatest song Black women have *never* heard. In the midst of the constant demands on Black life in the US, it's difficult to even catch our breath, hard to sing our redemption songs. Often what we need is quiet, a time to reflect, meditate, and listen to our spirits. In his book *The Sovereignty of Quiet*, Kevin Quashie explores what the concept of quiet could mean to how we think about Black lives and culture. He speaks of how the long struggle for freedom has been a necessarily *public* resistance. As such, Black lives in outward, loud, and public protest has been the character of resistance assigned to Black people. He states that this is the "dominant expectation we have of Black culture."[19] But he also suggests that sometimes when we speak of resistance, Black lives and culture deserve a finer analysis, a "broader picture of the humanity of the people who were enslaved."[20] Most importantly, he argues that a missing piece of our analysis needs to hold a space for quiet and for what quiet provides as a way to see reflections of the inner lives of Black people, our spirits: "Quiet is a metaphor for the full range of one's inner life—one's desires, ambitions, hungers, vulnerabilities, fears. . . . It has its own sovereignty. It is hard to see, even harder to describe, but no less potent in its ineffability. Quiet."[21] Quashie goes on to suggest that quiet, as an aesthetic, is not incompatible with Black culture. But in order to notice it, we need a shift—a (re)search—into how we read and understand what we see and feel, what we look for, what we expect. That is what (re)search requires and that is what our time in Ghana provided: a searching again not only from the connected space of the US and Ghana but, equally important, at a *distance* from the US.

For many Black American people in our history, such distance was a way to survive and to nurture one's spirit and one's consciousness. In his arresting book *Giovanni's Room*, James Baldwin conjured the concept of merciful distance in speaking of his own Black consciousness and the need for the distance that his personhood required. He described this distance as necessary, as a way to be in solidarity with and respectful of revolutions in Black consciousness in the 1960s but done at a distance that allowed for quiet, for living in a particular kind of freedom as a Black gay man. And Baldwin lived most of his adult life at a merciful distance from the US, not only in Paris but in places like Istanbul, the United Kingdom, and Germany. We see this same merciful distance in the life of amazing visual artist and sculptor Elizabeth Catlett, a Black woman who gave up her US citizenship and lived in Mexico at a merciful distance from the constant harassment of the US government. Merciful distance was also a part of the long and productive lives of Dr. W. E. B. Du Bois and Shirley Graham Du Bois, who emigrated to Ghana to work on the multi-volume *Encyclopedia Africana* and other projects of (re)membering Africa and her diaspora. This concept of merciful distance is also useful in thinking about what Ghana provided for Black women teachers over the years: a spiritual space of revolutionary quiet where we could (re)member who we are from the inside out and (re)member who we are from our rightful beginnings. This was the hope and the homeplace that was often uttered in class, a place where we could feel secure in the sometimes difficult knowing that our (re)membering required and, at the same time, embraced by abundant love and care. It was this merciful distance that we hoped, as Black American women, would allow us, as poet nayyirah waheed wrote in 2014, to be "held and set free at the same time."[22] Ghana was *that place*. It was that place to be quiet with our minds, bodies, and spirits as Black women at a merciful distance from what we "knew" in order to be able to see visions of what we *could* know more fully.

# CHAPTER 3

# THE EVIDENCE OF THINGS UNSEEN

## *(Re)visioning*

*Through [her] life, Africa is once more reinvested with worth, the continent is no longer fractured from human history but restored to consciousness with valid meaning. Through the healing of one of Africa's lost daughters, a scattered people are made whole again, and the question "What is your nation?" is no longer a bewildering and devastating mystery.*

—Abena Busia, "What Is Your Nation"[1]

Sometimes a bus ride is not a bus ride but a portal that can transport you to places you had never imagined. Such was an afternoon in December, as our group traveled from the Ashanti Region capital of Kumasi on the long journey to Cape Coast. I always request that we take this journey in silence, in sacred memory of those enslaved Africans who traveled this exact same path through the bush some four-hundred-plus years ago, barefoot, near naked, and shackled. We traveled in silence in memory of those who had possibly traveled hundreds of miles from wherever they had been brutally captured to the place where we were traveling, joining the long march of Black people to places they did not know. We moved in silence in memory of the fathers, mothers, sisters, brothers, aunties, uncles, and children who perished along the way. We traveled in memory of and bearing witness to those who survived these horrible degradations so that we could be alive and sit in our air-conditioned bus on that day.

In our silent travel, some of us reflected with our eyes closed, listening through our headphones to whatever musical inspiration we had chosen to accompany our journey. Some of us slept, much needed rest behind the jet lag of our arrival two days prior and the lullaby of the engine of the bus. Others intently read one of the highly recommended books from our course, *Homegoing*, a 2016 novel by Yaa Gyasi. This stunning text echoed in fiction some of the exact places in Ghana that we were experiencing in the Ghana Study Abroad in Education program. Captivated by our own inner worlds and wrestling with our unsettled spirits, some of us simply watched the scenery go by and tried to imagine what that journey must have been like for our ancestors. Such witnessing was heavy, a mix of deep respect and incredible humility for their strength, courage, and will to live.

Unbeknownst to me, this bus ride would be different from any I'd ever taken before on study abroad trips. As usual, I heeded the advice I had given the participants just moments before: "Allow yourself to feel and experience *everything*," I said. "Be open to whatever Ghana is trying to tell you." As is often the case on this memorial bus ride, I put on my headphones and closed my eyes. I was listening to Jonathan Butler, a South African musician, sing about God's grace, about the need to lift the Creator's name on high. I realized in that moment that our travel on the path of our ancestors was itself worthy of being "lifted on high." As many of the Black women teachers across the years had mentioned, we were being blessed to bear witness to the very long and treacherous journey taken by our ancestors as captive human beings. In fact, this journey was the beginning of *our* journey as a people in diaspora, the journey of people who became African American.

Eyes closed, I let my mind wander, trying to imagine that walk of the ancestors. How frightened they must have been, not knowing why they had been so brutally kidnapped from their families and where they were being so inhumanely made to walk. It was as if time stood still in those moments, as if past, present, and future were one connected moment. Yes, my body could feel the bus moving me along, even with my eyes closed. But I was also "seeing" in my mind's eye. I saw a funeral procession of hundreds of Ghanaians in bright red and black cloth adorned with adinkra symbols, beautiful Black women with silky black scarves worn only during times of mourning. Some of the older men wore traditional black cloth, some of the younger brothers donned bright red soccer jerseys. I was moving with them, even as I didn't know consciously how that movement was happening. I could feel my tears, warm and wet, running unabated down my cheeks, as Jonathan Butler's words sang in my ears: "You are worthy of my praise." "Yes, you are," I replied, possibly out loud. Then, in gratitude, I quietly repeated: "Kind ancestors, you are worthy of my praise." And even as I felt these moments of mourning, I could also see that women are still working. There is a woman in black with taga nuts on her head. She comes by the window, calling for us to buy. Two men ride by on an aboboya filled to the rim with freshly cut firewood. The one with the machete in his hand smiles at me, as this story runs in my head and touches my heart too. I see coconut trees and big plantain plants, their beautiful fronds and big leaves waving in the breeze like gigantic fans. Then, I spot in the distance one of my favorite trees in Ghana. It's called the tree of life. Like the baobab, it is a treasured tree in Ghana, given its wide sweeping branches that provide abundant shade and a necessary place to gather for moments of cool respite from the scorching sun. In my vision, my head turns and my eyes now face the other side of the road. There is a young Ghanaian sister, using both hands to turn freshly harvested cocoa beans on a woven mat so that they might dry evenly in the sun. Eyes still closed, I see myself looking out farther on the horizon past the sister. Something is moving. Squinting, I catch my breath: the movement in the bush is a long line of Black people, shackled at the necks, hands, and ankles, trudging along, heads bowed, spirits too. My eyes shoot open and I am more than a little shaken. I immediately grab my journal to write it all down.

Clearly, there were not enslaved Africans on that horizon. However, I share this story to illustrate a larger point. When one (re)members, one will have experiences with time, space, and spirit that are different from anything else one may have previously experienced, a new way of imagining and seeing life that does not move you further from it but instead moves you more deeply into its possibilities. That was definitely the case for us, as Black women teachers in Ghana. Kwame Onwuachi in his memoir *Notes from a Young Black Chef* describes being in the company of his grandfather and other village elders on his very first trip to his heritage homeland of Nigeria. He describes his process of (re)membering this way:

> This was different than anything I had experienced in America. The air, hot and windless, was also heavy with the past. The Igbo had been holding councils like these for thousands of years, gathering for meals like this for thousands of years, living in households like this for thousands of years. The past connected to the present without a rupture, without a seam, with no distinct lines between then and now.[2]

We have all had experiences that we cannot explain, the moments of déjà vu that make us tilt our heads a bit, sometimes in wonder or reflection, other times in disbelief. This is the work of our spirit. Most of us have also had moments of great clarity, helped by our visions or dreams of people who have mattered to us, long passed on to the other side, and who appear to us again. Again, this is the work of our spirit. While one can literally have these experiences wherever one is on the planet, *it's our attention to those moments of (re)membering and the lessons they bring that are important to teachers' lives.* What being in Ghana provided for Black women teachers is the time, space, and support for imagining and creating new visions of ourselves and Black people without the ruptures and breaks that usually mark our learning (and teaching) of the story of Black people. This learning is not solely about African Americans but a fuller story of Black people. You heard some of these fragments in the previous chapter, in the ways Black people in diaspora are always seeking and gathering bits and pieces of our stories—and the ways that those stories never, ever felt whole. Too often our stories of Black life and legacy start on the shores of the Americas as enslaved people. Truncated in this way, these stories rarely embody the beauty and struggle and joy and love of Black people's lives that we ourselves heard at the knee of our parents, their parents, their parents, and their parents. They are stories that always have us yearning for the rest of the story. Being in Ghana allowed us space to put some of the fragments of ourselves and our stories as Black people back together, a sometimes difficult but often amazing invitation to (re)vision who we are as Black women on our own terms and within our own timelines. It felt a bit like we have the time and space to stitch our story together into a new vision of the beautiful kente that we are. In the words of our esteemed Black feminist scholars, this defining ourselves for ourselves is very important to understanding and being more fully human as Black women, as we live all of the intersections of our social and cultural identities.[3]

While all of the processes of (re)membering require us to look anew both inside and outside of ourselves, (re)visioning very specifically asks that we narrate and articulate an expanded vision of Black peoples and our cultural and heritage knowledges beyond the people, places, and things we have seen in our current life experiences. (Re)visioning is to engage what Oyèrónké Oyěwùmí describes as our *world sense*.[4] In other words, (re)visioning involves an awakening to our senses that includes an awakening to our spirit and spiritual knowledge. It involves and invites us to move beyond what we think we have "known" through our physical senses, beyond what we have only touched, felt, thought, and experienced. (Re)visioning involves attention to the deeper, often more just knowings that Black people have used to survive and thrive for millennia. For Black women teachers in the GSAE, our (re)visioning of what counts as knowledge—and who the holders of knowledge *really* are—included an overt attention to spiritual knowledge, the "evidence of things unseen." This (re)vision included careful attention to what was inside our hearts, to how our hearts were feeling. It involved learning how to *trust* what we felt, intuited, and "just knew" in our spirits as Black women who teach. Developing the ability to trust our spirits, we could let go, break free of the taken-for-granted visions of who we had been. We could set aside familiar definitions of ourselves and of others that may have been comfortable because we were used to them but that no longer fit our expanding spiritual understandings of our selves and our power. (Re)visioning gave credence to alternative realities that, in Ghana, we found were often deeply connected to our incomplete realities in the US. We began to imagine *otherwise*—our lives, our work, ourselves. As Maxine Greene states eloquently in her breathtaking book *Releasing the Imagination: Essays on Education, the Arts, and Social Change*, as we encountered things in and about Ghana that we perceived as new, imagination was critical: "We are called upon to use our imaginations to enter into that world, to discover how it looks and feels from the vantage point of the person whose world it is. That does not mean we approve it or even necessarily appreciate it. It does mean that we extend our experience sufficiently to grasp it as a human possibility."[5]

As Black women teachers in Ghana, we faced the hard work of clearing our minds of the lies, distortions, and untruths of what we had been taught and shown about Africans generally, Ghanaians particularly, and by extension, about who we were as African or Black Americans. As Black women, it was our relationship to what we were seeing all around us in Ghana that told us otherwise every day. In our minds and by our passports, we were all Black women who were US-born nationals. As such, what we were seeing in Ghana wasn't what we were accustomed to seeing in the US. But what we also struggled with was that it was not what we had expected, not what we had been told it was either! The following are representative of the rather distorted and sometimes stereotypical visions and perspectives that began our (re)visions, visions that, for Black women from the US, were captured in our responses to what "surprised" us upon our arrival in Ghana:

> "I was surprised with the amount of cars on the road. There is so much traffic, yet still so many people walking. The last thing that surprised me were the people on the side and in the street actually selling items." (Jacqueline)

> "I was shocked by how much construction there is and also how many tall buildings there are." (Olivia)

> "I was surprised by the advertising. I'm surprised by how the Black women are in the ads—almost all have straight hair, and

there were a ton of advertisements for hair products that gave the illusion that their use would turn a Ghanaian woman into a newer, better version of herself. I guess it's just surprising because African Americans had to fight against this for so long. I guess I had a romanticized view of how this would be on the continent." (Denice)

"As our group set off in the tour bus, we immediately hit traffic, there was so much congestion that it felt like we were right in the middle of New York City. There were so many cars, nice cars on the road. The media's portrayal of Africa and African people were wrong, well at least in this area. My preconceived notions of what I expected Africa to look like were misguided." (Jacqueline)

As we talked each day we realized the very problematic nature of the education we had received and that served as the foundations of our own teaching. We came to see that the white supremacist education and societal and cultural norms that we carried from the US got in our way as Black women in Ghana as we attempted to make sense of what we were seeing, who Black people were in this place, how Black life mattered here. In conversations on the bus, in meetings, at cultural and education sites, we realized how white supremacy and racist schooling contexts in the US had quite thoroughly done their work of dehumanizing Black women: white supremacy had perpetrated its stories of our origins, origins we now had come face-to-face with in Ghana and could viscerally feel as lies. The hardest part was realizing that, to varying degrees, we had learned and taken up many of these lies as Black American women as well. But we were also increasingly clear about the fact that these lies and lessons of anti-Blackness had not served us well. What was so frightening was that we realized that in accommodating to and often tacitly accepting the white supremacy and anti-Blackness that typified our own schooling experiences, we were also carrying in our bodies, minds, and spirits the *expectation* of pain, as Black women. In other words, we had come to see pain—whether in the form of racism, sexism, homophobia, etc., as part and parcel of what it meant to be Black women in the

US, what it meant to be ourselves. We believed through generations and generations of Black women's experiences that, as Zora Neale Hurston describes in *Their Eyes Were Watching God*, Black women were the "mules of the world."[6] But the contradictions with what we were seeing and experiencing in Ghana were simply too great, as we watched Ghanaian women move about their everyday lives. We saw women doing the backbreaking work of gathering water for the day's washing and walking miles back to their homes or villages, or working over a hot fire stirring kenkey or banku in big black pots with a long wooden paddle. We saw Black women brilliantly teaching in schools, often in classes of thirty to forty children, sometimes with one of the schoolchildren, one who needed to be close to her, swaddled on her back as she taught the others. We saw Black women serving as Supreme Court judges, electoral officials, nurses, doctors, women chiefs, queen mothers, and broadcasters on the evening news. And in all of these various places and roles where Black Ghanaian women lived their lives and did their work, we realized we had rarely seen a whole country of Black women doing "all the things!" There was a dignity in the work that showed up in their straight backs and their collective support of the other Black women gathered around them. It was rare to see a Ghanaian woman alone. She was always surrounded by other women (and a few men) who were Black and proud, even amidst the harsh economic conditions that represent everyday life in Ghana. Built into the very fabric of the country is the fact that her life exists in *community*. It is guided by the concept of Ubuntu, which is deeply grounded in community as a philosophy: *I am because you are.* While modernization and the push for globalism are also shifting this philosophy in Ghana's cultural milieu, we could still feel it strongly in the cool glasses of water we were offered whenever we visited someone's home or place of business or in the ways we were always cared for. But being in Ghana still had us wrestling with tensions in our minds, bodies, and spirits, given the disproportionate lack of economic opportunities, lack of access to education and healthcare there, and the relative privilege of our everyday working-, middle-, and upper-class realities that our international study abroad represented. I often navigate these many tensions through meditation and writing. And as an endarkened feminist scholar, writing itself is a meditative practice that often yields texts like the one below. While I wrote this as a way to better understand the tensions I wrestled with in one of my earliest trips to Ghana in the mid-1990s, it serves here as testimonial and tribute to our collective wrestling with these tensions as Black American women in the GSAE.

> *Resting*
> How can I rest,
> *As an African of the world,*
> *When the world so close around me*
> *Is working so hard?*
> *This is the question*
> *I ask myself every day here in Ghana:*
> *How can I rest?*
> How can I rest
> *When request after request*
> *Touch my heart so deeply.*
> *"Madam, please can you help me?"*
> *I want to weep—and do so often.*
> How can I rest
> *As I look out from my modest but cozy*
> *Air-conditioned room,*
> *To the village outside my window*
> *And see school-aged children*
> *Who have never stepped foot*
> *Inside a school?*
> How can I rest
> *When the call to wake each morning*
> *Is the sound of a man with a machete*
> *Cutting the grass or*
> *The swish, swish of a broom,*
> *A sister readying the home for the day?*
> How can I rest

*When I know*
*That the young man who cleans my room each day*
*Earns for his six-day work week about*
*$15 per month, from which*
*he has expenses to pay just like I do?*
How can I rest
*When I know that part of the reason*
*For the struggle of my Ghanaian brothers and sisters*
*Is intimately tied to the economic hardship and*
*Material desire created by the likes of CNN*
*And perpetrated by the country in which I have an address?*
How can I rest
*As a sister passes me on the street,*
*Balancing heavy aluminum pans*
*Full of fish*
*On her head,*
*A child tied to her back*
*And another one holding her hand?*
And it is this very sister, Lord
*Her back so straight,*
*Her strength so apparent*
*That has been sent*
*As the answer to my question.*
*I can rest in knowing that in every situation,*
*I too can find balance,*
*I can rest because I know*
*That I am not*
*my sister or brother's keeper,*
*I am in fact my sister or brother,*
*Each of us responsible,*
*for what we do with our circumstances,*
*Your gifts.*
*I can rest in identifying,*
*not with malice*
*But joyously*

*with those who are suffering around me,*
*I can rest in the love*
*That is the wave of the sister's hand,*
*And the sister's smile from under the pan on her head,*
*I can rest in the love*
*Of a life of service*
*And gratitude for the divinity of Your hand,*
*Knowing that each soul*
*Will have to give its own account*
*For itself.*

Ghana was the context where we could start to unlearn the detrimental lessons of our education about how Africa wasn't a part of us. We could (re)member who we really were as part of the larger African story in diaspora. We had to face our preconceived notions and stereotypes about Africa generally and Ghana particularly, part of what we carried (even unknowingly) within our minds, bodies, and spirits. As Black women teachers who have grown, learned, and now teach in racially integrated schools in the US, I shared a few examples in the previous chapter that illustrated the reason why Black women, in very conscious ways, chose to (re)search Black identity and culture and, thus, selected the GSAE program: consciously choosing to study abroad in a Black country was an important step in our personal and professional understanding as Black women teachers, to our healing as Black women, and ultimately to healing education.[7] But while we could understand in our minds where our ideas about Ghana may have come from, we ultimately had to face the fact that we had carried these distorted visions of Ghana in our souls and spirits. Increasingly, these old visions felt like a pair of pants that we may have been able to wear at one time in our lives but now didn't fit. Yes, we could keep them, but they were of no real use as functional garments. And if we were to leave our house fully clothed, we would need a new pair of pants that actually fit us. We had to be open and willing to physically and spiritually challenge our own misinformation, lack of knowledge, low expectations, and images of Ghana that we'd been fed through our education and socialization in order to "see" the origin of the beauty and brilliance of Blackness that was taken away from African shores—and that their relations were never supposed to see or experience. That was the work of our (re)visioning. It was about trying to understand our own identities in a Black context that was both different and hauntingly similar to what we already knew. In other words, even if we didn't fully know how, we could see ourselves as Black women in relation to and with Blackness in Ghana.

Interestingly, this shift in perspective and vision usually began even before arriving on the ground in Ghana, very particularly as we gathered at JFK airport for our flight to Ghana. As one teacher shared, her personal view as a Black woman was shifted simply by being in the racial majority of passengers on the plane, a predominately Black presence she had never experienced: "[It was] on the connector flight from JFK in New York to Accra, Ghana, that I realized I was no longer the 'minority.'" Another teacher, Olivia, shared how important that flight was in relation to the known and unknown nature of the experience she was yet to have in Ghana:

> The first thing that inspired me was when the Black flight attendant said to lift the shade and look out the window at the beautiful Mother Africa. I received this overwhelming and unexplained feeling of be-longingness, one I have never gotten when traveling anywhere else. Those words, this feeling inspires me to use this opportunity to do something great, even if that great thing is solely becoming a better, more humble person.

The flight itself gave participants a chance to imagine Blackness as prevalent, numerically powerful, and beautiful. More importantly it gave us all the chance to imagine and see, at that moment, that as Black women, we were part of a larger Black reality. For those who had grown up and been prepared as teachers in educational settings where Black women were considered and referred to as "minorities," being in the racial majority was an important experience. Seeing and feeling ourselves as Black women amongst Black people globally allowed us to begin to challenge another idea that many had lived and learned in the US—that Black people are a "minority" at all! On that plane, on the ground in Ghana, on this earth as Black people, we are the majority of people in the world. Having the opportunity to experience Black identity globally was the beginning of our (re)visioning.

## GHANA AS A SPIRITUAL CONTEXT

I have written previously about the ways that Ghana has been a continual space of what W. E. B. Du Bois called our spiritual strivings.[8] For me, that striving embraces the yearning for my work and life as an educator to be as much a spiritual pursuit as it is an intellectual one. This has not necessarily been spiritual striving guided by religion or dogma experienced in churches or other organized religious settings. Instead this is spiritual striving toward a deeper sense of our minds, bodies, and spirits as Black women. Now, it might show up as a calling or a feeling, a notice or maybe even a whisper. But what we could hear, see, and intuit in Ghana was central to opening a way for shifts in our visions of Black life and pathways for being more closely aligned with our spirits. Again, I am suggesting that Black women's spirituality is wrapped up in the ways that we consciously connect and are connected to an energy larger than ourselves, one that both sustains and guides our lives. While our spirituality emerges from our collective experiences as Black American women, in diaspora, it is also connected and informed by Africa, whether we are conscious of it or not. I lean on Akasha Hull, who suggests that our spirituality is not simply tied to religion, although it may be deeply informed by it.[9] She suggests that our spirituality brings together three interlocking dimensions from which we enact and engage our lives: (1) a strong political and social awareness, (2) a spiritual consciousness that may bring together religious traditions as well as traditional ancestral practices, and (3) an enhanced creativity and ability to imagine. Ghana provided a context for us to explore all of these as we (re)visioned our connections to that place, as we learned to (re)member the things we had learned to forget about ourselves, and especially about our spirits.

## EVERYDAY SPIRITUALITY IN GHANA

When we think about spirituality and its relationship to education, we often substitute religion or religious practices for spirituality. I am arguing here not against religion but for a spirituality that is more expansive than religion, that allows and supports the integration, inclusion, and understanding of aspects of life that affirm our humanity and provide guidance and wisdom. This was one of the most profound (re)memberings for Black women teachers, as we engaged and discussed our learnings in Ghana; that our spirituality, as African people, is quite literally woven into the fabric of our everyday lives. According to a number of African-centered scholars, there is no separation of spirituality from Black people's everyday existence.[10] In fact, spirituality is a central element of the cosmology of African people and is the way that African people order the world, wherever we might find ourselves. According to Dona Marimba Richards, spirituality is not a rationalistic concept that can be measured, explained, or reduced to neat conceptual categories.[11] Instead, as Iyanla Vanzant suggests, it is "the truth of who we are at the core of our being, . . . the consciously active means by which we can recognize, activate, and live the impartial, nonjudgmental, consistent *truth* of who we are."[12] Thinking back on Stuart Hall's ideas from chapter 2, which suggest that African people create Africa again and again wherever we find ourselves, I am also suggesting that spirituality exists inside Black women teachers in *everything* that we are and everything that we do. Coming to this realization was central to our (re)visioning, as our spirituality is the truth of who we are as human beings and who we are as Black women teachers, regardless of our involvement with organized religions.

However, those religions did matter in our spiritual lives as Black women teachers, especially as we saw familiar iterations of those religions in Ghana. A bit about the religious contexts in Ghana might be important here. Islam and Christianity are the primary organized religions, having arrived in the place now known as Ghana in the tenth and fifteenth centuries, respectively. Both religions were well established through early trade in goods by Africans across the continent of Africa and later by the exploitation of Africans by Europeans. Both religions are also ever present in everyday life in Ghana and deeply rooted in the culture of the country today. Our GSAE Black women teachers very quickly (and often unexpectedly) witnessed religious practices, sacred sites, and cultural ways of being in Ghana that were familiar to their own understandings of a spiritual life and similarities in their practice that often mirrored the central place of spirituality in their everyday lives as Black people in the United States. Here are just some of those similarities: (1) the strong regard and honored ways of (re)membering familial ancestors; (2) the deep sorrow of memorial practices that are central to the ways we honor our dead as Black Americans, especially in wake-keeping in Ghana, which does the same sacred, memorializing work as the wake in the US and throughout the diaspora; (3) the ways that GSAE participants were requested and even expected to ask for divine favor, guidance, and care through prayers by our bus driver, in school ceremonies, and at formal dinners; and (4) the centrality of immense joy (and cuttin' up) in gatherings of intergenerational families, made up of kin people by blood, by deed, and by name with no distinction between them. These are but a few examples.

What became an important contrast in Ghana was where, when, and how these spiritual practices showed up as we traveled. Across the years of GSAE, all of the Black women teachers who participated were either practicing Christians or grew up in various Christian denominations including the African Methodist Episcopal (AME), Baptist, Church of God in Christ, Presbyterian, and other evangelical religious spaces. But what was also true? In Ghana, there was a syncretism between spirit and life that was largely absent in our lives in the US, especially in our professional lives within educational institutions. The strong demarcations between church and state as Black women educators in the US also served to further fragment us from the very powerful tools that Black people have used for millennia to survive and to thrive. But in Ghana, it was the lack of separation between the spiritual and physical world and the ease with which life flowed between them that became a productive space for figuring out how our spirituality mattered to us, to our lives as educators, and how it might matter to the lives of the students we teach.

### BEYOND RELIGION: WHEN THE ANCESTORS SHOW UP

Blink. Blink. Pause.

That was the response on the face of Olivia, an undergraduate public relations major at the university, when I asked her to talk to me about her spirituality. Most often, across the years and GSAE participants, when our discussions explicitly turned to spirituality, there was some version of the same: a very pregnant pause for most, a hesitant pause for some. Blink. Blink. Pause. It seemed as if any talk of spirituality was to be hushed if we were also talking about education, especially if we were on the university campus. It was as if the word "spirituality" itself could conjure something both sacred and clandestine, especially as an educator. I specifically chose Olivia to explicate the process of (re)visioning, as she was one of the few undergraduate Black women who was studying in a major outside of education. She was also one of the few Black women across the years who did not grow up affiliated with any organized religion.

So it was not surprising that Olivia began expressing her distaste for all of the religious references that we immediately saw when we landed in Ghana. For example, on the back of nearly every taxi are Christian references, verses, and declarations in bold letters that might include sayings like "In God's Favor," "The Lord Provides," or "Gye Nyame" (Except God). A small kiosk or shipping container that serves as a neighborhood barbershop might have a signboard that exclaims "No Weapon Formed Against Me Barber Shop." And the overwhelming presence of Jesus portrayed as a white man—on billboards, in Ghanaian homes, in infomercials on television—raised strong negative emotions for many of the Black women teachers.

But for Olivia, the overt portrayals of white Jesus that she was seeing all around her as we traveled the country were incongruent with her understandings of and desires for her own spirituality: "I didn't grow up religious but have always believed in a higher power. In the southern United States, religion is ingrained. I have traveled from Costa Rica to Ghana. And in every place, Christianity is a tool of manipulation. Seeing that white Jesus really bothers me. And I'm in Africa seeing that." Interestingly, she contrasts this version of spirituality (i.e., the racist depictions of Jesus) with a very different experience of spirituality in the Cape Coast slave dungeon. As we stood on the sacred ground of the dungeons that once held the bodies of our enslaved African ancestors, a Ghanaian traditional priest prayed and poured libations to Nana Tabo, a large gray rock considered a sacred god to the Fante people of Cape Coast. Prior to the invasion of Europeans, the Fante of Cape Coast had for millennia prayed to Nana as an intermediary God to Nyame, the Almighty God. Nyame is rendered similarly to the ways God is portrayed in Christianity. Scholars believe this synchronicity is why Christianity so easily took hold in Ghana and other parts of Africa; the belief in a Supreme God was a belief that Africans *already* held, a deep spiritual relationship that existed long before the arrival of Christian missionaries and colonizers.[13] The Cape Coast dungeon was built in various stages and through multiple takeovers by the Danish, the Dutch, and finally by the British. Before ground was broken to build the dungeon, Nana Tabo was moved to the center of Cape Coast. Once the transatlantic slave trade was abolished, the townspeople brought Nana Tabo back and created the shrine in the bowels of the dungeon that visitors see when they tour and experience the dungeon. And for Olivia, the organic and traditional practice of spirituality engaged by the priest at that shrine felt right to her, as he spoke in the local language of Fante, prayed for us, and poured libations to the ancestors. She stated, "In the dungeon, we saw prayer in a different way. The priest prayed to the ancestors and prayed for us too. It became closer to the way that I pray without religion."

Olivia could see her own spiritual practices in those offered by the priest, an important affirmation of the African roots of her spirituality. She often wondered aloud if she had missed something by not going to church and about how others tended to look at her sideways as if something was wrong with her because she was not "raised in the church." To be able to bear witness to what she does as a Black woman on the other side of the Atlantic Ocean as having roots in African traditional practice lifted, broadened, and affirmed her understandings of herself as a Black woman engaged in a *spiritual* life. This acknowledgment was also rooted in her ability to (re)member the spiritual practices she saw on that day in the dungeons.

However, the majority of the Black women in the GSAE across the years were born and raised in the southern United States. This also meant that nearly all of them had grown up steeped in the religious roots of the Christian Bible Belt and most often in predominately Black church settings. Such was the depth of religious upbringing of Dr. Denice, who had grown up in Baptist and United Methodist denominations and still regularly attended her home church at the time of her sojourn to Ghana. Academically, she had earned her master's degree and was completing a doctoral degree in social studies education, the first PhD in her family. Dr. Denice had an outstanding reputation as a middle school social studies teacher, having taught in the local community for three years. Known by a great number of her students' parents over her years of teaching, she was a determined advocate, especially for Black and Brown students. As a full-time doctoral student at the time of GSAE, she was also being exposed to theories and literature from Black critical and feminist traditions, bodies of literature that were challenging all that she knew about her place in the world as a Black woman and how she envisioned her work as an educator. She was also questioning the theories, structures, and purposes of her Christian religion, both historically and contemporarily. In an interview after the program, we can see her (re)visioning process and how she was creating new ways to think about her spirituality after being, for example, in the Cape Coast slave dungeons. For everyone in the GSAE (and for most Black people from throughout the world who have had the chance to step into the dungeons), they are deeply moving sites of (re)membering. I will share more about the impact of that site in later chapters of this book.

For Dr. Denice, her deep political consciousness as a teacher of history was intertwined with an equally deep spiritual consciousness.

Both were key to seeing connections in Ghana and to (re)visioning her spirituality in a way that more deeply centered Black people. Her resistance to the stories she had been told about our ancestors in the lessons she'd learned in school as a Black woman were palpable:

> When I went to Ghana, I ain't gonna lie. I was wrestling with some questions about Christianity. I am a Black woman from the South. I grew up in the church, right? But the more I learned . . . about whiteness in Christianity and what it had essentially done to African people across the globe, I had all these questions [because] this doesn't make any sense, it doesn't resonate with what I know about Christianity or about Jesus. Then we went to the church above the dungeons [at Cape Coast]. And I came to the understanding that our ancestors knew God in a way that their captors did not. Even though their captors would tell them X, Y, Z about God, they knew better. And that history runs all the way from the continent, all the way through slavery and beyond. . . . So I'm like in awe of them and how they came, how they knew that God wasn't what these people were telling them God was. . . . Ultimately my faith in God was reaffirmed, but my skepticism for whiteness and the fact that it will use any tool including God to oppress people has been sharpened.

During this same interview, she and I had a moment of levity that further demonstrated the way she was (re)visioning, where she began to see the connections between her growing Black feminist consciousness, her Christianity, and what she was coming to know as spiritual practices in Ghana. Our moment began when, during the interview, I opened a bottle of water and took a long, deep drink. Like previously with Olivia, I had just asked her to describe her spirituality. And like Olivia, Dr. Denice's version of blink, blink, pause gave me just enough time to swallow the water before she sort of jumped up in her chair. And it was clear that she was eager to speak:

> Dr. Denice: I know what it is! My spirituality. It's a Black feminist spirituality. That's what I have. It's me attempting to be well so the community can be well.

In my own excitement, I quickly put the bottle on the table and replied:

Dr. D.: To that, I might even pour some on the ground for the ancestors.

Dr. Denice: But Dr. D., this is not just libations—it's rooted in connection, in community, in us as Black women.

Another crucial element of (re)visioning a spiritual life beyond religion for these Black women educators in the GSAE was the important and continuous (re)cognition of the ancestors in every element of Black life in Ghana. Our biggest realization? That the ancestors we witnessed Ghanaian brothers and sisters calling on and honoring in Ghana were, in actual fact, our ancestors too. This was revelatory for us as Black women teachers. We were seeing and experiencing the story of our ancestors unfolding right in front of our eyes, past, present, and future. Dr. Denice described this experience of her (re)visioning this way:

> We were able to be there. Being on the ground in Ghana and being able to make connections that a Black American can't make without being on the ground. There are things about us as Black Americans that we know and feel Black people do, but we don't know *why* we do them. Putting my feet on the ground allowed me to make connections with the ancestors because sometimes Black Americans can write ourselves off because we don't know the roots of some of those things that we do. Knowing that we are connected to our African-ness makes me want to hold dear to those things.

## WHO AM I, BLACK WOMAN?

One of my favorite films of all times is the adaptation of Alice Walker's *The Color Purple*. But there was something about being in the third row to see the theatrical adaptation of the novel that had me up nearly all night after the performance, unable to sleep until I ordered the recording of the music from the Broadway production I'd just seen. The experience of seeing *The Color Purple* in live theatre was an embodied one for me. I felt every emotion, from sorrow to elation; my soul and spirit were so deeply touched. I wanted to (re)member that feeling and that story, a complex look at everyday rural Black life and relationships that are playful, even magical. At the same time, Black life and relationships in the story were also haunting, painful, and certainly complicated. In the play, Celie's sister, Nettie, travels with a pastor and his family to Africa as missionaries. This is the same pastor to whom Celie's children (who had been taken away from her at childbirth by her slave owners) had been given in secret by Celie's father in order to save their lives. In the song "African Homeland," Nettie sings of arriving on the African continent as a Black woman who'd grown up in the United States, the child of Black sharecroppers. The first line of the song perfectly captures the (re)visioning that was happening for the Black women teachers in the GSAE program, especially as we began to engage more deeply with schools, children and teachers, and Ghanaian people more broadly. *It was like Black seeing Black for the first time.* In the second part of that same song, Celie sings of the tragic lack of access and opportunity for Black people in the United States in the early to mid-1900s. But this was exactly what Black women teachers in the GSAE were experiencing over one hundred years later, overwhelmed by what we had not learned about Black people and our stories, coupled with what we were experiencing in Ghana in our minds, bodies, and spirits as loss, as sorrow. Nettie sings of how everything Black children in schools are taught about themselves could fit in a thimble. How, as she stepped on the African continent, the little bit that she did know about Black history and culture didn't resemble and was totally disconnected from the pride, the culture, and the historical knowing and being that she could see and feel through the people there. *It was like Black seeing Black for the first time* was a perfect description of what we were experiencing in everything around us, within us.

Here we were: *Black* women amongst Black people on the continent of Africa. *Black* women who could so clearly see the lies told to us about Black ingenuity, Black governance, and the depth and breadth of Black education in this place called Ghana. *Black* women whose hearts were breaking for our African ancestors, their enslavement, and their long walk to the coast of Ghana. *Black* women wrestling with our religious upbringings and their connection to the suffering we were seeing. *Black* women who realized that, while we have "richer" material and economic conditions in our everyday lives as citizens of the US and in our classrooms as teachers there, we might be the ones who were in fact "missin somethin. Somethin so important."[14]

How does one make sense of these awakenings as Black women, our (re)visions of ourselves and others that were happening in real time in our bodies, minds, and spirits? Maybe the clearest answer to that question is another question, related specifically to our identities as Black American women: *Who am I as a Black American woman in this place called Ghana?* For these participants, seeing and being with other Black women—both those who were part of the GSAE group and Ghanaian women with whom we met and shared precious time and space—was absolutely key to how we made sense of what we were seeing and how we were (re)visioning ourselves and our lives as Black women. These ways included, for the first time, seeing Black people beyond the paltriness that had been our education as Black women in diaspora. Seeing images and roles of powerful Black women was central to how we as Black women (re)visioned, developing more deeply our senses about the history of Black American people in relation with our brothers and sisters in Ghana. This (re)visioning amongst Black women educators was also the process of "endarkening" the vision of who we were as Black women.[15] In other words, our insights and encounters with Blackness and Black women, particularly while in Ghana, allowed us to articulate how reality is known when based against the Black backdrop of the historical roots and lives of Black women on the continent of Africa and alongside our known histories as Black *American* women. That powerful (re)vision presented new possibilities for us.

## TO BE A BLACK WOMAN WITH ROOTS AND ROUTES

(Re)visioning requires a shift in consciousness, the capacity to ask new questions as one reflects on all that is being experienced in the now, in place and space. As Maxine Greene suggests: "Human consciousness, moreover, is always situated; and the situated person, inevitably engaged with others, reaches out and grasps the phenomena surrounding him/her from a particular vantage point and against a particular background consciousness."[16] She goes on to say that consciousness is always partial, always changing, as human beings gather bits and pieces of new information and new realities. Maybe most importantly, she suggests that within the notion of consciousness lies a strong sense of vision, the ability "to look at things *as if they could be otherwise*."[17]

As Black women in the American context, we have historically been denied the opportunity for such self-consciousness to develop within our formal education. We have existed in what Du Bois so accurately described as double consciousness, "a world which yields [the African American] no true self consciousness but only lets [her] see [her]self through the revelation of the other world."[18] In Ghana, we continually experienced Du Bois's notion of double consciousness as we attempted to move with respect and grace as Black women. But we were also trying to answer the question that Du Bois asked so eloquently in his essay titled "On Our Spiritual Strivings": "As I face Africa, I ask myself: What is it between us that constitutes a tie that I can *feel* better than I can explain?"[19] In Ghana, we were Black women coming face-to-face not with another world that was white (as we were deeply accustomed to in our default position in the United States). For most of us, it was the first time in our lives that another world was *Black* and African. Intellectually, culturally, spiritually, we were coming face-to-face with Ghanaian consciousness and culture, a continental African space of understanding, identity, and knowledge that did not emerge from a space of striving, limitation, or yearning. This is not to suggest that white supremacy, capitalism, white standards of beauty, and Western culture had somehow skipped over Ghana. In nearly twenty-five years of regularly being in the country, I find the distortions that make anti-Blackness familiar to us as Black Americans are also slowly creeping into Ghanaian culture as well, as the country opens its doors wider and invites "development" in. What I am suggesting here is that, despite these shifts in the Ghanaian cultural context, the consciousness we were developing as Black American women came from engagement with a place and a people who had deep roots and an overwhelming richness in the meanings and abundance of history that we could *feel* in the present. Our collective identities as Black American women now rested in (and wrestled with) a social and cultural context where we were not defined (at least in the same way) as the "problem."[20] We did not feel the weight of being those who were always "measuring one's soul by the tape of the world that looks on in amused contempt and pity."[21] Instead, the meanings of our Black American woman identities had come to meet Ghanaian consciousness which required us to deeply interrogate what we meant when we called ourselves African (American) or Black or Black American. And being in Ghanaian schools and communities together with other Black women was fertile ground for that pursuit.

Being seen by Black women in Ghana as being *of* Africa was a key part of this process of (re)visioning. It provided affirmation and the spiritual ground for us to begin to imagine and explicitly (re)vise our identities as Black women as also being connected to and of a common African cultural identity. As Janet, an English education doctoral student at the time and former high school English teacher, shared:

> I think overall, if you were to say that there's a thing for me that has impacted me about identity, it's about this idea that as African Americans, we are African. And we're African in our movements, in our speech, and how we interact in spaces with each other. Let me think, there are so many! I would say that when we went to the last school in Mpeasem . . . interacting with the mothers there was very powerful for me in the sense that, it was almost as if I was at home [in the US] interacting with

mothers. And, they encouraged us to move, they would yell out in joy about how we danced. It was almost as if they could identify us as being African, too, because there's just certain things that our bodies do [pause], that people try their whole lives to try to emulate, I believe. So when they would yell out "Aye!" real loud, it was what we do when we're with our own families. So that has been really helpful in shaping my identity. I see it. Yeah.

What is important here is that, prior to arriving in Ghana, we had every expectation that we would be perceived as strangers in Ghana, given our own education that offered few identity or cultural connections between ourselves as Black American women and Ghanaians, particularly Ghanaian women. But even before we traveled, as we read, discussed, and critically studied, we could feel those connections. As we talked of what we wanted this experience to be for us, we described (often through rivers of tears) a deep longing for a place where as Black women we would be seen and loved just as we are. And the (re)visioning that we hear in Janet's words above came through directly *experiencing* the connected and cultural space between herself and Ghanaian children, mothers, and teachers. Similarly, after a demonstration and field experience in Bonwire, a small village well known for kente weaving in Ghana, Jacqueline shares:

Here, I understood that it was not just the children that gave titles but the adults too. "Sister, let me show you." One man gently took my hand and brought me to his station. And he showed me how he weaves as he taught me. The technique is incredible and they have to be so meticulous, precise, and agile to make these beautiful pieces in such a timely manner. As I took off my shoes, the weaver placed my toes in the handmade loom. The process required a plethora of hand-eye-coordination as well as multitasking, involving your feet and hands. It was hard and he encouraged me. . . . My inability to master his craft [made me] quickly get off the machine to purchase many pieces of this magnificent cloth.

Seeing ourselves as a sister, a mother, or an auntie to people we met in Ghana and to "other people's children" was especially important in our (re)visioning as Black women.[22] Such (re)membering literally allowed us to *see* ourselves bigger, filling out our identities and roles as Black women in ways familiar and different. But regardless of our encounters, our circle of Black family continued to grow in Ghana, allowing us to see ourselves in the eyes of a sister, a brother, an uncle, and an auntie there. It was an echo of Tom Feelings's stunning illustrations and Kwame Dawes's beautiful words in the children's book *I Saw Your Face*.[23] As he articulates in his drawings, ours was a spiritual connection of Blackness and relation, as we saw a mirror of the family and relations we knew and loved in the US reflected in the faces and hearts of Ghanaians we were meeting on a continent over ten thousand miles from where we had grown up:

> *I saw your face in Benin*
> *And in Ghana near Takoradi*
> *Then there on the plains of Bahia*
> *Your gentle eyes said hi*[24]

Olivia echoes these words in a moment of (re)visioning the nature of relationship and how she felt as a Black woman in a marketplace in Ghana: "There was this seller, a young brother selling. He just gave me a bag, looked me straight in the eye, and said, 'Because you're my sister.' He helped me to reshape my story that day. He was my brother too. That brought me back to my power as a sister, that power before we were colonized."

In Ghana, we began to see ourselves more clearly as Black women, with expanded possibilities in our roles and identities, possibilities that could be valued not only while in Ghana but in our roles as educators in the US as well. For example, each student in the program was required to do a small-scale inquiry during their time in Ghana. Interestingly for Jacqueline, her self-selected topic was about the role of mothers in Ghanaian culture and their influence on the role of teachers. Specifically, her goal was to "assess the different roles that students give adult [women] in their lives . . . and how these specific roles change or alter the way that the teacher teaches." Part of the power of Jacqueline's (re)vision of herself had to do with the ways that Ghanaian women entrusted their children to other women that included her, as a Black American woman. We were visiting a school designed for abused, neglected, and abandoned children and were present on the last day of school before the Christmas holiday. Given the day before the holiday, the majority of our time was spent playing with the young primary-age children. Jacqueline described her experience with the various identities that the children gave her:

> We got the chance to interact and play with kindergarteners during their recess time. As soon as we started walking toward the playground, children's laughter echoed as we watched a myriad of children running toward the playground all smiling from ear to ear! At that moment I realized these children just looked "normal" [her hands gesturing quotes], playing and having fun, not orphans with ripped dirty clothing, pot bellies, and sunken cheeks from lack of food that is so heavily portrayed in commercials in the US. I loved seeing the excitement in their eyes playing with us. I remember racing with huge groups of children, dodging children. All of us running so fast and crashing into the fence. "And the winner is . . . EVERYONE!!!" After playing so hard in the scorching heat I heard, "Mommy, Mommy. I need some water." I heard one child say it, then five, then ten, all calling me mommy. A mother's job is to provide the basic needs (food, water, shelter) for her children. The mother is such a strong and respected role in Ghanaian culture. I felt a huge sense of honor given the role of "mommy" because it is held in such high regard. And I am not even one yet! But maybe I am?

Just as Jacqueline experienced, I found that in the school I established in the village of Mpeasem, and in most schools around the world, children quite explicitly tell you who they need you to be. And if we listen carefully (and all of these Black women teachers were keen listeners), Black children in the US also tell us what they need, as in Dr.

Denice's reflections on her teaching experiences with Black American middle school students:

> In teaching middle school, I jumped right in and became a part of people's lives in community. Most of the teachers in my school including me were not from Collegetown. . . . I am essentially like an outsider, right? I told them "I'm not from here but I'm about to teach y'all." I don't know if it's just my nature or if it's what Black women teachers especially do. We just love on em. And like on the third day of school, kids were calling me auntie or mama just like here [in Ghana].

In response to that last line, she often joked with other teachers in her school about "not being old enough to be their mother." But Dr. Denice also began to see the ways that being a Black teacher in the US was not the same as being a Black teacher in Ghana, especially as it related to mothers and their presence in the lives of the school and community. In her dissertation study on the ways Black teachers prepared their Black students for racism they would inevitably face in the US cultural context, Dr. Denice found herself needing to reflect on her past experiences as a teacher in order to establish meaning and direction in the study and to make sense of the work of mothers that she was seeing all around her in Ghana. She clearly understood the very problematic ways that schools in the US rarely provide the cultural and spiritual supports or structures for Black and Brown children and their teachers to engage in education in culturally relevant ways. However, given what she was witnessing in Ghana, she could also begin to see the ways that US schools were also not only anti-Black but *anti-spiritual* in their lack of attention to the fundamental place of mothers in the communal and collective community for Black children in the US. She says:

> So US schools operate as if like the nuclear family is the one structure that should exist and support students equally, even though most students don't live in such families. It seems to me that Ghanaians figured that out a long time ago that it takes a lot of people to support our kids and help them get to where they need to be. But our systems aren't set

up that way. But in every school we've seen in Ghana—from SOS to your school to Montessori—every time we went, we also saw parents there. We saw mothers there. Multiple people in that room along with the students and the teachers that children could go to. There seemed a clear relationship that the school had with parents and mothers as well.

The (re)visioning for US teachers in schools in Ghana was based in experiencing that the spirit of schools—from the teachers, to the culture, to the languages, to the presence of parents and community members—was not only racially Black but *culturally* Black. More profoundly, we could see that whatever it meant for schools to be a part of a community, it included a focus on spirit and spirituality where neither was separated out or set aside in the curriculum, pedagogies, or ways of being in the school. In Ghana, there was an inherent understanding and consequent behavior that as humans, "we" were not in control; it was the collective spirit of the community that served as leader and guide for everyone in the community, showing up explicitly in the shared rituals and prayers, in the culture, and in the songs and language. Related to parents and children, Sobonfu Somé says, "To create a community . . . there is a need to look carefully at some of the fundamentals of a healthy community—spirit, children, elders, responsibility, gift-giving, accountability, ancestors, and ritual. These elements form the base of a community. And it doesn't have to start with a lot of people."[25] She also speaks about how this is so important in the care and development of our children: "When you have a child, for instance, it's not just your child, it's the child of the community. From birth onward, the mother is not the only one who is responsible for a child. Anybody else can feed and nurture the child. . . . And it's perfectly all right."[26] Somé echoes what Dr. Denice said earlier, about the inherent need for a village or community to be the foundation for Black and Brown children and those who love them: "Giving a child a broader sense of community helps her not to rely on one person. Then the child can go to the person of her choice and if that person cannot fix her problem, she can go to someone else. . . . So in raising children, we will definitely need the support of other people."[27]

Patricia Hill Collins refers to this work of foregrounding community survival, empowerment, and caring identity as *motherwork*, the collective effort to create and maintain family life in the face of forces that might undermine the integrity of the family or community:

> Motherwork . . . softens the dichotomies in feminist theorizing about motherhood that posit rigid distinctions . . . between family and work, the individual and the collective, identity as individual autonomy and identity growing from a collective self-determination of one's group. . . . "Work for the day to come" is motherwork, whether it is on behalf of one's own biological children, children of one's racial or ethnic community, or children who are yet unborn.[28]

So what we were seeing and experiencing in Ghana—and what many of us experience as we teach all children, but very particularly Black children, and as we work to survive and thrive in US public institutions—is a kind of motherwork. Motherwork in the spirit of Black women who love and teach Black children is what animates our village and provides nourishment for our teaching, politics, spiritual consciousness, creativity, and ultimately our lives. Yes, we are always responsible for our children's lives and spirits, but in Ghana, we experienced that responsibility beyond the rhetorical way the phrase is used in the US: it really *does* take a whole village to raise a child, including our mothers, other caretakers, and our elders. And it takes a whole village to educate them too.

## TO CREATE A VILLAGE THAT LOVES THE SPIRIT OF BLACK CHILDREN

The meaning of community and spirituality and their relation to school was under constant and continuous (re)vision in Ghana. We could see how profound it was to fundamentally ground education in humanizing ways and place that at the center of teaching, learning, and living for Ghanaian children. And the focus on children's inherent competence, the value of love and collective caretaking and the natural centering of culturally relevant and sustained teaching was what awaited children in classrooms in Ghana. And their parents and their community were *always* present. It was all love in the village.

The way that life in Ghana is structured around village and community was not new to us as Black American women. Many of us had grown up in tight family and extended family circles that were our villages, particularly those who had grown up in rural settings in the US. But there was something about seeing the freedom of Black children and families in the context of the village community that was a sight to behold. I will try to paint a portrait of what school in a village community in Ghana looks like, using my own Cynthia B. Dillard International School as an example. It is truly a labor of love familiar to me and to the Black women teachers who have visited this school over the years through our study abroad program.

Our school is located in the village of Mpeasem, in the Central Region of Ghana, to the west of the historic town of Elmina. What you see when you enter the grounds of our school is the spirit of Black children who feel *full* of themselves, whose spirits have never been separated from the cultural ways of being for Black people. Children who can call generations of their ancestors while standing on the land of the birth of those ancestors and their own. Children who have language that connects and embodies the meanings they wish to convey to the ancestors and to others, that flows like water from them. Sometimes when I speak with my children in Mpeasem in the only language I know well (and which they are learning in school, along with French and written Fante), I feel a strong combination of guilt and sorrow as I (re)cognize the deep sense of loss of my heritage language, wherever it lives on the African continent. So learning English? It is additive in our school and does not and will not serve as a substitute for children's home language. From the body of the Akan languages in Ghana, Fante rings out boldly in classrooms at our school: in songs, dances, games, and in the ways that teachers check for meaning and understanding of the foreign languages of English and French in their daily lessons. That language from home is also present as the school connects and affirms the spiritual lives of the children, their teachers, and their community. Fante is embodied with everyone's spiritual understanding of the world. God—whether in the form of Allah, Nyame, or a Christian God—comes right up into the school with them and is celebrated as part and parcel of *everything* they are. The children learn to understand science in relation to ancestors and the uni(one)verse, an echo of the lessons they learn from their farming grandparents and their teachers. They pray for strength and wisdom as they begin and end their days, in multiple ways and to multiple versions of deity or divine energy, without confusion or strife. They (re)member the moral lessons of the proverbs that undergird the Ghanaian symbolic language of adinkra that has been a foundational part of Ghanaian literacy practices and discourse for millennia. They celebrate through indigenous (and contemporary) foods, songs, dance, music, and forms of speaking. As a visitor to our school, "you are invited" is what the children will say to you (and what every visitor says they *feel*), whether through a child's hand that lovingly grabs yours to show you the way to their school and its practices, or in the invitation to eat right alongside them from the same bowl. *I am because you are.* I understand my world by understanding and inviting you and yours into mine.

These children (like all children) will lead us. But what the Black women teachers talked about after having visited several schools in Ghana was the need for schools and teachers to be spiritually ready for Black children. To teach in ways that are worthy of them *requires* that their teachers examine our own inner lives, those places in our hearts where we may harbor mischaracterizations and misunderstandings of the spirit and power of Black children. This examination invariably raised fundamental questions as we unpacked and examined our spirits as teachers, (re)visioning how we might be more willing, able, and ready for the invitations that Black children are giving us every day in the US. We were humbled by a question that puzzled us as we went to school after school in Ghana, seeing joyous spaces of education where Black children and community were inextricably woven together: *How might we create similar educational spaces relevant to the spirit of Black children and communities in the US?* Having grown up in the racially divided United States of America, I was certainly more ignorant than I should have been about the length and breadth of global Black life when I first started traveling to Ghana nearly three decades ago and sometimes even today. Growing up in the US, I had been forcibly socialized and separated (sometimes by my own will) from African ways of knowing and being. As Black Americans we often do not understand, see, or feel that Africa is a part of us—and we a part *of* her. Like everyone in our group, I too learned in school that my people began in slavery on the US side of the waters. But what physically being in Ghana let us know is a profound truth: *as enslaved persons in the new world is not where we began.* Our story as Black women had an origin, a root and a route. What the children in the school in Mpeasem taught us (and Ghanaian knowledges and cultural ways taught us more broadly) is that African children and people on the continent can still mostly see Black Americans as African people. Yes, we are seen differently, sometimes problematically, given the ways that global capitalism has positioned us one to another. But in time spent together, we experienced something much more relational and more loving, the company of our brothers and sisters. Let us be (re)minded: four-hundred-plus years and scores of oppressions on both sides of the water is a lot to unlearn and a long context within which to (re)member beyond the lies we have been told and that we have learned. But the bottom line is that African or Black Americans are still a part of a Pan-African community, unbounded by temporal or physical limits. Africans belong to the African community, even when not residing in a predominately African town or community.[29] In the ways we were invited in and took up our invitations as Black women teachers, we *belonged* to Mpeasem. We could see ourselves as Black women teachers in the spirit of the village of Mpeasem, in this homeplace that Ghana had become for us.

(Re)visioning for these teachers in Ghana was about being a student of the spirit of Black community of which children are central. It was also about being a student of the length and breadth of Black history from the continent of Africa through its diaspora. We were connecting the unfamiliar in Ghana (whether language, traditions, or other cultural ways of knowing) to our US communities, communities that were becoming more expansive and generative in the process, given a deeper understanding of the connections across the African or Black world. I bore witness to Black women educators from the US being fully present in sites of Black trauma in the slave dungeons in Ghana, and in sites of great joy like the classrooms of our school. In both places, their sense of connection and meaning of Black identity and spirit became understandable when their bodies, minds, and spirits were placed in context of a long line of African people, starting at its root. The ties between our cultural and racial understandings as *African* Americans and the conditions of our brothers and sisters on the continent of Africa became both clearer and stronger in our interactions with Ghanaian ways of knowing and being and became the basis upon which we could see our spiritual connections and responsibilities as educators as well. Through this process of honoring the spirit of Black children on both sides of the water, we ultimately embodied the spirit of Ubuntu by (re)membering our *own* spirits, histories, and ways of being as a collective part of the African family. What my scholarship and experiences in Ghana have taught me is that it is the attention to the spirit that has supported and affirmed (and continues to support and affirm) culturally relevant and sustaining practices in educational spaces with Black children and their teachers. In other words, educators must be well enough to (re)member who they are from the inside out as a central part of the ability to engage in meaningful ways with what cultural relevant and sustaining practices *require*. This also demands a new sense of what schools can be. As teachers of Black children, the education we need comes not from the often anemic educational experiences that we receive as Black women students in the US but from experiences that allow us to (re)imagine and (re)vision what's possible as Black women teachers.

That brings me back to Olivia. Her words and her story (re)mind me of the power of seeing spirituality and community embodied in Ghanaian teachers and the possibilities of seeing a (re)vision of what a Black woman teacher can be. She says: "I realized how powerful education can be! How important the village is. It can affirm, transform, and must empower young people. Seeing Black teachers of all stripes who did not fit molds of 'educator' was so important to me. They were competitive and silly. Some were very young leaders. And they were often Black women like me." As previously mentioned, Olivia was one of the few non-education majors across the years of the GSAE program. Her words of (re)visioning are a foreshadowing of major shifts to come in her own life and work:

> Umm, okay, so unlike a lot of other people on this trip, I have never really worked in a classroom before, and, I'm not an education major. But what I've learned is that teaching doesn't have to necessarily mean always being in a classroom. You can be a teacher and be a role model. You can be a teacher by just walking right. So, the most impact that I've had is being able to—when my friends back home ask me, "Well how was your trip?" and I'm able to tell them you know, how I was empowered and what I've learned, that's being a teacher without being in a classroom. So, that's what empowers me.

Olivia graduated from the university with a degree in public relations in 2014 and returned to New York City, where she was born and raised. But her time in Ghana quite literally (re)vised her entire career path. Upon (re)turning to New York, she actually took a job as a teacher in a new charter high school:

> I think that if we could get to the place where school is in the kids' culture and the teachers who educate our kids who created the culture would teach it, that would be amazing. If we teach from a strength-based perspective in the way I saw in Ghana? The opportunities for our kids would be endless. It was so important for me to be able to see Black identity in other spaces where it was not racist, so ingrained in everything we do. And to see someone who looks like you in various positions was very powerful. I don't know why it was so transformational for me, but it was. Like to see the president of Ghana be Black but also look in the streets and see people. . . . To talk about experiences with others. Also it was like unlearning a lot of the things that I thought were true for Africa. . . . It was really transformational. . . . So thank you. I don't think that if I went to Ghana, I would have been an educator honestly.

Seeing anew, (re)visioning in Ghana, was so profound that it led Olivia to choose an entirely different profession! Instead of public relations, she chose to commit herself to the lives of Black and Brown students when she (re)turned to the US after GSAE. And she has served as a teacher at a charter high school for six years, recently accepting a leadership position as the school's academic dean. In our interview seven years after her GSAE experience, I could hardly believe how deeply Olivia had committed to ways of imagining her *whole* self: as a Black woman who is deeply engaged and spiritually conscious and as a teacher, leader, and mentor for young Black and Brown girls at her school. There was no blink, blink, pause when we spoke of the place of spirituality in her everyday life and work. Olivia, her back straight in her chair, looked regal in a simple black tank, hair pulled up into a top knot the morning of our interview over Zoom. She wasn't wearing any makeup and was simply radiant, defying what most of us might look like on a Saturday morning. Midway through our conversation, I asked the same question I'd asked before: How do you describe your spirituality? This time there was no blink, blink, pause. With confidence that belied her young age, she looked directly into my eyes and said: "I can now speak things into existence. If my heart is good and pure, I can manifest things in my life. And that's what I teach my girls. Now [in this new position as academic dean], I lead from a place of 'I can do anything I want to do' as long as it's in service to the higher power or in service to others, which is the higher power essentially. That's kinda how I've been leading my life [since Ghana]."

Black children will benefit from that kind of conjuring, the kind of deep reflection and lessons engaged by Black women teachers that draw on the strength of our spirits and the length of Black life. These are the lessons that give new meaning to spirit, to self, to work that arises from the origins of Africa and brings those lessons to a life of building in community.

CHAPTER 4

# A CHANGE OF MIND AND HEART

## (Re)cognizing

*The smell was unbearable. In the corner a woman was crying so hard that it seemed her bones would break from her convulsions. . . . Esi had been in the women's dungeon of the Cape Coast Castle for two weeks. She spent her 15th birthday there. On her fourteenth birthday, she was in the heart of Asanteland, in her father's compound. . . . When she wanted to forget the Castle, she thought of those things, but she did not expect joy. Hell was a place of remembering, each beautiful moment passed through the mind's eye until it fell to the ground like a rotten mango, perfectly useless, uselessly perfect.*

—Yaa Gyasi, *Homegoing*[1]

*I know that they are not gone, but have merely entered a different phase of life. I know this because I hear their voices. Voices that advise me, that forewarn me, that embrace me. They are always with me.*

—Fleda Mask Jackson, *My Soul Is a Witness*[2]

Being in Ghana provided time and space for Black women teachers to (re)member who we were and who we could become. It was an experience that gave us precious and sacred time and space to engage in a (re)search for the heritage knowledge and origins of Black people's stories from the continent to the diaspora. Time and space to better understand how encounters with Ghana helped us to imagine Black womanhood in different but connected ways to our diasporic lives. These processes of (re)membering are processes of becoming aware of the spiritual nature of Black life, especially in relation to the education of Black children and community. And these processes provided the opportunity to (re)vise our lives and embrace our spirits as guiding energies within and outside of our lives as Black women educators.

When I think about my own schooling experience as a young Black American, one of my fondest and most culturally relevant experiences was as a member of my high school debate team. Unlike in most of my classes, debate allowed the rare opportunity for me to choose authors I wanted to read and engage with. This was critical for me as a debater who focused mostly on the category of expository speaking. In order to be convincing in expository, I had to be able to passionately conjure the spirit of the original speaker or writer. As might be expected, I chose legendary Black women like Sojourner Truth, Ntozake Shange, and Maya Angelou whose words quite literally gave me life in the all-white spaces of my schooling. I recently (re)watched the film *The Great Debaters*, based on the true story of the all-Black Wiley College team's brilliant debate strategies and success against the Harvard University team in the 1930s. Denzel Washington plays Mr. Melvin Tolson, the Wiley debate coach. In one scene, Mr. Tolson's lesson is about the Willie Lynch letter, a now infamous text that described the ways that the enslavement of Black people was maintained by white slave owners by "keeping the Black body strong and taking the Black mind." But Mr. Tolson's lesson was also an admonishment of the ways that one of his students was not taking his debate studies seriously, not *honoring* the genius that he was. Embedded in his scolding of the debater, he also spoke of how his central commitment and purpose as a debate coach was intimately tied to their success as his students and as Black people. This purpose and commitment is fundamental to many Black educators today, a covenant embodied in the words that Mr. Tolson poignantly shared with his truculent student: "*I and every other professor on this campus are here to help you to find, take back, and keep your righteous minds.*"

(Re)cognizing is a similar pursuit: the work of "finding," "taking back," and "keeping" one's righteous mind. In Ghana, our process of (re)cognizing was about Black women teachers changing our minds and thinking *again* about who Black people *really* are. It was about thinking *again* of the incredible feats that Black people have accomplished across time and space at great risk to our lives and liberties. It was thinking *again* about the intellectual, cultural, and social brilliance of Black people from the African continent to the diaspora and back again. (Re)cognizing was manifest not only as a change of mind in a cognitive way but as a change of heart or feelings as well, as illustrated in the spiritual need for righteous minds that Mr. Tolson shared with his student. Key to (re)cognizing is understanding again how, as Black women teachers, we *already* know. We already have within us a righteous and just knowing, especially in our work as teachers of Black students, our children. The stories of (re)cognizing in this chapter are the ways that Ghana (re)minded us—made us think *again*—about who we were as Black women, with freedom on our minds and in our hearts. (Re)cognizing is embodied work that helps us fill in the gaps in Black cultural and heritage knowledge that were quite deliberately omitted from our educational experiences as Black women. And (re)cognizing is also about seeing these lessons manifest in our being and our behavior. As my father used to say, it is to *know* better so we can do and be better. However tentative, when one begins to (re)cognize, one also begins to be and exist in line with that knowing.

In our time in Ghana, one of the most profound experiences of (re)cognition over the years has often happened when we encountered the slave dungeons. There are over thirty-two forts and dungeons along the coast of Ghana alone. Many were used solely as forts; some, however, were used as dungeons for enslaved African people and today are often referred to as castles (as in the opening quote of this chapter). But believing that names and accurate naming is important, I refer to them as dungeons. This was especially important in explicitly centering Blackness and Black identity in the Ghana Study Abroad in Education program, especially since we would have the opportunity to be in these sites of Black trauma while in Ghana. We needed to call them by their true names.

Learning about the dungeons that held enslaved African people—
our ancestors—began as we read and engaged in our pre-trip class
sessions with Maya Angelou's stunning memoir of her time spent in
Ghana, *All God's Children Need Traveling Shoes*. I selected this text for
the GSAE for several reasons. The first is that, in Angelou's (re)count-
ing her own time living in Ghana with her son, we came to know
something about the country through the eyes of a Black American
woman. Second, Dr. Angelou provided us a particular point of view
of the first country in Africa on the cusp of freeing itself from British colonial rule in 1957. Third, throughout the book, Dr. Angelou
introduces us to the steady stream of Black Americans who were
visiting, living, and learning from Ghana, often at the invitation of
then-soon-to-be president of the independent African country, Osa-
gyefo Dr. Kwame Nkrumah. This stream of Black American sisters
and brothers was a roll call of esteemed civil rights leaders, intellec-
tuals and others: Muhammad Ali (then Cassius Clay), W. E. B. Du
Bois and Shirley Graham Du Bois (both of whom were by that time
permanently residing in Ghana and served as the sort of informal
welcome committee for those visiting from the African diaspora), the
Reverend Dr. Martin Luther King Jr., Malcolm X, and others. Their
visits around the time of Ghana's independence from colonial rule
provided insight into what our study abroad experience might also be
like as Black Americans (re)turning to Ghana. Finally, *All God's Children* provided a useful metaphor to ponder throughout our journey:
that of traveling shoes. One of the many meanings that was shared
about this metaphor was that traveling shoes are *necessary* for Black
people because, as one educator suggested, "they let us know where
we've been and where we are going." I still carry her words foremost
in my mind and heart, having heard this message on repeat from participants across the years of GSAE.

On the night before our visit to the Cape Coast slave dungeon, I
often provide a brief (re)minder to educators that we will be going
to the dungeons the next day. Given the slipperiness of the grounds
there, I advise them to put on walking shoes (versus sandals or other
open-toe shoes) in preparation. "Think of these as your traveling

shoes," I often say to them. "You are going to *need* them." But in my spirit, I am also (re)minded *why* I say this, aside from their personal safety. It is an echo of what brilliant poet Nikky Finney suggests in her book *Head Off and Split*: I already *know* that every step we take in those dungeons will be "from the breath of the dead to the hands of the living."[3] And this living will not be easy.

To (re)cognize our spiritual and material connections in the dungeons was *healing* work. I have said in other writings that healing methods for Black people are always situated, sacred, and spiritual, and arise from indigenous and endarkened healing traditions.[4] I lean into the brilliance of Asa Hilliard who spoke of African Indigenous teachers like us as being "selfless healer[s], intent on inspiring, transforming, and propelling students to a higher spiritual level."[5] To (re)member the spirit of Indigenous Black thought and being, I have suggested further that there are three engagements that are critical to "endarkening" and healing both teacher and taught:

1. A person must be drawn into and be present in a spiritual homeplace.
2. A person must be engaged with/in the rituals, people, places in intimate, authentic (and humble) ways.
3. A person must be open to being transformed by all that is encountered and recognize those encounters as purposeful and expansive, as healing methodologies.[6]

In other words, returning to a sacred place like the Cape Coast dungeons—a place implicated in our complex relationships as African or Black Americans past, present, and future—had the possibility to both center the spirit and to shift the epistemological and cultural location of our thought and action in the world as Black people. From a spiritual perspective, we were engaged in a pilgrimage that was simultaneously sacred, secular, and spiritual.[7] As Ghanaian writer Abena Busia describes in her analysis of Paule Marshall's landmark book *Praisesong for the Widow*, we engaged our journey "in the same active process of recognizing and reassembling cultural signs of a past littered along our roads of doubtful progress. The challenge therefore is not to look at this [journey] as abstraction, but as a concrete aspect of our lives where our meaning—our story—becomes what we can read and what we can no longer, or never could, read about ourselves and others."[8]

As in *Praisesong*, our visitation to the dungeons of our ancestors in Ghana was *not* our journey's "end" as Black Americans: our journey's end in that moment was *Africa*, as we were "symbolically reversing the diasporic journey and recross[ing]" both symbolically and physically, coming *back* through the door of no return in Ghana.[9] This movement in West Africa also necessitated (re)cognizing our positionality in the world (physically, intellectually, and spiritually) and examining the implications, transformations, and healings of our minds, bodies, and spirits that arose through being in that space and place of (re)turn. As we were always in community with other Black women in the GSAE program (meaning that every cohort had multiple Black women participants), these acts also provided a collective healing for Black American women. And our collective hurt, harm, pain, and joy were by necessity (re)cognized in our (re)turn through those doors in Ghana that we were never supposed to (re)turn through. According to scholar Dionne Brand, being at that door of no return was not merely a physical location: it was a *spiritual* location. "It was about healing a rupture of history, a rupture in the quality of being. It was also a physical rupture, a rupture of geography. . . . The place where all names were forgotten and all beginnings recast. In some desolate sense, it was the creation place of Blacks in the New World diaspora at the same time that it signified the end of traceable beginnings."[10]

(Re)cognizing in mind, body, and spirit on the sacred ground where centuries before, and in such violent ways, our ancestors had not voluntarily left these same shores was a powerful place of reckoning for Black American women. It was our creation place.

Our experience was a response to the ancestors calling us. We were answering in a way that our politics, spiritual consciousness, and creativity as Black women teachers were coming face-to-face with the beginnings of who we have become as Africans in diaspora.

The door of no return in the Cape Coast dungeon was our place of reckoning. But as Brand suggests: "No amount of denial, however, dislodged this place, this self, and no amount of forgetting obscured the Door of No Return."[11] We were standing in the place where only God and the land knew the Truth.

## SPIRITUAL RECKONING: (RE)COGNIZING IN THE CAPE COAST DUNGEON

It's hard to know that you have reached the Cape Coast dungeon. It is nestled among kiosks busy with artists and craftspeople selling their goods, and stands in stark contrast to commercial banks and neighboring buildings. Our bus pulled up to a parking space alongside a white wall. At first glance, we were taken aback by the overwhelming scale of the building covering several city blocks. Made of solid stones and cement blocks, this dungeon, like all along the western coast of Africa, was as imposing as it was impenetrable. But even with what we knew had happened there, Cape Coast dungeon was somehow also stunningly beautiful, a majestic building, dazzlingly white against the blue sky and equally blue sea. As we heard the waves crash on the shore, we could feel the tears well up behind our eyes in (re)cognition. We were (re)minded that our ancestors did not see beauty in this place.

After purchasing our tickets, we met our tour guide, a young Ghanaian man named Patrick (a pseudonym). He took us first to an open and airy room on the very top floor of the dungeons that was formerly the market, the room reserved for the auctioning of captured Africans to various slave traders from Holland, England, and from "the New World," as the United States was often nostalgically called. The irony? At the time of our visit, the space was being used as an art gallery, filled with contemporary paintings by a Ghanaian artist. In later conversations, we wrestled with the commercialization of what seemed sacred space and the economic needs of the brother artist to make a living. But this irony added to the heaviness of all of the ironies in that dungeon and what felt to us like a (re)appropriation of memorial space. Along with the brutal Ghana heat, it felt almost debilitating.

In this room, Patrick shared the overall history of the Cape Coast slave dungeon. It was initially built by the Swedish in 1654 as a small fortress, and it exchanged hands several times among competing European nations and their interests. The dungeon was taken over by the British in 1665, who developed it from a fortress into a "castle." It took more than two hundred years of additions and demolitions for this dungeon to be constructed as it stands today (with mostly African labor, of course). Hearing that the dungeon itself was over 350 years old really situated the transatlantic trade and slavery in the Americas as a much more real and protracted historical event for us as Black women. Within the walls of this dungeon, itself a historical site, we could see and feel a different beginning of capitalism and the imperialism that is America. Something about that moment and the depth of reality it provided was "new," deeper, *real* for us in a visceral way.

In our own educational experiences in the US, the study of slavery was a brief and truncated one. As Black women teachers, most of us had learned that our ancestors were slaves brought from Africa to pick cotton and serve white people. None of the pictures we saw in texts included the images we were seeing on this day in the place where we now stood. The sights and feelings swirling around us moved far beyond the sketchy nature of our social studies textbooks and their pitiful and inaccurate depictions of our people. We could feel and see in these moments that slavery in the US and African diaspora was a part of a long stretch of time that involved many people: White men from then "developing" Western nations, African chiefs, some in search of opportunities for their people and others in search of trinkets, drink, and material goods for themselves. The catchers, traders, and ship's crew. Those in charge of the auction blocks. Slavers in what we now call the Caribbean and the Americas. But the bottom line? Slavery remained in place for hundreds of years because it was a profitable business based in the subjugation of Black human beings. And this trade begot us as African American women.

Historically, the Cape Coast dungeon started as a fort for the profitable trade in gold, diamonds, and ivory. But in that space, we learned how the sale of Black human beings was part of a larger, longer capitalistic system that not only forever changed Ghana and other African nations, but that forever *changed the relationship between African people worldwide.* Not only did African kingdoms within and beyond Ghana lose a significant portion of future generations through this barbaric trade, but major companies that continue to reproduce wealth today in the United States have their very history and roots in this brutal economic system.[12] In the dungeon where we stood, we asked ourselves: How could such an ethical and moral line shift in white human beings from selling and trading objects to selling and trading humans who look like us? As a Black person in the dungeons, this question remains from the moment you step onto these grounds. And emotionally, it created feelings beyond pain, feelings that became heavier and heavier as we continued through the tour. It was that feeling that our hearts were breaking wide open, that feeling that brought uncontrollable weeping for some, tears of rage that could not be wept for others, and all of the feelings in between.

These same Europeans who held enslaved Africans in these dungeons came to spread the Gospel, to "civilize" those considered uncivilized. As Black American women, many with roots and personal histories in the Christian church, we wrestled with the complexities and tensions between capitalism, religion, and our spirituality. Throughout the journey, a very troubling relationship between slavery and "spirituality" based in organized religion confronted us. For example, the church that the English built as their place of worship within the Cape Coast dungeon was directly atop the male slave dungeon. Adjacent to the church door was a spy hole. As Europeans went to pray and worship, they could literally both listen to and look down upon enslaved African males in the dungeons below. Even if they could ignore the sound in their ears, couldn't they hear the screams and moans in their hearts? Did they have hearts? What must it have felt like for our ancestors to know that others were profiting off their suffering and pain? What was the condition of the spiritual consciousness of those who existed in the castle, both free and captive? We learned that many of the slave ships had names such as *Jesus, God Is Great,* and *Santa Maria.* And while it was tempting to demonize Europeans engaged in these barbaric atrocities against Black human beings, we tried hard to sit in the complexities, to consider the spiritual nature of their choices, and the spiritual conditions that allowed (and still allows) human slavery to exist. We wrestled with the capacities that humans have to wield such misery and death over others. We considered the place of forgiveness in our (re)membering, particularly given the often multiracial nature of our GSAE groups. These were not easy thoughts, and they were certainly not easy conversations.

Our GSAE groups have been predominately made up of those who identify as women. And as we visited both the male and the female slave dungeons, Black women participants generally described the female dungeons as the place that resonated most strongly with their bodies, minds, and spirits. We entered these dungeons and descended down a slight but dark and uneven incline, grasping at the brick wall for balance, or holding on to others to steady ourselves, both physically and emotionally. As we went from the bright, sunny Ghana day down into this dark, dank place, the very nature of the air changed, became putrid and fetid. Our breathing changed too, often shallow, rapid, and anxious. The longer we were in the female dungeons, the more uneasy we felt. Our bodies and spirits seemed to have minds of their own. My own legs and body shook, uncontrollably. Some felt their stomachs churning or felt faint. In a very small space, over 120 enslaved Black women had been held, Patrick shared. Black women like us, forced to urinate, defecate, vomit, menstruate in the same place where they had to lay their heads to rest. *In the same place where we now stood.* In excavating the floors of the dungeon, the chains and residue of vomit, hair, feces, and blood found on the floor surface were more than eight inches thick in places. *In the same place where we now stood.* We tried to imagine the daily existence for these enslaved women. No. We tried to imagine the daily existence for our *sisters,* the darkness and smells mixing up the past, present, future. When we closed our eyes, we could see our sisters' faces in agony, in this overcrowded and inhumane place, uncertain and not knowing what they had done to deserve this punishment. Some of us could hear their voices wail and moan. Sometimes we realized those voices were also our own. The sheer physicality and the spiritual meshing of time were often overwhelming, beyond the ability to describe them adequately in words. But what we experienced as Black women in various ways was that time and space changed in those dungeons. Where our personhood stopped and our sisters' personhoods began became blurry, unclear to us. Where is that sound coming from? Is that my voice or my sisters' voices who wail and moan here? And at times, the memorial dirge was in fact coming from *our* own bodies, collectively and uncontrollably, a spiritual response, a reflex of memory.

And, there we stood, facing the past in the present as Black women. Living the past of our ancestors in the dungeons, the present of our (re)memberings as "free" Black Americans, and the future of those who will read this story and maybe even make a pilgrimage to the dungeons themselves. As the teller of this story, I find it so difficult to find the right tense to write it in.

Our final visiting place in the dungeons was a location and fixture common to all of the dungeons that dot the western coast of Africa: the door of no return. Patrick shared that once a captured African went through these doors, they lost all contact with Africa. The transatlantic slave trade lasted nearly five hundred years. Five hundred years of captives through this door of no return. The estimate is that over two million enslaved Africans passed through Cape Coast slave dungeon alone, about one-third of whom, after the long journey by foot and in shackles that it took to get to the dungeons, did not survive the inhuman conditions within the dungeons. To really (re)member this number hurts to the soul even as I write and (re)member again. At the door of no return, we could imagine our ancestors as they walked, often crawled through this door, the hard sand and rocks beneath their feet grinding into their knees. Big iron cannons stood facing the sea, looking out over the ocean like huge black binoculars, seemingly watching the waves. How could something so beautiful represent so inhumane a history as the carrying of millions of humans away from their homeland? Patrick, our guide, says that outside the slave dungeons, visitors are met with the beautiful stature of the castle. Yet inside, a very different reality exists. Complexity emerges: beauty on the exterior, yet beneath its layers, fundamental questions of what makes us human. Questions that turn a gaze inward, both to the spirit and to the inner workings of the spirit of human slavery that are often incomprehensible.

## HEARING THE VOICES OF THE ANCESTORS

Enslaved African people were dispersed widely in the slave trade and the making of capitalism and nations that followed. About one-third were taken to South America and Brazil. The West Indies and Caribbean received the second largest number, and North America received the fewest. Standing in the courtyard of the dungeon in Ghana, the African diaspora became deeply understandable and located *inside* us. Prior to this experience, many Black Americans struggle to connect (both consciously and unconsciously) to the African continent, to explore the deeper meanings of the Africanness in our Americanness and our identities as Black people. Slavery, as we were taught (and admittedly, as we have sometimes repeated to our own students as their teachers), was something that happened a long time ago. As we were growing up, it seemed a thin thread of a distant African heritage, mysterious and fuzzy. However, in this moment in the Cape Coast dungeon, we could not only feel our history in our spirits, but we could see and experience this thread as the *foundation* of our very existence. We really were, in fact, part of the African body, throughout the transatlantic world. Through the door of no return, our ancestors were taken with the ancestors of many Africans *from one soil, from one homeland* to many different parts of the world. Whatever doubts concerning our place and relationship to African people globally were dismissed on that day. Here, in the dungeons, our spirits (re)oriented themselves to the world, metaphorically turning those slave ships around. Walking through the door of no return, and then turning around to walk back through the same door of (re)turn, was symbolic of a (re)turn that generations after slavery was *not* supposed to happen. A revolutionary (re)turn. Yes, the name of that door embodied the desires of the slave traders. But nothing can keep a people from their home forever. And even if Black people never step foot on the African continent, Black people still belong to the African family.[13] And family will always be family.

In my first experience at this same dungeon in 1995, I wrote a letter of gratitude to my ancestors that carried the profound new vision of my own work and life as an *African* American woman educator. The sentiment of this piece and the gratitude for the profound experience of (re)cognizing have consistently been shared in the many conversations I've had with Black women teachers after our time in the dungeon and even years later. I share it here.

*Dear and Wonder-Full Ancestors,*

*We come before you on this day,*
*in deep gratitude,*
*to honor you,*
*upon whose underground cells*
*we sit,*
*the sun on our shoulders,*
*free to look out over the blue sea,*
*free to make decisions about our work,*
*our purpose,*
*our bodies and how they will move in the world.*
*We come to you today,*
*grateful for your sacrifices,*
*the lack of liberty and freedom you suffered,*
*the injustices you were dealt,*
*that have enabled us, as Africa's children,*
*to be in this place on this day,*
*to be educated,*
*to be able to work,*
*for the very things that were taken from you.*
*We render ourselves humble*

*for your lives,*
*and we recommit ourselves*
*to the hard work*
*Of justice*
*Of freedom*
*Of the human right*
*to become more fully* human.
*We are reminded today*
*of our privilege, Dear Ones,*
*received only through your*
choice
*to survive.*
*We pledge to our Creator today*
*and to you, our Dear Guides,*
*to continue your work*
Our *work,*
*With renewed vigor,*
*With wonder and awe,*
*With a joyful heart.*
*Ayeeko!*
*Amen.*

## THE PRIVILEGE OF THE STRUGGLE, THE PRIVILEGE OF THE KNOWING

To (re)cognize is to struggle. But it is also to *reckon*, to consider what it means when something is so important that it can't be ignored, when something is so important that it must be taken into account in our bodies, minds, and spirits. In those dungeons in Ghana, we were forced to reckon in our minds and hearts with the various ways that this experience on and with the sacred grounds of the Cape Coast dungeon *mattered* in our lives as Black women educators. But it was also the case that we had to reckon with how it might matter in the lives of our students, in our abilities to tell this connected narrative of Black people that we were (re)membering.

As we sit by the ocean to dialogue after our experience in the dungeon, there is often a sort of hush that falls over the conversation. It is the kind of hush you might experience at a solemn occasion like a funeral or a wake. From my view, it represents a sort of mourning, an exhaustion from the mental, emotional, and spiritual labor of the experience in the dungeon as Black women. In our multiracial cohorts, it is usually the Black women who speak first. Embodied in their words is a deep sense of (re)cognition both painful and profound. As I have listened carefully over the years, their shifts and articulations came from understanding more deeply not only the enormous trauma experienced by our ancestors given the transatlantic slave trade and the diaspora experience, but the pride and the *privilege* of our legacy as Black women. While not mutually exclusive, it is important to tease out the ways that the notion of privilege was shared by this group of educators. But it is also important to understand that (re)cognition of our privilege as Black American women began even before our experiences to the shores of Ghana. But there was something in our embodied experience at the dungeons that made both pride and privilege as Black women much more poignant for us. These salient lessons about pride and privilege as Black women are shared below.

### Lesson 1: In the dungeons and in Ghana, we had the privilege to be *with* our ancestors, to hear their suffering, to feel their presence, and to "*stand* on their shoulders."

There is no way to really prepare for the experience with the dungeons in Ghana and for the ways that our bodies, minds, and spirits engage with and react to the spirit of the space and place. It is unique and different for each person. Having curated this experience for decades at two different universities and as a private retreat leader, I do what I can to create a space for each person to come to their own knowings and to have space for their own emotional and spiritual engagements, regardless of the types or the intensity of those experiences. In our travel on the bus to the dungeons, I share two parameters that are important for participants to keep in mind and heart. The first is to (re)mind them that they are having their *own* very personal and spiritual experience in these dungeons. How they engage, what they feel, the depth of those feelings are theirs to learn from. But

I also encourage them to stay open and aware of their bodies, minds, and spirits. This encouragement is intended to set the stage for the experience to be both sacred and meditative. I request that they not push down or away the feelings or reactions that the body, mind, and spirit are having. In other words, whether "good" or "bad," the work is to (re)cognize all of our feelings or thoughts in a nonjudgmental way and stay or sit with them *all*. Second, I (re)mind participants that everyone will have their experience with and in the dungeons *differently*: in order to respect each other, we must let each other grieve and mourn as we individually need to. Finally, I (re)mind them that as a collective, we will have plenty of time to care for one another on the other side of the dungeon experience. So I request that while each person is having their experience and engagement in the dungeons, that they do not walk up on each other to try to console or ask questions about how the person is feeling or doing, even if the person is crying or having some other emotional response. Respectfully, we simply must allow each other to "be." I assured them that I would keep watch and respond to situations in which any person might be in danger, unsafe, or not well. Over the years, we have encountered a number of emotional and spiritual responses in the dungeons, from uncontrollable shaking, weeping, and moaning to hyperventilation and panic attacks. So I am always aware and prepared to serve as caretaker. But these reactions speak to how powerful the spiritual nature of this sacred memorial space can be, especially for the Black men and women. It is understandable that (re)membering the suffering of our ancestors—our *family*—that happens in that space often brings the most vivid reckoning and reactions.

Grace is a former elementary teacher and a doctoral student. In the past two years, she served as my graduate research assistant. She also had the good fortune to travel to Ghana with two different cohorts of the GSAE. "My first experience in the dungeons was powerful because it was my first time being there," she states. But the experience in her second year in Ghana typified the spiritual connections of the ancestors so often felt by Black women educators, and it serves as an example of the depth of the process of (re)cognizing in both the mind and the spirit an experience that remains with educators years later. In an interview, Grace talked about being in the dungeons. As she begins telling the story, I can see the tears begin to well up in her eyes. "It was just something that happened in that women's dungeon, just entering in there," she says. "It felt like the physical world was just silent. Everything was still. I don't know why (re)calling this experience is super emotional for me, but it was that earthshaking." Those same tears begin to run down her face as she grabs a tissue, wipes her eyes, and continues:

> I was trying not to cry in those dungeons. But just being in Ghana, those tears meant something different too. It was very healing. So being in that women's dungeon, I just felt like everything around me was silent and still and I felt like the spirits of our ancestors, those women, reached up and grabbed my ankles. . . . Their hands were shackled on my ankles and I could not move. I just felt something, their voices, that just said "Sit with us. Just sit with us." And I felt like I mourned with them and I thanked them for their survival. And I had never considered the ancestors like that. Ever. Not ever considered it. Never talked to them. Never thought about them and communed with them like that. And I am because you were, because you survived, because . . . I'm literally here because of you. Thank you! The reverence that I have for Black women, Black people in general, the diaspora in general, but man! The reverence that I have and gained for Black *women*, that kind of changed.

Being in the dungeons was not a metaphorical experience for us as Black American women: we (re)cognized that we were *literally* standing on the flesh, blood, bones, and remains of those who came before us. This gave new meaning to the oft-used phrase that, as Black women, we "stand on the shoulders" of those who go before us. But being there also provided the privilege of changing our minds and hearts about whose "shoulders" we had been referencing when we used that phrase in our daily lives and our teaching. Here were the remains of our ancestors in the Cape Coast dungeon. And we had the *privilege* of engaging body, mind, and spirit with the depth and length of ancestral Black suffering and struggle in those dungeons. But we also had the privilege to bear witness to the strength of our legacy of survival and thriving as Black people. As Black women educators, we (re)cognized a much longer timeline of our legacy as Black people: that legacy now included the voices and stories of ancestors and family whom we "met" in the dungeon on that day and throughout our GSAE experience.

### Lesson 2: In the dungeons and in Ghana, we (re)cognized both the privilege and the spiritual importance of our (re)turn as Black women, only possible *because* of the sacrifices of our ancestors.

I often spoke with Black women in the GSAE program about how powerful it was to be in Ghana. Together we also fully (re)cognized the privilege of the journey, one that many in our own families, friend circles, and communities might never be able to take. This was clearly both an economic and a national privilege as Black women from the US. We also wrestled with the ironies that being in those dungeons also raised for us as spiritual women who will continue to navigate the contours of race, gender, sexualities, and multiple intersections of our identities every day in the US. These wrestlings can be seen in the voice of the now Dr. Janet:

> Being a Black woman of faith from the South who is also American meant that I had to acknowledge the privilege of being American in Ghana. Acknowledge how horrible you feel, what it means for you to be an American. . . . But it is so interesting to get them [white people] to understand like how ironic that is: how Black folks came over [to Ghana] and then how privileged we are when we return, even if we don't have many of the same privileges [as white people]. . . . But that American privilege meant that my folks came over to the US probably from an area much like Ghana, my ancestors did. They left in chains and then I come back, not in chains. I come back here in this freedom or liberation . . . but I still don't have that same freedom in the context of America.

But what if we fully embraced the notion of privilege that Dr. Janet alludes to as Black women? What if we leaned into the idea that we have the privilege of the spirit as we experienced it in the dungeons, a privilege that doesn't just reside in this moment but in all the moments past, in the moments that are to come? Then even in the horror of our ancestors' experiences, we find joy and hope in the fact that the ancestors dreamed and imagined *us*, imagined and maybe even hoped for our (re)turn: that (re)membering gave life to our really being our "ancestors' wildest dreams."

And what if we considered it our privilege to hear them speak and then bear witness to their voices? We might hear something like this, something that I hear in my own heart nearly every time I encounter the dungeons, that sounds something like this: *Children, we know this dehumanization isn't our way as African people. But we will go through this degradation so that you and your children and your children's children who are always our children will survive, even thrive. Because we know that the struggle of Black people has always been about being on our way to something better, right?* What we so very humbly (re)cognized deep down in our souls and in our spirits was that our ancestors thought about us even in the horror they were going through. And we (re)cognized their strength and hope in the privilege of standing on that solemn ground in the dungeons in Ghana.

### Lesson 3: In the dungeons and in Ghana, we had the privilege to see and engage our righteous rage as Black American women.

Imagine trying to reckon with the brutalities against an estimated fifty million Black people, forcibly stripped from our civilization and our families, our homes, languages, and ways of being while standing in the very place of those brutalities? In the place where your ancestors were viciously uprooted from the motherland and taken by slave ships on the agonizing journey across the Atlantic that gave birth to you? We stand in the dungeons that held our people, chained and shackled, ankle to ankle, wrist to wrist, often with "the living and the dead fastened together."[14] I am still often overwhelmed by an incredible and complex set of emotions inside myself when I visit the Cape Coast dungeon or other dungeons like it. But two emotions seem important to name, as they also always rise to the top for Black teachers who study abroad with me in Ghana. Interestingly, in my conversations with Black teachers in US schools, in witnessing the ongoing Black Lives Matter protests in news around the world, and as we interrogate and critique oppressive systems of educating our children, the emotions felt by Black people in the dungeons are also instructive. The first emotion that we often feel deeply as Black women in the dungeons in Ghana is anger, the kind that can be debilitating if left unexamined. The kind that really weighs us down, ties us in knots and contortions so great that we struggle to see humanity clearly, both our own as Black women and the humanity of the descendants of white people who enslaved us. But greater than anger was a second felt emotion: a deep sense of mourning as Black American women, an emptiness that rumbled all up and through our lives. This grief has been something I have only recently been able to name as such. It is a grief born of displacements and dismemberments, echoed in school practices and experiences that ignore our desires as Black people to know the place from where we come and the spirit that animates our being. What we felt and knew in bearing witness in the dungeons was how the sheer brutalization of African people set the stage for continued brutalization through chattel slavery in the "New World" and our continued dehumanization in the ongoing criminalization of Black American men and women through inhumane policing and the prison industrial complex.[15] We felt how the suffering and dehumanization of Black life in those dungeons continues today in the traumatization of Black children in education, the adultification of young Black girls, and the inequitable state of health and social services in the US. It is one thing to read about the root of such evils; it's another to see and feel their beginnings and to allow yourself to mourn, as Dr. Janet recounts:

> What resonated with me [in the dungeons]? The unexcavated floor. Why not use the word holocaust? The brutalization of Black men drinking water from each other's hair. The death of unborn and living children.

It was not only the beginnings of racial trauma but the sickness of white privilege. These spaces were orchestrated, designed to dehumanize and kill. It did exactly what it was designed to do. But what can I do about the design, the sickness that overtakes the mind, that allows us to inflict harm upon others, in the name of God and country? Black folks are used to creating, taking what is evil and doing a remix in a way that is honorable and just to those who have suffered. It makes me think about how cultural appropriation is done with no dignity in the US. But in those dungeons, we had to do something with our minds, to combat the hell we were dealing with. And anything we could do or believe in could mean some type of relief. They even might have listened from below . . . to the Christian hymns above, all with the purpose of trying to get some relief. We took those songs and made them our own.

For Black American women, being in those dungeons was its own trauma, forcing a reckoning that was unlike any other. We were angry at what we were seeing, learning, and (re)membering. But we were also in a sacred space of mourning. As a Black woman educator and as the leader of the group, I carry this anger as well. Fortunately, after a number of years of the GSAE (and the nearly two decades before it), I can now also walk through this space as a pedagogue who has had the privilege of bearing witness to these experiences with my sisters and others as the tremendous gift of (re)membering that it is. Anger is replaced by a kind of healing as I hear their lessons mirrored back to me, like here with Dr. Janet: "What does it mean that you're drawing from what you are experiencing versus drawing from the frustration and the anger? I remember, when we were reflecting, you saying, 'What does it mean *essentially*? What is the meaning you are drawing from the dungeons?' . . . You can get so caught up in the frustration and the anger that you're not drawing and learning from it, right? You block yourself from learning."

The privilege for these Black women in Ghana is in the learning provided through (re)membering. In learning to (re)member that our ancestors resisted, fought, and loved hard, we also (re)membered that the same spirit resides inside us as women of Africa.

**Lesson 4: In the dungeons and in Ghana, we had the privilege to see our resilience as Black people and realize there is nothing that we cannot do or be. We (re)cognized and measured our Black women identities in millennia of resilience and strength. We (re)cognized ourselves as part of the African family, regardless of what we call ourselves.**

Being in the slave dungeon at Cape Coast was a point of demarcation for Black women educators, a sort of proverbial line in the sand. (Re)cognizing was illustrated most powerfully by shifts in language and positionality that demonstrated how (re)membering was, as one participant described, "molecule shifting." And the process of (re)cognizing was also one of the elements of (re)membering that clearly illuminated the racialized nature of the process of (re)membering, an outcome of having been born and raised in the racialized context of the US. What I mean is that (re)cognizing was different for racialized participants in our groups across the years of the study abroad programs. In the case of the Black educators (including myself as director of the program), this process of (re)cognizing or changing our minds and hearts was largely about (re)covering parts of our identities as Black women and making connections to our larger stories and legacies as Black people. As mentioned, the prefix *re-* means "back" or "again." Woven into the very design of the GSAE program was an explicit assumption that there is a cohesive, coherent (albeit dynamic and ever-changing) cultural history of and for Black people from the African continent to her diaspora and sometimes back again. Thus, Black participants' (re)cognizing processes centered on (re)covering pieces of Black identity, stories, and culture for themselves while in Ghana. Using Freire's notions of oppressor and oppressed, a major assumption related to racial and cultural identity here is that the racially and culturally oppressed must seek their *own* stories and endeavor to create identities that are empowering and powerful, often in solidarity with others who have experienced similar oppressions.

This work of (re)cognizing for Black women is deeply embedded in the act of (re)membering what is already inside us that has been pushed down or forgotten, our cultural memories.[16] Tom Feelings suggests that such memories, from a spiritual framework, have the potential to connect those on the continent of Africa to those in the diaspora through the traumatic acts and aftermath of the transatlantic slave trade.[17] This is the first central characteristic of racial and cultural memories for Black people in diaspora: they are memories that acknowledge an ever-present link between the diaspora and the continent, an acknowledgment of a heritage homeplace. Second, racial/cultural memories are intimate. Whether good or bad, they make you want to find out the deeper meanings and matters in your life and in the world. Third, racial/cultural memories change our ways of being (culture) and the nature and ways of our knowing (epistemology) in what we call the present. They are inspirational, breathing new life into the work of teaching, inquiry, and living. They are memories that can transform us, that feed our ability to engage new metaphors and practices in our work.[18]

So the dungeon in Ghana provided a powerful site for such (re)cognizing, for examining the racial and cultural memories that, in some cases, were not conscious or had not been thought or felt before. I'll use Jacqueline's words here to illustrate the beginnings of a shift in her thinking and positionality, her (re)covery. As a Black woman experiencing the dungeons, she quite literally began to see herself as part of the "we" that is connected to Black women ancestors who were strong and resilient, full of humanity and love. These connections became a source of inspiration for her and other Black women educators to stand in their Blackness and woman-ness not only *because* of the ancestors but also *with* them. Below, we see this shift for Jacqueline in the collective "we" that had not been a part of her descriptions of her identity as a Black woman before her encounter with the Cape Coast dungeon:

> Yeah, again, like the slave dungeons. When we went and saw how *we* were treated. I mean, we learned about it but actually being in there and seeing it for ourselves, the inhumane way *we* were treated. There

was barely a window; I couldn't hardly breathe in there. And it was that, but that was the realness for me. . . . And actually being in there, it just put everything in perspective and showed how strong of a people *we* actually are to where *we* made it through that. I'm a descendant of all that.

Or in the words of Olivia, who similarly begins to situate herself within the longer narrative of African history:

In America, again like, we just—coming from, I came from New York, where I went to a charter school in Harlem, and most of the people there were minority students. So, we were taught a lot about Black culture early on, so I knew that I had a history, and I knew I had a culture. But when I moved down to Georgia where I was the only Black child in my class, and the only history that was taught to me was about slavery, it kind of took away from me that sense of history and culture that I once had when I was a child. So, just coming here kind of reminded me—it kind of reminds me of Dr. D.'s book title, *Learning to (Re)member*. It proved that *we* didn't just—our history didn't just happen when *we* walked on the shores of the other side of the Atlantic Ocean, in chains and shackles. That's not where our history started. Our history started in Africa, where *we* were kings and queens and *we* knew how to do things with our hands, and *we* knew how to live off the land. That's where *our* history started, and it's kind of just amazing to have gone and come full circle—come back to the door of no return and return where *my* ancestors were taken from to learn that *we* do have a powerful history.

### Lesson 5: In the dungeons and in Ghana, we had the privilege as Black women teachers to (re)cognize our origin stories, value them, and begin to think about how to both walk and work with them as educators.

Throughout our time in the dungeons and in Ghana more generally, we naturally talked about teaching. About how being in Ghana was a privilege not afforded all Black people in diaspora or Black teachers, but how it *should* be. We spoke in the spirit of such experiences being *necessary* pilgrimages to (re)member the origins of our stories as Black people. There is something very powerful about a people who can (re)member their own stories that feels like our balm in Gilead as a people who have been separated from our origin stories, having heard only those narrated by those with histories of conquest and oppression and disregard for the humanity of those whom they oppressed. Nadia Yala Kisukidi's words in Felwine Sarr's epic book *Afrotopia* help us understand why the (re)cognition of shared and connected heritage and culture matters to the power of a people, in this case to the power of Black women educators:

> It is about creating new critical epistemologies . . . which take into account the situation of utterances of the subjects who were once colonized, dominated not only within the order of pre-constituted forms of knowledge but also within their own open and active tradition. . . . It is found in rethinking historical experiences founded on domination in order to reform them within a shared history; a hope for reciprocal recognition, giving back to everyone their history, culture and dignity.[19]

The privilege of the reciprocal (re)cognition of Black heritage connections in those coastal dungeons was all about what becomes possible when we realize in our bodies, minds, and spirits that we also have the gifts of power, strength, and resilience that allowed our ancestors to survive. It exists inside us too. This was an important lesson that Black women teachers brought back to our students. And this was not just a lesson in history but a lesson about the spirit of Black people. For the Black women teachers in GSAE, this lesson also pointed the way to what our work as educators, gifted with the privilege of this experience, must be, echoed in the brilliant words of Dr. Maya Angelou: "Once you are healed, go out and heal somebody else." Having learned and experienced those dungeons in our minds and hearts, creating experiences for our students that echoed such transformations became a central focus of our teaching work and new guidance for our lives. As a literacy educator, Dr. Janet speaks of the power she felt and knew after her encounters with/in the dungeons. And the spirit of her voice, and the work she planned to do as a result, was an echo of the rest of the Black women on that day and beyond, about the responsibility to share what she has learned with others:

> A lot of my work deals with focusing on the empowerment and really the uplifting and just making sure the people hear the voices of Black girls and women. And I like to do that through writing. And so, when you hear about slave narratives, which is usually how in literature we study slavery is through slave narratives, most of them are written by men. And not to say that there's none out there about women, but very few that I know of. It makes me want to research that idea more, and it makes me want to research what happens when you actually use your voice just to tell your story. And although we were in those slave dungeons, and we were in that female dungeon, you know, that energy and that space had a lot of stories there. And I want to explore what that means now, because in a way, we're—Black women are still in this metaphorical dungeon where you cannot—there's a tension. You can't win for losing. . . . There's a lot of people out there that don't care about Black women, and it shows. So what can I do in my work to make sure that we are talking about standing on the backs, the literal backs of these women. . . . How we can empower Black girls to know who they are. And the thing is, they know who they are. That's the trick. They already know, but it's the point of them understanding that what they know is okay. Because they will be ostracized for being that Black girl, that mean girl, that bitch, that welfare queen, that Jezebel, that ho. I mean it's always that we're pushed into some category that makes us feel bad about every part of ourselves. And it's like how can we really take it back? Just like those Black people outside the door of no return taking care of their families. They took back that piece. How can we take back the struggle of Black women?

This (re)cognition in solidarity and kinship with African heritage and culture had and continues to have profound influence in the lives of these Black women educators. And what animated the lives and work of these teachers shifted in the dungeons on that day and made what my dad said earlier even more powerful for us as Black women teachers: now that we knew better, we had to *do* better.

# CHAPTER 5

# THE TRUTH WILL SET US FREE

## (Re)presenting

*Let us be ourselves now as we define us. We are not a figment of your
imagination or an exotic answer to your desires. We are not some button
on the pocket of your longing. . . . We are the hyphenated people of the
Diaspora whose self-defined identities are no longer shameful secrets in the
countries of our origins, but rather declarations of strength and solidarity.
We are an increasingly united front from which the world has not yet heard.*

—Audre Lorde, *Sister Outsider*[1]

There is a Zimbabwean proverb that prophetically states: *Until the
lion tells [her] side of the story, the tale of the hunt will always glorify the hunter.* This chapter focuses on the process of (re)present-
ing the lioness's story. It focuses on the ways that, as a result of our
experiences in and with Ghana, Black women teachers (re)mem-
bered, literally putting ourselves and our understandings of Black
identities, notions of Black womanhood, and culture back together
and into the world in new and fuller ways. Given the depth of this
(re)membering, our lives and work as Black women teachers also
(re)presented a kind of truth-telling for us, a reckoning with and a
righting of historical wrongs for ourselves, our students, and our
communities. Our (re)presentations embodied what Gloria Anzaldúa
speaks of in AnaLouise Keating's edited volume *Light in the Dark/Luz*

*en lo oscuro: Rewriting Identity, Spirituality, Reality* as a type of spiritual activism. This is an activism that is not only about the need to know the lessons of our heritage stories but also about being and doing better on behalf of Black people as a result of *living* those lessons.

For Black women educators in Ghana, our process of (re)presenting also acted as a praisesong to ourselves as Black women, a letting go of what we had learned and embodied that had harmed us and a picking up of Black womanhood in ways that (re)presented a studied and embodied expansion of our culture and identity as Black women. Praisesongs are traditional types of poems, sung in various locations all over the continent of Africa and beyond. They are ceremonial and social poems, recited or sung at public celebrations such as outdoorings (where the birth of a new baby is celebrated, named, and brought "outdoors" for all to admire), anniversaries, or funerals. Embracing the long stories, rituals, and traditions of a community of people, praisesongs have traditionally been used by Black people on the continent of Africa and her diaspora to celebrate or affirm our triumph over adversity and our bravery and courage both in life and death. Praisesongs can also mark social transition and upward movement culturally, socially, or spiritually. The pertinent question of these praisesongs as forms of (re)presentation for Black women educators in Ghana was this: *How can our experiences and their (re)presentations in and with Ghana act as praisesongs in the world as we (re)turn to our lives and work in the US?* What we came to understand through our time in Ghana is that whether our work as educators was primarily centered in teaching, conducting research, and/ or examining and creating "texts" (whether the research narrative, the lesson plan, the interview transcript, the representational text in publication), our sense of who we are, our identities, our very selves and spirits were seen, understood, (re)cognized, and grounded in our past. They made sense to us *today* based on something that *had* already happened in the long collective memory of Black people. I suggest here that it is from these memories that we can (re)member and better answer the question: "Who am I?" and collectively "Who are we?" by being able to answer the question "Who have I *been*?" This isn't just about being able to (re)cognize times past on a calendar or in a datebook; this is to fundamentally see that our known, unknown, and yet-to-be-known lives as human beings are deeply imbued with meaning based in our memories. W. James Booth, in his stunning book *Communities of Memory: On Witness, Identity and Justice*, suggests that, in order to answer the question of who we were, we have to go deep into the well of memory "to draw a boundary between group members and others; to provide a basis for collective action; and to call attention to life-in-common, a shared history and future. . . . All of these involve claims about identity across time and change, and about identity and responsibility as well. . . . Statement[s] of identity turn out to involve a strong *temporal* dimension."[2] This temporality is also fundamental to an African cosmology, one that is based on understanding one's place, space, and purpose in time through (re)cognition of a common or communal destiny: I am because we are. And as we embraced deeper and deeper memories within ourselves as Black women in Ghana, we (re)membered African knowledges and sensibilities and experienced them as spaces that felt really good to our spirits. We delighted in the shifts and changes that we were experiencing in ourselves, feeling and seeing and experiencing our (re)memberings.

While each day had a plan or a schedule while in Ghana, it was beholden less to what time it was than to what our spirits, minds, and bodies needed and wanted on any given day. We moved *with* time, continually seeing it as the fluid human construct that it was. Time was what had happened, what continued to happen, and our intentionality in honoring "the relationships that linger [there]" in Ghana and beyond.[3] This is one of the major ways that African cosmology constantly challenged our Western conceptions of time, space, and location while in Ghana. In Ghana, time was circular, based in past, present, and future as intricate connective and collective webs of meaning making. As Black American women, we not only felt that circle; we also felt the freedom that the circle opened for us and in us, from the inside out. And when our spirits had space to be more free our bodies and minds became more free, too, especially when it came to how we (re)presented ourselves as Black women who embodied and embraced a growing African aesthetic. And we cultivated and celebrated this freedom. To put it into words, this was a (re)membered aesthetic for the Black women, what bell hooks describes as "an aesthetic of existence, rooted in the idea that no degree of material lack could keep one from learning how to look at the world with a critical eye, how to recognize beauty, or how to use it as a force to enhance inner well-being."[4] We were, in ways that felt new to us as Black American women, (re)membering and inhabiting space in Ghana that helped us to become more beautiful from both the inside out and the outside in.

But writer Rosalind Shaw (re)minds us: "There are other ways of (re)membering the past than by speaking of it."[5] In Ghana, there were all around us sophisticated Ghanaian fashion and style, cultural traditions, and identity markers with long histories, and always full of deep meanings. From African bead traditions to Ghanaian textiles to other styles of African and Ghanaian fashion, we studied their meanings. I focused very particularly on styles, textiles, and adornments that many of us, as Black Americans, might already be a bit familiar with. This was our starting place to explore connections that had traveled full circle in various forms. As scholar Stuart Hall teaches us: Black people go about creating versions of Africa wherever we are in the world.[6] For example, whether to classes in the US or in Ghana, I often wore what is commonly referred to in the US as a dashiki. The roots of this garment were not lost on the Black women educators in the Ghana Study Abroad in Education program, nor on anyone who saw me wearing this particular shirt. It is an unmistakably African cloth. But according to culture writer and journalist Damola Durosomo, the symbolic and aesthetic significance of the dashiki, while it is African, was created thousands of miles *outside* Africa:

> It was those of African descent, whose ancestors were hauled to North America in chains, who carried this torch. The Civil Rights and Black Panther Movements of the 1960s and early 70s gave the dashiki its

political potency. African Americans adopted the article as a means of rejecting Western cultural norms. This is when the dashiki moved beyond style and functionality to become an emblem of Black pride, as illustrative of the beauty of blackness as an afro or a raised fist.[7]

Ironically, Durosomo goes on to suggest that like Pan-Africanism and Rastafarianism, the birth of this garment with a distinctly African aesthetic outside of continental Africa helped shaped some of the fiercest understandings about African identity and the politics of Blackness:

> Many of these outward concepts of African identity adopted by Black Americans were once again reinforced by people on the actual continent. Principles taught by Civil Rights leaders were widely embraced by leaders of African liberation movements, and the revolutionary politics of Malcolm X and the Black Panthers, helped transform Fela Kuti's relaxed highlife into the socially-charged afrobeat that he's lauded for today. This transference of ideas is much less odd than it seems—perhaps such philosophies could have only been nurtured within the context of the Black American and Caribbean experience. The "promised land" could be more clearly envisioned by those savagely removed from its promise, and the dashiki could become something greater than itself when worn by Black folks who were, for hundreds of years, denied the opportunity to embrace anything that represented their African heritage.

Like those of us who wore this shirt in the 1960s and '70s, the dashiki is no less African because its identity was shaped outside of Africa. The dashiki, whether worn in Negril or Accra or Washington, DC, links the continent of Africa and the diaspora, characterized "by a shared assertion of the value of an original Black creation. . . . When a Black person dons a dashiki they are sporting one of the most universally understood interpretations of the phrase 'I'm Black and I'm proud,' without having to utter a word."[8]

So this process of (re)presenting a Black aesthetic for the Black women educators in GSAE was about the ways we understand and embrace an African aesthetic. In Ghana, we often found ourselves first drawn to cloth, clothing, and adornments that we may have seen in the diaspora but that we were now coming to (re)member through (re)cognizing as part of a longer narrative of Black culture, a part of a collective Black heritage. As Black American women in Ghana, we began to put ourselves, our identities, and our understandings of Black affirmation in the world in new and expansive ways. Being in Ghana allowed us to see ourselves and our beauty as Black women differently and to (re)present ourselves in ways that may have been new to us but that have also been a part of an African aesthetic for millennia. This included intentionally choosing African styles of clothing and adornment. Most importantly, there were numerous examples of how we were invited by Ghanaian women, by our spirits, and by being in the place and culture of Ghana to enter into new ways of being and (re)presenting ourselves more expansively as Black American woman teachers in the world. These invitations to be seen fully were crucial to how we (re)membered our selves and thus to greater, truer possibilities of how we could (re)present our selves as well.

### AFRICAN AESTHETIC (RE)PRESENTS A BOLDER VERSION OF ME

One way this (re)presentation showed up was in our physical appearance as Black women teachers in the GSAE. Aside from the occasional accessory like an earring or a bracelet, few Black women in GSAE groups over the years had a well-established or strong African aesthetic that guided their personal appearance. This might be best understood not as an anti-African aesthetic related to apparel or style but instead as something that had been previously unexplored (and often unavailable) for most Black people in the African diaspora. In discussions, we unpacked the ways that we all had simply not explored deeply what was African about us. In some cases, this included needing to unlearn many negative lessons that we had learned as little Black girls about Blackness, from stories of staying out of the sun so as not to become darker, the desirability of good (straight) hair, and the need to cover up and rein in ample hips, full breasts, and thick thighs. As we took in the gorgeousness and confidence surrounding Black women's bodies in Ghana, we were constantly faced with reconciling the negative lessons we had learned with the stunning confidence and bold freedom in Ghanaian women that we were seeing and experiencing as Black American women in Ghana. Those childhood lessons contradicted what we could now see as African about us, arising out of an aesthetic that we were now coming to see and feel as beautiful on its own terms, on our terms as Black women. Now, several of the women over the years had certainly embraced the Black women's natural hair movement that had grown widely in the US. A handful of us rocked locs or short and long Afros. However, except for the occasional African Sunday at church or Africa Day at school or conferences, as general practice, most participants wore Western clothing because that was what was deemed acceptable or professional by our various fields within education, as well as in our families and communities in the US. However, in Ghana, we began to make shifts and take risks in (re)presenting our looks in line with our growing (re)memberings of African heritage, culture, and beauty.

Let's take Jacqueline as an example. From the time we began the program and throughout her time in Ghana, Jacqueline only wore Western clothing. In fact, she was very fond of university logo T-shirts and wore them nearly every day. One of the activities we do in the GSAE is to select beautiful pieces of African cloth from which we have clothing tailored just for us. These pieces of clothing were custom-made for our Black women's bodies and not ready-to-wear, which we had always bought in the States and elsewhere in the world. For most of us, this was our first experience of meeting or being with a tailor, in this case a Ghanaian woman who knew *how* to create outfits designed to fit our bodies and our styles. Jacqueline, in her thoughtful way, carefully selected a very traditional Ghanaian wax print. This cloth would be her outfit for our final formal banquet and was a combination of yellow and blue, with images of eyes printed into the fabric. It was by far more patterned and certainly brighter than anything I had ever seen her wear. On the day of the banquet, there is always much excitement as we all get dressed, showing up and showing out in our custom-made outfits. Fashion models on real runways have nothing on the Black women in every cohort group of the GSAE! We created our own imaginary runways and fashion shows, walked our own red carpets, held our own photo shoots, and served plenty of face for this gala banquet.

Later that evening, as I was organizing last-minute details for the banquet with the restaurant staff, I turned to see Jacqueline walk into the banquet area. She absolutely took my breath away. I swear that her back was straighter too as she walked, stunningly resplendent in her off-the-shoulder long kaba-style dress. She wore a matching head wrap, which she had tied to perfection. As I stood there, in awe of how beautiful she looked, she walked toward me and smiled, almost coyly. "This is my first time," she said as she touched her head wrap, her head bowed a bit in respect, reminiscent of the way it had been in my campus office long before she began the GSAE experience. "I hope I did it okay."

It was clear she was waiting for my approval and I was over-whelmed as I gave it. "You look stunning, Jacqueline," I replied.

She asked for a photo to be taken of the two of us and she held her-self the rest of the evening as the queen that she was. But her story of (re)presentation becomes even more clear in what happened the next day as the group was departing Ghana to (re)turn to the US. Jacque-line came to the lobby wearing the same head wrap, this time with a T-shirt and jeans. I noticed and commented on the repeat of the head wrap, to which she replied, "I am going home a different person as a Black woman—and I need everyone to know that I have changed. I am not the same person who left America. So I called my boyfriend and told him that he has to know that I am returning more confident and full of self-esteem. He better get ready! Everyone needs to know I am different so I am wearing this home." Jacqueline chose to (re)pre-sent herself "as a new person" with her Ghanaian cloth head wrap as the symbol of how she now chooses to show up to the world as a Black woman. To be clear: this was not a mere flirtation with a (re)presen-tion of self that drew more deeply on an African aesthetic. At the final colloquium of the GSAE program, she showed up in this same gorgeous outfit with the head wrap tied just so. About a year later, when she was working as an elementary teacher in a school district near Atlanta, I asked her to come and speak to my upcoming group of students and to share her perspectives as an alumna of the GSAE. She arrived rocking natural hair, a brick-colored lipstick that accented her beautiful full lips, and an African-inspired print skirt. On her right arm was a recycled glass-bead bracelet from Ghana. About four years later, I received an invitation to attend Jacqueline's wedding (to the same young Black man whom she called from Ghana to let him know about her transformations). In their engagement photo (on the card that I still have on my refrigerator), Jacqueline stands forehead to forehead with her beloved in a burgundy rose shirt, gorgeous natural ringlet braids down her back, lips full of color. I saw her again the next year at a benefit sale for our school in Ghana, where she and her mother came to buy new Ghanaian clothing for themselves and African art for her new classroom. My point in sharing such detail of Jacqueline's (re)presentations is this: whatever affirmation of an African aesthetic happened for Jacqueline and every other Black woman in their time in Ghana, it has been *enduring*. For all of the Black women teachers, an embrace of Ghana in our everyday aesthetic may be at differing levels, but it signals and signifies something enduring, life-changing. Our (re)presentations are not another version of the anthropologist trope of "going native." The ways we (re)present our learnings in Ghana show up in ways subtle, bold, and all-out. What distinguishes our (re)presentations of self is in our consciousness in deciding *how* we want to show up as Black American women and knowing the creative source and meanings of the aesthetic we now consciously choose to marshal and to *be*. We show up on purpose in a way that lifts our African aesthetic to a purposeful empowerment. Sometimes we show up in a warrior smock at a faculty meeting when we know that we are going into that room to do battle. Other times, we may put on Western clothing, but we match it up with a piece of kente over the shoulder as we give a keynote talk to (re)mind ourselves that what is woven together can't easily be torn apart. We show up, as one young sister shared, "in my Angelina [the dashiki

I spoke of earlier]—and I know what's up even if they don't." As we (re)member, we are able to put on our crowns and take to our runways on our terms, in greater knowledge of the meanings of our choices and our presence. We show up as our Ghanaian sisters (re)minded us in Ghana: gorgeous, beautiful, regal, as Black women marshaling a greater story in our spirits.

## THE BODY (RE)PRESENTS, TOO

Dr. Doreen is a faculty member at the university and has traveled with me to Ghana three times: once as a participant in the GSAE program, once as a participant in a Full Circle Writing Retreat that I held in Ghana, and another time as a faculty coordinator who led the group when I was on leave of absence. One of the most brilliant voices in her field, Dr. Doreen speaks often through very strong identities as a Black woman, a teacher educator, and a single mother. Her professional life as a researcher are echoes of these identities as well. On her first trip to Ghana, she focused her individual inquiry on the link between families, communities, and education, something she also studies in the contexts of the US. She was particularly interested in how Ghanaian women whom we would call "single mothers" in the US parented their children and the ways that perceptions of motherhood can either distort or lift up the tremendously powerful ways that Black women mother. Our group visited a village community and school designed for abused, neglected, and abandoned children called the SOS Children's Village and Primary School in the suburb of Accra called Tema. These children at SOS were supported by being brought together into families with a single mother hired to serve as their mother within the village community. The mothers (and hired aunties who take over for the mothers when they go on leave) are responsible for every aspect of their children's lives, including supporting their learning, which takes place at several of the finest schools in all of Ghana. Every child in the village has access and opportunity to these excellent schools by virtue of being in the village community. Dr. Doreen shared her observations:

When we went to the SOS primary school, I got to see how a single mother can be valued and that this is a family, a *whole* family. But here in the US we're considered broken. That—that was life changing. Because you're told you're broken and you go to Ghana and you find out you're . . . you're whole and it's beautiful. Absolutely beautiful. And let's talk about my weight. Each time I went [to Ghana], I was complimented on my body. My fat specifically. People will say "I like your fat."

The shift of the conversation from SOS to her body and weight caught me off guard a bit, and I asked Dr. Doreen to tell me more. A huge smile shot across her face:

The time I remember most is when we were at the Goil Station spot, and I had on a dress, a red and white dress that was horizontally striped. Now I wanna tell you, I don't know, I would never wear those horizontal stripes over here in America. That's just a lounging-around kind of thing. But we were walking to the bathroom that night, I think it was me and Grace, and someone, a woman, said: "I like your fat." I was stunned. What does that mean? But I knew what it meant because it wasn't the first time I heard it in Ghana. But wow!

I (re)member that evening vividly, watching Doreen on her way back from the restroom: I was facing her as she was making her way back to the group. The joy all over Dr. Doreen's body was palpable, as she nearly jogged back to the table to tell us what had just happened! I (re)call her putting her hand on her hip, something I had never seen her do before. There was a sassiness about her, an exuberance that was so evident that I knew even before she (re)counted the story in our interview that whatever had happened, it brought her great joy. She laughed and continued telling about other experiences of (re)presenting in Ghana that she enacted and embodied when she (re)turned to the US:

What happened? Yeah, yeah, I looked good. I could hold my head up. I could hold my head up. And you know what else? The billboards. I started taking pictures of the billboards as we rode around to different places. Because when you look at those billboards, there are voluptuous, beautiful women. And what I love about them is that they are always clothed. You can be voluptuous, large, fully clothed and still be beautiful, admired and sexy. . . . I wanted to take that home with me because we don't see that here in the US. That's not who is on TV. That's not who is on billboards. That's not who is in the magazines typically. Especially if it's us [Black women]. . . . One part of my work [since Ghana] is specifically making women aware of their beauty and I don't mean in the superficial way. Their wisdom, their grace, their value, the importance of their work with their families and communities. . . . Sometimes it's about the way we talk to ourselves. . . . But when I remember how I felt so affirmed, I am able to give the same grace to them.

In her (re)membering (in this case, of the beauty of her body regardless of size), Dr. Doreen felt affirmed in the grace that Ghana provided. She could see that "queen" is a verb, a way of being that we need only (re)member. Like Jacqueline, Dr. Doreen now shows up queen-being much more often, wearing a regal caftan in the hallowed halls of the academy, recycled glass beads just because, headgear to an interview. She wears clothes that fit her body and that beautifully gesture at what's underneath, hair done to the nines. Being in Ghana lifted her body and spirit as it did all of us, Black women in all of our splendor. And we came back to our US classrooms, meetings, keynotes, and projects with all kinds of regal armor in the battles of sexism, racism, dismissal, and erasure that we knew we would face. But we are here. Every last inch of us. And we slay.

### MODERN-DAY GRIOTS WITH TRUTH TO TELL: TEACHING AS (RE)PRESENTATION

We always hold a final conference on the last day of the GSAE experiences in Ghana, as a way to gather ourselves and to begin turning our heads in transition back toward the US. In preparation, I ask each person to bring an artifact that (re)presents what they have learned in Ghana and who they were now as they (often reluctantly) prepare to (re)turn from Ghana to the US. Here are a few examples of the stories they shared, (re)presentations of deep learnings in Ghana and the spiritual nature of their transitions back to the US:

> I feel a deep transformation, like in my spirit. So I brought a beautiful piece of adinkra cloth that I got in Ntonso. It really represents my journey of learning about my Blackness. As funeral cloth, this cloth affirms my work of living in Blackness and what I'm supposed to do. It asks (as she gestures to the entire group): How are we spending our time on earth? This piece of cloth is the foundation of me learning who I am and why I am here, as a Black woman. (Dr. Janet)

> I brought this mask because it's really beautiful and it's really sturdy. I feel empowered, mostly. I had to completely remake myself here in Ghana. As some of you know, I have always been the only Black girl in school and I never learned anything about Black people. I remember hearing about Mildred Taylor and I always wanted to read her books. Here, I have learned about adinkra, about kente, about *our* people, about *our* power. We *are* something. I feel empowered as a Black woman, so I brought this mask. (Jacqueline)

> Mine is kind of funny, a little odd, but I brought a bottle of Voltic water. We have all become familiar with these bottles during our time here in Ghana. And it is what has kept us alive, it is life. And I brought it because I feel like in Ghana, I have been made whole (she begins to cry). I feel whole. So this water bottle is unopened with an unbroken seal and it represents the trip making me as whole as this bottle of water. (Dr. Denice)

What became clear in their words was that we were Black women teachers who were also modern-day storytellers. In the traditions of our ancestors and our griots, we could now tell old stories in new ways. We could name our cloth and its meanings as in Janet's story.

We could address the wrongs of our educational experiences as Black women in the US with new educational possibilities through knowing our cultural traditions as in Jacqueline's story. We could literally remix a symbolic version of baptism, our reverence for the water of life to make ourselves anew as in Dr. Denice's story. In all cases, Black women teachers had old stories to tell in new ways, old songs to sing in new ways, using our bodies, minds, and spirits to show up in new ways in our work.

But to be a griot is not simply to be a person who tells stories. According to Sobonfu Somé, Black women have always been keepers of the cultural and moral heritage of Africa and by extension in African American diasporic spaces as well. These cultural lessons are often embodied in our stories. And we share stories not simply for entertainment purposes but to teach and guide through the moral, ethical, and cultural lessons embedded within the tale.[9] But the way these transformations and (re)presentations were embodied by Black American women teachers in Ghana was different for each person, especially as we contemplated the spirit of our own teaching or what animated us to be and do our work as teachers and modern-day griots. For most of us, this process of (re)presentation, once we (re)turned back to the US, was a gradual and ongoing process. For others, the process of (re)presentation post-Ghana was immediate, unwavering, and bold. But in all cases, storytelling was a huge part of how we thought about and used our experiences as Black women teachers and how we (re) presented what we had come to know about our bodies, minds, and spirits. Multimedia journalist and essayist Andrea Collier speaks to why and how this (re)presentation of ourselves as Black Americans is an imperative and not a luxury: "Storytelling is our roots and wings. No matter who you are or where you come from, the human spirit wants—no, needs—to be validated. While story means so much in every culture and ethnicity, I know that Black folk, no matter how they got here, are planted in story and shared lived experience. It's the way we witness."[10]

Behind the transformations in our bodies, minds, and spirits in Ghana, we had "new" stories to tell, stories that not only resisted the ways that we as Black women had been characterized in our lives against the backdrop of school and society in the US but that shed light on who we *really* were and are, that bore witness to the strong, enduring spirit of our people. And while we knew of the lynchings of Black Americans and the violence still perpetrated against Black Americans and other Black people worldwide, we could now make the link in our bodies, minds, and spirits between the white supremacy and brutality that led to our even being part of an African *diaspora*—as part of the same inhumanity that existed in the minds, bodies, and spirits of white people who claimed another human being as property. We could link the same white supremacy that incarcerates Black people in the US at alarming rates to its inception in the brutalities of slave raiding in so many places on the continent of Africa. The same inhumanity that killed Breonna Taylor as she slept and put a knee on George Floyd's neck, murdering him in broad daylight, is the same spirit that stacked us in rooms in a dungeon, in the bowels of ships, and measured our teeth on auction blocks. We (re)membered that the same mindsets and spiritual deprivation that make it acceptable to continue to oppress and do violence to the minds, bodies, and spirits of Black people everywhere are the same mindsets and spiritual deprivation that took our ancestors from where we stood on the coast of Africa. This is the same mindset and spiritual deprivation today that we, as Black American women teachers and our Black students, are living within. Christina Sharpe, in her stunning book *In the Wake: On Blackness and Being*, brilliantly describes this reality that the GSAE teachers were now facing as they (re)turned to the US as "the ways our individual lives are always swept up in the wake produced and determined, though not absolutely, by the afterlives of slavery."[11] As Black women who always already live in this afterlife, whether in Ghana or the US, we could now feel way down deep inside our spirits the residue of the inhumanity that had defined us as Black women in the afterlife of slavery and that showed up in our teaching, learning, and living. We understood that it could not continue; we could not (re)turn to what we had done before or the way that we were. It was as if we were required by what we now knew and witnessed in Ghana to be responsible to ourselves and others. Our experiences in Ghana (re)minded us that we were Black American women teachers and that every last part of that being *mattered*. What had been reinforced for us was that the very lives we were living were witness to stories that Black people had been telling and living for millennia. We went to Ghana to learn more of our heritage stories for our students and communities, *but we came back with so much more.* I turn to Collier again as she describes the work of a Black women's summit she attended where sisters came together to talk of strategies and social action. These echoed our thoughts and hearts as Black women teachers who were turning back toward the US and reflecting on our experiences in Ghana: "It was an opportunity for these women, of all stages and ages, to tell stories about their stress, their pain, their hopes for the future. Even when they sang and danced and cried, they were bearing witness to not just the stories of their past but the stories of their future."[12]

So, though we were thousands of miles away from the US, being and learning together in Ghana were not silver bullets that protected us from our lives as Black women in the US. We were (re)turning to those lives. And the processes of (re)presenting our learnings and our lives in ways that demonstrated the influence of that (re)membering was itself a process.

Take Rita, a doctoral student in higher education whose work will eventually include teaching at the collegiate level as a faculty member in student affairs. With a level of vulnerability that often typified our conversations, she reflected on the spirit of her work before she went to Ghana and after: "I think before, I was just going through the motions. Getting through it as a doctoral student, doing what I had to do. But my posture has changed. It's like I could see myself more clearly in the mirrors I saw myself in Ghana. Gorgeous. Confident and Black. I want to go back. I am now journaling, using new theories, Black theories. It is like I went back and I found my purpose for being here as a Black woman."

But being a *Black* woman on purpose for a purpose and (re)presenting oneself in line with the weight of our legacy as Black women is not always easy. As I chatted at my dining room table with Dr. Doreen about her experiences in Ghana, the look on her face and the eyes full of sadness told me that she was not as satisfied with how her learnings from Ghana were showing up in her (re)presentations of self and in her teaching back in the US after her third trip. This dissatisfaction was also evident in the self-deprecating language she used to describe how she had expected to do or be something different, given three trips to Ghana. I could sense that something was not well with her spirit, as she reached for her Ghana journal inside her tote bag. With a sense of reverence, she gently turned to a page in the journal. It was as if she was gathering herself, wanting to share with a kind of exactness that casual conversation did not always allow. Watching her carefully open the journal and leaf through it reminded me of the way one turns to a passage in the Bible or a hymnal in church, in search of the kind of strength or answers that we often turn to those texts for. She began:

> The themes across the schools in Ghana were so important to me. They affirm what we need here. The trips have influenced the things that I was passionate about already. Now it's almost like, I know what I know. But now I know it *longer*. And I have even more evidence that I'm right. So professionally, the idea of bearing witness to what I saw there, I ask, . . . "What am I doing with it?" I started by reading Christina Sharpe's *In the Wake: On Blackness and Being*. That has kind of helped to answer why I've been silenced and why I have been stymied in some ways.

Her last line is in reference to several years of slow academic productions and projects not fulfilled. She had talked a lot about what she wanted to do but had not being able to move forward, especially on a book project that was still undone. I pushed a bit and asked her to talk further about what it meant to be stymied or silenced. "I don't know if I can do this without crying," she said. I assured her of the goodness of her tears and gently pushed the box of tissue closer to her. She continued, tears now running down her cheeks:

> I think the structure of the academy doesn't fit me as a Black woman. I am a daughter of the help. And I don't belong. There are all kinds of messages that say that, that have said that, and I've allowed that lingering impact of slavery to affect me. "You're Black," but I am acceptable because I went to Emory? Because I'm from the North? Because I don't like to argue? Because I look the way I do? I'm acceptable because of something. . . . And I have silenced myself because I am also not a person who seeks power. My power is my God. So my spirituality keeps me centered and humble.

Dr. Doreen continues to talk. What I am bearing witness to is what bell hooks and Cornel West describe, in their book *Breaking Bread: Insurgent Black Intellectual Life*, as the work of breaking down to break through. And I (re)member how, during her third and most recent trip to Ghana, she was constantly in tears. Whether we were in Ghanaian schools, looking at fabric, talking to other Black American visitors from the US who were also in Ghana, standing in the dungeons or at the water's edge, Dr. Doreen was crying. Her tearful witness continued in this interview:

> So I have read Christina Sharpe, I am now reading Melissa Harris-Perry's notion of the crooked room . . . and I'm understanding more [about Black womanhood]. But I think going to Ghana showed me that I come from strength. . . . The story of slavery, the way it is told here? We miss so much. . . . One thing that really surprised me, going for a third time, was breaking down the way I did. It's not like I hadn't been to these places before. . . . But I think it was the reality of it. . . . When I went the third time, I think what was going through my mind was the time between the first, second, and third time. What have I done?

There was a pause. I got up to get some more tissues, as I sensed there was more to be said about the deeper meaning of the question she'd just asked herself. So I asked her what she meant, if she felt a sense of guilt about things she had not done or accomplished after three trips to Ghana. Her answer was no. Instead, she offered that what she felt was a sense of shame. I prodded gently: "Is it still with you?" She moved nervously in her chair, the slump in her shoulders suggesting that she was still deeply troubled. "I think it's a part of me. I think I need to work more on my self-care. I've abandoned my self-care. . . . This is my natural tendency to beat myself up."

We rested quietly behind that exchange for a bit, both of us writing notes to ourselves. Dr. Doreen shared that the challenge for her was in really feeling like she was enough. That if she could "come back to the book [journal] and write it down" she was more aware of the negative things that she said to herself, especially as she considered how she wanted to fully embody and (re)present what she'd learned in her work in Ghana. But the origins of these wrestlings toward healthy self-esteem as Black women arise directly from the constant barrage of what we should be or what we were not, especially in the context of the US. And sometimes participants believe that this process of (re)membering and particularly of (re)presentation of self as a Black woman teacher is as easy as going to Ghana and "finding" oneself. But (re)membering is a kind of praxis: (re)presenting, the process of integrating all that we had come to know in Ghana within ourselves, about ourselves, and about others was, in essence, the *beginning* of our moments of praxis. It was the space where we had the opportunity to bear witness to our triumphs as Black American women and use them as catalysts for what we would do *next*. We all started in different places. We had all been through experiences in Ghana. And even in our commonality as Black women, our praxis, our stories, and our thoughtful actions after the GSAE would be something we would go through *differently*. As Collier suggests, "The silences gave way to the triggered cries and in some cases wailing. . . . The stories hurt us but they freed us and moved us. Good storytelling in [our] community is measured by the response. You know that you made your point only by the reaction or lack thereof." Like the griots of old, we were teachers who were also more explicitly becoming storytellers, praise singers, and poets as we (re)turned to our work in the US. And, as Jacqueline explains, being in Ghana was an intensive master class, rooted in Black truth-telling on both sides of the Atlantic: "I want my students to know what I learned in Ghana: that we (Black people) stand on a mighty past, we have accomplished great things. I am reading Dr. Love's book *We Want to Do More Than Survive* now, and I have ordered Dr. Gholdy Muhammad's book *Cultivating Genius*. I am hoping to use that framework for my classroom lessons. I'm still growing, Dr. Dillard, but Ghana started it."

But Ghana *started* it. As Black women teachers, we had our voices and our spirits when we arrived in Ghana. But being there helped us learn how to *trust* them. We learned that our truth matters as Black women. And that if we speak from the breadth and length of our truth as Black women, other people and especially our students will be our witnesses. And if we reach back to Sharpe's notions of the wake as an existential place where Black people live today in all of our complexities to do *wake work*,[13] we can (re)cognize that part of the wake work we were doing in Ghana was also about the experience of joy that comes from gathering yourself, from seeing your beauty and your stories and a vision of Black womanhood that centers itself in "the beauty that exists before they even knew what beauty was."[14] Sharpe describes the difficult work that her mother did in making a small path through the wake for her family. Her words were at the heart of our learnings and experiences in Ghana that now showed up as acts of (re)presenting ourselves, our stories, and our spirits as Black women:

> She brought beauty into the house in every way that she could; she worked at joy; and she made livable moments, spaces, and places in the midst of all that was unlivable there, in the town we lived in; in the schools we attended; in the violence we saw and felt inside the home

while my father was living and outside it in the larger white world be-fore, during and after his death. In other words, even as we experi-enced, recognized, and lived subjugation, we did not *simply* or *only* live *in* subjugation and *as* the subjugated.[15]

(Re)presenting is about putting ourselves and our knowings in the world in new ways. I turn now to the fruits of that labor, to the ways we (re)claimed ourselves and our heritage knowings and began to *be* the living legacies that we are as Black women, as women of Africa.

# CHAPTER 6

# THE INVITATION, SANCTUARY, AND LIVING LEGACY

## *(Re)claiming*

*I am not free while any woman is unfree, even when her shackles are very different from my own.*

—Audre Lorde, *Sister Outsider*[1]

Imagine what it might have been like to be a Black woman in the 1600s, living in West Africa. You are minding your business, your family, your life, and your responsibilities in community with others. And for generations—*all* of your natural life and beyond—you also live with the fear that slave raiders will come into your village and steal away your daughters or sons, your partners, relatives, or friends. For hundreds of years, mothers like you live this fear and the continual grief that accompanies it, as you also try to carve out a life for yourself and your family. You wonder and pray against the inevitability that this day might be the last day that you will see your loved ones in this world. And even as you attempt to (re)construct life after a loved one has been brutally kidnapped, you would surely wonder every day what happened to your beloveds. You would wonder about the place your family member or friend had been taken, about that world they now occupied that you yourself had never seen, could not imagine, and had never experienced. Your questions about their disappearance would require you to reckon with the loss of your loved ones *in your spirit*. As Sandra Jackson-Opoku ponders from the perspective of the ancestors:

> What new world awaits them? How many worlds can there be under the same sun? This is something we have not seen. We have seen people captured, but never yoked and shackled. We have seen people taken against their will, but never transplanted in such numbers. We have seen blood sacrifice, but not mass suicide. And perhaps those who lie in underwater graves are the lucky ones. What greater horror awaits our first-born daughter and her first-born daughter [and her first-born daughter . . . ] on the other side? What hope can there be with life mate gone, father unknown? *Still they are not beyond our aid.* It is not the nature of fresh water to cross salt water, for a river to traverse an ocean. But our daughters are headed for a world they call New. And we, their ancestor mothers, are alive in their blood. *They are not alone, the ones who cross over. They take us along.*[2]

*They take us along.* And even if their physical bodies do not (re)turn to us, their spirit is always with us, as ours is always with them. This is the belief of African people, our need and desire to be with our families and communities, to know ourselves *together*. But when your people have been flung to parts of the world unknown to you, you must imagine them and their lives in a strange and mysterious blurriness. And sometimes, just sometimes, you meet once again.

As shared throughout this book, (re)membering always requires a looking back. This was on full display by the Black women teachers in their GSAE class time, in their engagements in Ghana, and afterward. (Re)membering involves sankofa, which, in the Akan languages of Ghana, means going back to your roots to get what you need for the present conditions and circumstances of your life, as well as the future. Here, I share stories of (re)claiming, of how Black women teachers, with (re)membered cultural, spiritual, and historical knowledge are able and willing to (re)claim the legacy of Black African people and to take our place in living this legacy in our work as educators. These narratives speak directly to the difference that (re)claiming makes in the lives of the Black women educators in the GSAE: in our spirits, for our activism, for our well-being and the well-being of those whom we teach. And that (re)claiming started with an invitation.

## THE INVITATION

Hospitality and laying out a good meal has always been a part of Black women's stories. Whether creating feasts from what others discarded or spending all day making that perfect pot of gumbo, gathering and preparing food that feeds the body, mind, and spirit has been an important part of African legacy. Spiritually, Black people often pray (and hope) that whatever we prepared with our blood, sweat, and tears would be multiplied to feed any and all who showed up at our tables—and we usually plan and prepare for the whole community to show up and be fed! In the Akan traditions in Ghana, food was and often still is served in a collective bowl, and all who gather around that bowl—and others who show up at just that right time—are still today greeted by the phrase "You are invited." Only after this invitation is given is it appropriate to begin eating.

But when you are a Black woman and anti-Black racism and sexism have structured both your educational experiences and the context of your profession as an educator, what is necessary to create affirming Black spaces is the kind of invitation we encountered in Ghana: a table that centers who you are, who you've been, and what you might dream for your life in community with others. In gathering around this table, the possibility exists for healing and (re)claiming that reflects what you may have always felt but didn't have words for or may have experienced but did not have a context to demonstrate that experience. I am suggesting very explicitly here that the table for Black women—like those in the GSAE who were (re)membering the longer stories and exemplars of Black excellence and brilliance—is a table where Black women educators are willing *and* able to pull up a chair with a fierceness and take a seat. It is the kind of fierceness of purpose that Beyoncé suggested in her call to graduating seniors in the midst of the 2020 global pandemic:

> I know how hard it is to step out and bet on yourself. There was a pivotal turning point in my life when I chose to build my own company many years ago. I had to trust that I was ready, and that my parents and mentors provided me with the tools I needed to be successful. But that was terrifying. The entertainment business is still very sexist. It's still very male-dominated. And as a woman, I did not see enough female role models given the opportunity to do what I knew I had to do. To run my label and manage my company. To direct my films and produce my tours. That meant ownership. Owning my masters. Owning my art. Owning my future, and writing my own story. Not enough Black women had a seat at the table, so *I had to go and chop down that wood and build my own table. Then I had to invite the best there was to have a seat.* That meant hiring women, men, outsiders, underdogs, people that were overlooked and waiting to be seen.[3]

If we think of our work as teachers in the spirit of Beyoncé's words, then the invitation for Black teachers must include the breadth and depth of Black life and the ways that Black life has influenced and been influenced by other lives as well. That would be the table that feeds us so that we might feed others.

The table also serves as a perfect image for the GSAE program for several other reasons. The kitchen table has been an enduring image in collective Black feminisms throughout the ages, an image of the serious and powerful theorizing, revolutionary thought, and sense-making that Black women have done for millennia around our kitchen tables. Such theorizing has too seldom been (re)cognized as intellectual until Black women made it so.[4] After decades of intellectual and spiritual work across two continents and the diaspora, my own development of the Ghana Study Abroad in Education program was the wood that I needed to chop as a Black woman teacher educator. It was the table I needed to build that was worthy of Black women teachers and others too. A table around which we could, in the fullness of our minds, bodies, and spirits—pull up a chair and sit a spell.

Where we could relax, release, exhale, and be free. To be clear, this was not a space that excluded those who were not Black women. But it was a space that unapologetically centered the spirit, culture, and intellect of Black women *and* served as a consistently sacred location for us, curated and designed for the nourishment of the legacy and heritage of Black women. And that required all of us to (re)member in order to (re)claim and walk in the spirit and pride of that legacy.

As I reflected on my own process of (re)claiming as an educator, I knew that the building and curation of the GSAE and the work of (re)membering had to be centered in a kind of hospitality. The program itself had to be an invitation centered in the spirit of educators' work and the ways that this spirit animates every decision we make as teachers. And it had to be an invitation centered in the love of Black people. In using *hospitality* here, I am (re)calling Black folks' traditions on both sides of the water where, as Christine Pohl writes, "the stranger is welcomed into a safe, personal and comfortable place, a place of respect and acceptance and friendship. Even if only briefly, the stranger is included in a life-giving and life-sustaining network of relations. Such welcome involves attentive listening and a mutual sharing of lives and life stories. It requires an openness of heart, a willingness to makes one's life visible to others, and a generosity of time and resources."[5] But here's what enlivens these spaces of welcome as spaces that are hospitable to Black women: there is an intentional focus by the one who invites on what actually *animates* the gathering. We can see this intentionality as a spirituality that sees our being and living as broader than a particular religious doctrine. As a scholar who pays close attention to the inner lives of Black women, I overtly resist (maybe to a fault) what is an over-reliance in US society on Christianity or other mandates of organized religion as the sole justification for righteous acts of kindness, love, or humility. In my mind and heart, one need not be "religious" to embrace these life-affirming acts as a human being animated by one's spirit. As I curated this experience to Ghana for my students in all of their ethnic, racial, gendered, and class identities, my invitation to learn and grow with them was fundamentally all about love and loving from an endarkened feminist epistemology. In other words, I sought to offer all who gathered an invitation to the spirit of love that Black women (re)present, and have always (re)presented, an echo of the definition of love that bell hooks offered up in her groundbreaking book *All About Love: New Visions*: "Love is the will to extend one's self for the purpose of nurturing one's own or another's spiritual growth. . . . Love is as love does. Love is an act of will—namely both an intention and an action. Will also implies choice. We do not have to love. *We chose to love*."[6]

What I realized is that with love as the organizing spirit of our table in this course and our experiences in Ghana, it was also my responsibility to pay attention to and center intentions and actions that loved Black women. And that kind of love will always (re)mind you of the truth that you knew in the first place. Given my own (re)membering over the years, I have (re)claimed the legacy of Black women as a legacy that is connected to and imbued by the spirit, culture, and wisdom of our origins, beginning on the continent of Africa. Having begun my own (re)membering with similar motivations and willingness to learn what Africa could teach me about Black heritage and being, this process of (re)claiming was, at its essence, an invitation to a much larger and longer memory of Blackness. As Black women teachers, we had all walked into our classrooms committed to loving the students who appeared before us and to embracing the diversity and brilliance of these students, whether we taught preschool children or adults. But we also came to (re)cognize that our work as teachers was not solely about learning and embracing the tenets of culturally relevant teaching, attending professional development on culturally sustained teaching, or marshaling other culturally based curriculum frameworks. It was about (re)claiming our *own* spirits and (re)membering the humanity and cultural traditions of Black women and people as a precursor to carrying out the deeper cultural and spiritual work of teaching that these frameworks *require*. It was to (re)claim wellness and wholeness and to invite others to place the lives and humanity of Black women and Black people squarely at the center of our teaching practices. But no one can teach what they do not know about the legacy of Black people. And that absence in our bodies, minds, and spirits continues to be felt today, especially in the call to serve an increasingly diverse population of students and families.

Being in Ghana allowed us to see, share, and experience so many invitations to know ourselves and to be included in life-giving and life-sustaining spaces for us, as Black women teachers. And what we learned in those spaces was that, for those offering the invitation, the experience was both deeply enriching and often times deeply demanding. The care we experienced there provided countless examples of how offering one's labor was crucial to building the larger community. With community foregrounded, the invitation was then made a *sacred* gesture, worthy of our reverence as well as our respect, which often came from deeper and deeper wells of understanding and gratitude for these lessons.

Acts of invitation in Ghana were also deeply inspired by reciprocity, in the truest sense of give and take. This was not a tit for tat (i.e., you give something to me, I give something back to you). Rather, the offering of hospitality we experienced in loving words and gestures and amidst joy and humility seemed to be as much a blessing to the person(s) giving as to the person(s) receiving the hospitality. Whatever was offered was given for the nourishment of our *collective* bodies, minds, and spirits. While some examples of the grace of the hospitality we experienced and engaged in Ghana have already been shared in other chapters of the book, the invitations to grow in love with Black women and families were critical to (re)claiming ourselves, the legacy of our hospitality, and embracing the spirit of Black legacy-making.

### Akuaaba Means *Welcome*

Over the years, I have had the good fortune to spend countless hours with Ghanaian families in homes and communities. As in gatherings in the US, every encounter in Ghana seemed an invitation to witness the ways that being in the company of Black women is a way of feeling at home that is physical, spiritual, and social nourishment for me, culturally nuanced in the way that only Black women can, no matter where you meet us on the globe. Take, for example, Auntie

Gifty, one of my oldest and dearest friends in Ghana. She also happens to be the extraordinary tailor who has sewn the custom clothing for *every* group I have led to Ghana for nearly three decades. I met Auntie Gifty, a smallish brown-skinned woman with beautiful eyes and a slight British accent, long before I started taking groups to Ghana, through another Ghanaian woman friend who recommended her to me. Yes, she is my tailor. But more than that, she is my sister. We have leaned on one another through deaths, divorces, and the challenges of building houses when money was not as plentiful as we would have liked. We know each other's families and children and have watched them grow up and have children of their own. We visit each other's homes and sit and talk for hours, often over a plate of fish stew and drinks. And after all of this time, she also has come to know my students in the intimate way that taking a measuring tape to someone's hips, chest, and waist requires. Long after groups have come and gone, requests come for Auntie Gifty to sew their wedding dresses, pastoral robes, and "another dress just like the other one." I am forever sharing photographs and photo albums with Auntie Gifty that my students send back to her, proudly posing at their graduation ceremonies or in front of their classrooms or meetings, fully embodied and stunning in their custom-made outfits.

On a typical trip to Ghana, we arrive along the coast of the country to the town of Elmina and check into the hotel on the day we go to be measured by Auntie Gifty (as my students also call her). Our newly purchased cloth is ready to be transformed (and to transform us) into something we have seen online or in a fashion magazine. Because Auntie Gifty also takes care of her now one-hundred-plus-year-old mother, we board the bus and go to her home, in the center of the historic town of Cape Coast. There, we crowd into the small room she uses for cutting and sewing, the ceiling fan whirling and plastic chairs waiting to accommodate only two to three people. As the majority of the group will not fit in the small room, the same plastic chairs also appear outside (with the swift help of one of Auntie Gifty's assistants), lined up in her home's courtyard for us to rest comfortably while we wait to create our dreamed outfits. There, we are also greeted by Auntie Gifty's mother, who is often outside catching the evening breeze, her back upright against the cool block wall. And from her perspective, our visit is an event curated for her entertainment and joy! I greet her warmly, happy to see her again, given her advanced age. "Ma, good evening. Ete sen?" I say partly in Fante. She replies enthusiastically: "Auntie Cynthia. Nyame adom. Oh, fine, fine, fine." Each English "fine" is punctuated with a firm handshake from this centenarian. I gesture for my students to come over, and she smiles and greets everyone with a handshake and the biggest smile ever. We go through a similar greeting for Auntie Gifty. But for her, I have a huge hug and a story to share with the group about our enduring friendship. While each person meets individually with Auntie Gifty to design their outfits and to get measured, her mother keeps everyone outside entertained, engaging with all who are in earshot. She asks questions about America and looks at photos of styles that the participants have brought to Auntie Gifty. The respect the Black women teachers from the US give to Auntie Gifty's mother is familiar and reminiscent of the rapt and joyful attention we often share with our grandmothers and elders whether we hail from Washington, South Carolina, Connecticut, or Georgia: wherever we are from in the US, that love looks the same. Auntie Gifty's mother often tells us how beautiful our cloth is and how beautiful it will look once it is sewn. She sometimes even offers her own style advice about a sleeve or a neckline. Amidst the happenings of the evening, a seller or visitor might also stop by the house, calling out "Ko koo ko" to announce their arrival before tentatively stepping over the threshold of the outside door into the courtyard. From inside the room, Auntie Gifty responds quickly, "Me mee me," her ears clearly attuned to everything happening around her, even amidst our loud chatter and excitement. Inside the sewing room, as Auntie Gifty is busy measuring, designing, and drawing, she asks questions about the styles that we have chosen or have dreamed up. She then renders what she hears us say or what we have shown her into a little book on her cutting table. Pencil moving swiftly on the lined page, she often points and asks whether she has the sleeve or the pant leg or the collar just right as each person looks on. The invitation to create outfits *with* her is important, and her reassurances and suggestions are comforting in this experience that is often unfamiliar to us. And by the attention she gives to each and every person, we know she wants to get it *just right*. Her pride and her work ethic are clear. She wants you to love the outfit sewn by her, and that comes from the creative work that the two of you have done *together*.

After everyone has been measured (typically for at least two outfits, sometimes more), it now feels like a party in the courtyard, everyone clearly comfortable in Auntie Gifty's home. Her mother is still chatting with whoever is sitting in the proximity of her quiet voice. Sometimes cold Fanta or Coke has arrived, compliments of Auntie Gifty and distributed by her assistant to the "guests." While groups each year have ranged in size, typically each group is between ten and sixteen people. Here's the amazing part: Auntie Gifty will have *all* of our outfits ready for fittings in just two to three days, before we leave for Accra to prepare for the final banquet before the group (re)turns to the US. And she has never left us disappointed, despite electrical outages, embroidery machines breaking, or other challenges. The hard work that this requires is not lost on anyone in the group, and everyone marvels at the miracles that go into the preparation of our outfits.

But the true awe comes when we arrive for our fittings. After the same ritual greetings, Auntie Gifty's labor and generosity of time and resources begin to show up, as outfit after outfit is modeled for the group to a chorus of ooohs and ahhhs. And I wish I could capture in words the look of the Black women as they see themselves in the mirror for the first time in *their* clothes. Not only are they wearing clothes that actually fit every part of their bodies but clothes that fit their spirits too. Their gaze into that mirror (as was my own years ago) is a combination of amazement and deep admiration: the excitement at the beauty of their reflection is palpable. Sometimes they turn and hug Auntie Gifty real tight, talking a mile a minute as they turn their gaze back to their image in the mirror, in awe of the sleeve, the fit, their beauty. And that usually occurs only minutes before they take their place on the impromptu runway that has been created in the courtyard, down the middle of their admiring GSAE colleagues (and sometimes to the applause and smiles of Auntie Gifty's mother, too). Auntie Gifty herself stands and smiles at the groups from the doorway of the little room, watching the shenanigans (when she isn't back inside, adjusting or pinning a few small alterations that might need to be made or being hugged again). The look of accomplishment and satisfaction on her face is real and has not diminished in decades of sewing for Black Americans. When the group has left Ghana and I (re)turn to Cape Coast where we live when we are in Ghana, Auntie Gifty and I often meet up and enjoy some post-departure conversations (and occasional gossip). And it is clear that she has always known intimately that the clothes she has made (re)present more than simple bodily covering. For her, they are also a (re)membering of her brothers and sisters that she knows is both fruitful for her and fertile ground for those Africans coming home to themselves, (re)claiming our clothing, textiles, and African styles. And as I have often heard Auntie Gifty say to me and to individual Black women in our groups over the years, as we stand in front of that mirror, stunned by the beauty of our own images in the mirror: "Akuaaba, my sister."

## FOOD IS FOR MORE THAN THE BODY

Visits to schools are a central part of the GSAE experience. But for the Black women teachers in the program, acts of hospitality in school settings are particular kinds of invitations. As places of learning, many of the meanings and symbols of schools and education were familiar to us, albeit rendered in line with the culture and communities in Ghana. We see school buildings and classrooms. We see books and learning materials, although often not as plentiful or prominent as in the US. We see teachers and children. A major difference? Both teachers and students are nearly all Ghanaian, and they are nearly all Black. It is important to note that a national mandate was issued from the Ministry of Education in Ghana that all schools teach the French language in 2019. So there are a growing number of teachers in Ghanaian schools who are African nationals from countries surrounding Ghana, including Sierra Leone, Ivory Coast, Burkina Faso, and Togo.

One of the schools we visited was a local Montessori school on the outskirts of Cape Coast. Many schools across the world follow the Montessori approach to teaching, developed in the early 1900s by Maria Montessori, who believed that instead of using traditional methods, educators should utilize child-centered educational theories to guide their teaching toward the developmental stages of their students. As all of the participants in the GSAE were relatively familiar with the Montessori method of teaching from our teacher preparation in the US (and some even from personal experience of having attended or having taught in a Montessori school in the US), we were all eager to see the ways this philosophy and approach to teaching were used in Ghana.

On the day of our visitation, we were immediately greeted by the headmistress, as the bus crossed through the school gates of the Montessori school. After an initial welcome by the headmistress (before we even got off the bus), we were ushered to chairs assembled under an outside canopy. All of us were grateful for the shade this canopy provided, as the Ghanaian sun can be ruthless in December when we visited. Children were busy, running from here to there or peeking through their classroom windows at these "visitors" who had just arrived but for whom they have clearly been waiting. One of the women staff members brought each of us a cool bottle of water, a customary gesture in Ghana when a visitor arrives at your home or school. This tradition assumes that visitors need a chance to catch their breath from their journey to your home or school, and it would be rude and inconsiderate to conduct any business before you attended to the humanity and health of your visitors. After we rested for about five to ten minutes, we were ushered into the office of the school's proprietress, another longtime friend of mine. Like Auntie Gifty's sewing room, the office was relatively small. But the staff managed to fit enough chairs for most of us to sit around the proprietress's wooden desk, while the rest of us stood near the walls. We heard a sweet voice outside the opposite door speaking in Fante, and we assumed from the tone that this person was giving directives for something to be taken care of right now. Then the proprietress entered. A tall, statuesque woman, she stood in the doorway as the dignitary that she was in that moment, wearing a kente-printed skirt and a turquoise-colored blouse, hair coifed just so.

The warmth of her spirit filled the room, touching each person as she twisted and turned through our cramped presence with an ease that defied the limited space between us. She stopped to give me a brief hug and asked a few questions about when we had arrived and such. She continued to shake hands with everyone and then settled onto the chair behind her wooden desk, smoothing her floor-length skirt. "Akuaaba," she said. "Welcome to the Montessori School of Cape Coast. Can I ask your mission?" Again, as is the custom in Ghana, once you have greeted someone arriving at your home or school and have served them water, you inquire as to why they have come, their mission. For the person sharing the mission, there is a need to briefly (re)call (1) when you last saw the person who has asked, (2) what major events have happened in your life since that time, and (3) why you are here or what your purpose is for being in the office or wherever you have arrived on that day. As the leader of the group, I responded to these questions, to which the proprietress responded that she had heard all that I have said and welcomed us to the school to carry out our mission. She reiterated her welcome, sharing how happy she was to see yet another GSAE group at her school. She gave a brief introduction about our history and relationship as friends, before sharing a bit about the school.

Part of our mission that day was to spend time observing and working in various classes of children, usually based on the levels of children we teach, have taught, or have an interest in the US. Teachers at the Montessori school were excited to host us. But I could see that the body language of the GSAE participants showed both excitement and nervousness, as they had no idea what they would be asked to do or little knowledge of the cultural norms of the school. But they all jumped right in. And immediately, what they realized was that they *did know*. Once they had been assigned to their classrooms, I walked around and watched GSAE participants engaging within the classroom. While not exclusive to the Black teachers in our groups over the years, intimate acts of caring and sharing were everywhere. Some GSAE teachers would be dancing with their children and teachers, people they'd met just moments ago. Some would be leaning into and learning the Fante language in a song or tradition that was important to the children in that particular classroom. Ghanaian teachers would sometimes be literally sitting on the sidelines while our GSAE teachers taught a math lesson or shared stories of what the US was like (the students at all levels had *lots* of questions). And after our allotted time in classrooms, I had to go and pull the GSAE teachers out! They did not want to leave "their kids." Some of the younger children at the school even cried when their visitors left them to return to the proprietress's office for our debriefing meeting.

Smiles were on every face as we gathered again. They said: "That was so fun!" "You should have heard how much they knew about the US. They were asking about the branches of government, about voting and stuff." The excitement of the GSAE teachers (re)minded me of children themselves, children who had just received an amazing gift. The proprietress directly asked them what kinds of things they saw and experienced during their visits and listened deeply to each and every response. And person after person shared some version of the profound acts of care and love they were shown as "visitors": From a special song that primary children sang just for them about their families to the invitation of the GSAE teacher to share with students what it's like to be a teacher in the US. Or junior high school students inviting our GSAE teachers to join into their dance or song or game or answering questions about how it feels to be a Black person in the US and to face racism or discrimination. In every voice, the meaning of these acts of care were surrounded and shaped by traditions that gave them meaning. The tradition of hospitality from the time we arrived until the time we left. The tradition of valuing various languages in addition to English, as children sang loud and strong in home languages *and* in English. The tradition of deep inquiry and careful global study, as typified by the depth of the questions rendered by junior high school students. The traditions of spirituality and nurturing kindness in the everyday. The tradition of life and well-being of yourself and others as being more important than your livelihood or roles or nationality. The tradition of seemingly random acts of unexpected hospitality. And on this day, we stayed nearly two hours longer than anticipated, sharing story after story with the proprietress. She mentioned that it was well past our lunchtime. And then a beautiful tray of scones that she had baked before our meeting appeared, along with some soft drinks. The proprietress did not eat. She simply smiled and watched as we enjoyed our treats. Once we finished, she walked with us to our bus as we prepared to leave the Montessori school. And imagine our surprise when individual boxed lunches of fish or chicken with fried rice had been prepared for our group and loaded onto the bus, including for our bus driver and tour guide, who had also been waiting for us and hadn't eaten all day.

Invitations—whether to teach, to learn, to dance, to sing—are always invitations to be in community with others, to know oneself in relation. Black tradition and heritage order the world in this way. Again, as Ubuntu teaches us: *I am because you are.* Building community "requires attention to good stories, wise mentors, and hard questions."[7] What Ghana continued to teach us and what ultimately Black women teachers (re)claimed in measure was just how important the spirit of the community is to living legacy as Black women teachers. We could not ignore the spirit embodied in all of the gestures of kindness and hospitality shown by Black women in communities we visited: from Auntie Gifty's awesome spirit and that of her assistants that mirrored the kindness of teachers and students we met in all of the schools we visited to the generosity of the headmistress, proprietress, and staff at the Montessori school, including the teachers and the students themselves. Their acts of hospitality were beautiful examples of the power of culture and community as a foundation for education. And as we talked, these invitations hit the Black women teachers just a little bit differently: they were also the invitations we needed to feel a sense of how school *could be* for Black students and teachers like us.

## EXPERIENCING SANCTUARY

Historically, a sanctuary is the holiest of holy places, often a temple, a church, or other consecrated place where sacred articles are kept and sacred rituals are practiced. While the word "sanctuary" has religious roots, its use has broadened to include anywhere people go for peaceful tranquility or introspection, like a beautiful spot in a quiet forest. Likewise, a car or home might be a person's sanctuary if that's where they can clear their head or lay down their burdens. Today, it is a word for anywhere a person feels especially safe and serene, a shelter from danger or hardship. A sanctuary is ultimately a place of comfort and security. As Black women teachers, we experienced Ghana as a sort of sanctuary, a place where we could become the sermon we needed to hear. In sanctuary, spiritual capacity is developed. And that is the power of a sanctuary as a space where we can use our minds, bodies, and spirits as tools to connect the outside world with the sacred world inside ourselves.

Black people in the US have always created sanctuary in the midst of a country that has not loved us. One historical example are the hush harbors created by enslaved African people from the beginning of slavery in the "New World." Hush harbors, sometimes called brush harbors, were places of freedom and worship for our ancestors, even after emancipation in the US and beyond. According to historian Paul Harvey, hush harbors were "secluded informal structures, often built with tree branches, set in places away from masters so that slaves could meet to worship in private."[8] Worship in hush harbors often included the Christian religious practices required by white slave masters in the segregated churches they created for enslaved Black people. These "churches" were designed by white slave owners for their enslaved and required worship of the Christian God as a way to "civilize" Black people.

However, unlike these segregated spaces created by white people, a hush harbor enabled Africans the freedom to combine African knowings, culture, and spiritual practices with the required practices of Christian religion they enacted in front of slave masters and white families.[9] In the hush harbor, far away from plantation life, Africans (re)membered the fields and forests of homelands and temporarily escaped the confines of segregation and degradation that was their condition as enslaved persons. They found joy and purpose in African rituals of praise in song, dance, and prayer. It was a place where one could testify, be affirmed in community with other Black people, and commune with the spirits of the ancestors. It was a space where bruised and wounded souls could be healed and a world that embraced Black *humanity* could be created again and (re)membered in the spirit. The value of Black humanity was already known by our people, and hush harbors were the *spaces* of that (re)membering. They served as a place to enact community and collective kinship that made the world right and fair, as well as a place to organize and develop resistance movements.[10] The everyday dehumanization of enslavement was not the reality in our hush harbors. It was there we could create a sanctuary for the humanity that we knew in our bones. It was the place where we created the world that loved Black people.

Hush harbors also embodied a secular function for Black people. They were spaces of Black abolition, revolution, and freedom dreaming. These aspects of hush harbors are useful concepts in theorizing how Black women teachers engaged in their own (re)claiming in and through experiences in Ghana. Julius Lester argues that "Africa's powerful celebratory rites acted as the spiritually strong balancing force to counter the pain of slavery."[11] If we see our historical hush harbors as spaces where Black cultural practices, freedom, and spirituality were sacred and central to our wholeness and (re)membering, then we might conceptualize and dream of schools as modern-day hush harbors, as affirming spaces to (re)claim Black heritage, story, and culture that our teachers and children *still* need as we navigate US schools and society.[12]

What Ghana taught us is that creating a sanctuary is an ongoing process, particularly for those of us in the African diaspora. In our process of (re)claiming—that is, in gathering what we needed from the great legacy of Black people as we moved toward wholeness—we were learning to draw on the strength of our stories, our community, our knowledge, and our spiritual reservoirs to burst out of where we were toward where we needed and wanted to go. But (re)claiming and living legacy happens only to the extent that we also (re)member our covenants with the ancestors, *trust* their guidance, and *trust* our spirits. The work of the sanctuary relies on the notion that the community is served best when we gather all of our selves and put our selves to work in service to building that community. It relies on our attention to living Ubuntu, living the philosophy of *I am because you are*. In that merciful distance from the US, we found sanctuary in the hush harbor that Ghana was for us. And while our lessons of (re)claiming focused on trusting each other and trusting the space around us, we were also learning to stand in the truth of what we already knew, felt, and even what we could not see. We were learning to trust our selves and learning to trust our spirits. What was required? As Rumi says: "*No more words. Hear only the voice within.*"[13] If you trust your spirit, you will open the way to what you and others need to know.

## I AM OK BACK IN THE CUT

Dr. Issa is a New Yorker from the inside out. Everything about her is New York, from her style and swagger to her unwavering loyalty to childhood friends who are still her village, to the cultural references she marshals in her teaching and invited lectures she gives all over the country. What is central to know about Dr. Issa? She loves Black women and will tell any and every one this fact of Blackness that guides her everyday living and being as a Black woman.

I tried to get Dr. Issa to come to Ghana with the GSAE for years. As a scholar of hip-hop, she would, I knew, find so many resonances and be deeply informed by the soul of the cultural traditions that she holds deep as she explored the Ghanaian highlife and hiplife that undergird much of the soundtrack of her life. But given a number of health issues and life circumstances, she put the trip off for a number of years. Then, after finally feeling strong and healthy enough for the required immunizations and at the divine right time, Dr. Issa came along as part of the 2018 cohort of the GSAE program. Given her popularity as an instructor at the university, undergraduates and graduate students could not hold their excitement in having Dr. Issa as a part of their GSAE experience in Ghana.

As a New Yorker, Dr. Issa was accustomed to reading contexts and knowing in her spirit when things just didn't seem quite right. But there was a comfort she felt in Ghana. She often said that things just "felt right to her." Often dressed in a Blackcentric T-shirt and long shorts, her fanny pack with the long black strap dangling behind her was the antithesis of the always sharp, always together Dr. Issa style that we were accustomed to seeing in the US. Amidst all the teasing about this "tail," Dr. Issa paid us no mind: she was at home, comfortable, unbothered.

She and I talked often about this newfound comfort and why she thought that sort of comfort was the case for her in Ghana. Here is but one example that seemed particularly striking. Our GSAE groups always visit the small town of Ntonso, made famous by its tradition of the stamping of adinkra cloth. We had studied the symbolic language of adinkra in our class sessions on campus. Like traditional kente cloth from Ghana, this particular textile is one that is often familiar to Black Americans and served as another connecting memory between Ghana and the US. Historically, adinkra was used for funeral ceremonies and memorial occasions and consisted of a plain cloth that is stamped with proverbial symbols, some of which have been used for centuries. The adinkra symbols reflect the complex social and spiritual nature of the Akan people and their social and cultural relations. In addition to the cultural life, the language of adinkra embodies communal values, codes of conduct, parables, and the like. They are an expression of the Akan worldview and reflect the complex wisdom and understandings of God, the importance of human relations, spirituality, life, and the inevitability of death. So this cloth is a Black history lesson in and of itself.

Each year, we visit this small village to learn these lessons and more. And on this day, Dr. Issa was with us. After initial invitations and stating our mission, we were ushered by our adinkra teacher through several little alleyways and around a few corners. Soon out of the view of the street, we were warmly ushered into the interior life of his family of craftsmen who are part of the generational tradition of adinkra clothmaking. In this space, we learned about adinkra not simply through our teacher's stories but through every one of our own senses. We smelled the smoke of the firewood and felt the heat of the fire that is central to how the ink is made. We touched and pounded the bark of the badie tree that creates the ink for stamping. We sometimes even tasted this same bark, as it is also used as medicine for menstrual cramps, malaria, and body pains. After these lessons, we stamped our own adinkra cloth under the careful tutelage of our teacher, who schooled us on the meanings of the symbols, shared contemporary symbols that have been created that were not on the charts we'd studied, and guided our hands as to the correct pressure needed to stamp clearly and well. Dr. Issa spoke passionately about the essence of that experience for her and the larger spiritual lessons she learned as a Black woman in this adinkra sanctuary:

> We was back in the cut. Now, I'm from the hood. I don't do back in the cut! I gotta have an exit plan, know where the exit is. But I felt so safe back in that cut. Mama sittin there watchin over us, goats and chickens running all around our feet, smoke from the fire. It was amazing. I somehow knew how to navigate out of my comfort zone. *And that was a comfort that I have never had.* It was remarkable, completely out of my comfort zone back in the cut. But I felt *safe*.

The idea of creating a safe space for Black women is central to creating sanctuary, as few places in the broader institutions and cultural life in the US have ever invited us in, offered us safety, and certainly have not ensured that we were cared for or loved. But being able to just feel safe is foundational to (re)claiming our whole selves, to moving out of our comfort zones by feeling secure enough to rest, to breathe, and, ultimately, to trust.

## (RE)CLAIMING GRACE

Often on the same day that we visit Ntonso, we also visit the town of Bonwire, the origin home of Ashanti kente weaving. Kente is a cloth that is often (re)membered on Black American graduation or choir robes worn by Black American sororities and fraternities. Kente designs are also contemporarily printed on cloth that is readily available around the world. Learning through kente was a crucial element of our GSAE experience in Ghana. And like in Ntonso, our learning was not only multisensory but was also imbued with the ability to transform our world sense as well. Bonwire was yet another sanctuary within which we experienced opportunities to trust ourselves in community with others. Dr. Doreen shares her experience at the kente-weaving village:

> I think about the first time I went to Ghana and I didn't want to do the weaving. It was at Bonwire. Some of the brothers were pulling us to go sit inside the loom and to try to weave. And I didn't think I would fit, so I kind of backed away. I don't know for sure, but I bet you could've seen me trying to hide so I wouldn't be seen. Well, somehow, someone saw me, two people, and I said, "Oh no, I won't fit." And they said, "Yes you will." And they made it work. And I did it. I felt the rhythm of the weaving and wow. That I thought I couldn't do it but they knew I could. And so when I see students who think they can't, that story empowers me. Yes you can. Let's make this work. Let's figure out how. Because those two gentlemen made that work for me. And I am grateful for that. Because I really, really didn't think I could fit in there. But that's the power of somebody else's vision.

She goes on to describe an elementary education student at the university whom she was supervising in their field placement at one of the local schools. This student was struggling in her placement and spoke anxiously about how *she* couldn't do what her mentor teacher was doing, like asking good questions in a way that kept the lesson moving or keeping the children engaged. Dr. Doreen weaves her role as a teacher educator together with the moments she lived and the lessons of trust and grace she learned in Bonwire:

> We talk about why she can't. Why can't you, what's stopping you . . . then what are we going to do? You know, I had another student in her first classroom and she sent me a text. "It's 20 days into the school. And I think I can't do this." WHAT? . . . We call and we talk about it. But that's it: When I talk to them, I'm (re)membering. I (re)member how I felt that way in Bonwire. And so I am able to give that same grace to them.

## OUR POSSIBILITIES ARE IN OUR RISK AND SACRIFICE

Audre Lorde's life-changing words about the transformation of silence into language and action come to mind in thinking about the trust, the risk, and the sacrifices that Black women have made to (re)claim ourselves and to begin to really live into our legacies, to acknowledge and (re)cognize the spiritual work of teaching and learning. Taken from her wise book *Sister Outsider*, Lorde has often served as a spiritual muse for my writing, her voice often pushing me to think or to breathe more deeply around a particular idea. Here, her voice is a cautionary one, about the need for Black people to speak, regardless of the attempts by others to silence us: "I was going to die, if not sooner then later, whether or not I had ever spoken myself. My silences had not protected me. Your silences will not protect you either."[14] She goes on to say what I believe is at the center of (re)claiming the truth of the legacy, brilliance, and beauty that has been rendered invisible about Black women in the US, that has distorted the truth of our humanity and that Ghana helped us to see and be again. And the power of the collective tale of the Black women's lives was becoming ours to tell, from root to tip, because, as Audre Lorde also suggests, "for every real word spoken, for every attempt I had ever made to speak those truths for which I am still seeking, I had made contact with other women, while we examined the words to fit a world in which we all believed, bridging our differences. And it was the concern and caring of all those women which gave me strength and enabled me to scrutinize the essentials of my living."

What Lorde was also saying was this: No matter how unsure, scared, or confused we might be, we were responsible to the ancestors to help build Black women's legacy. Regardless of what words had ever been said to us or against us, what we could now hear in Ghana were the ancestors' voices (re)minding each and every one of us. "You are not alone. You are safe. All you need is right there inside of you. Trust your spirit." What we also learned from Dr. Doreen's voice is that, as Black women, when we (re)claim and live our collective legacy, we give ourselves permission to be great. And in doing so, we also give ourselves permission to be free.

## LIVING LEGACY

This book was written during the global pandemic of 2020. Given inept and cruel national leadership in the US, death swirled around all of us like a bad dream that continues today, over one year after it began. Like for many, there were moments when the misery for Black people residing around the world and very particularly in the United States overwhelmed me. Waves of grief and incredible sadness became the spirit of days and then weeks, months, and years. We were locked in our houses. Brothers and sisters were locked in jails and prisons with no access to adequate PPE or ability to socially distance. Our elders were locked in nursing homes and care facilities and dying by the thousands. Schools were closed. Lives were being performed on Zoom and Facebook Live. But the rage of inequity too long endured—that rage that lives inside us—could not remain inside forever. And while Black death at the hands of those sworn to protect us has a long history of everyday terrorism for Black people in the US, it was the lynching of George Floyd that sent us, our allies, and even our detractors to the streets of the US and around the world. Black lives matter and we have had enough.

Given the pandemic, writing this book was my refuge, my sanctuary during difficult times. (Re)membering my students in Ghana and the wisdom, joy, and time for reflection that we had there was my safe haven. Then on Friday, August 28, 2020, actor Chadwick Boseman died, and I went into deep mourning again. But this time, it was a different kind of mourning. Among so many other things, the movie *Black Panther* showed us the culture and the spirit of African people so beautifully, its aesthetic and splendor drawn from across the entire continent of Africa for all to see. How is it possible to grieve our invincible Black superhero who saved Black utopian Wakanda? How do we say goodbye to *our* Black Panther, who saved the place where Black people (re)membered and lived out loud the brilliance, excellence, and beauty that we *inherently* are? While the characters and text of the film *Black Panther* will live on, the one who animated the spirit of our Black Panther in real life, Chadwick Boseman, had left this earth, as we all will, to walk with the ancestors. And we learned from the film the beauty and wisdom of the ancestral journey that allows us to be guided by this beautiful human still. And my spirit was lifted just a little from this state of profound sadness by a tweet that came a couple days after Boseman's death by comedian Trevor Noah when he said: "Yes this was our king. Not because we served him or because he ruled. But because of how he served us in everything he did. He played a hero on screen and lived like one in real life. He made so many of us proud of who we are. Hamba Chadwick. . . . Sizoku bona phambili."[15]

In this tweet, I was (re)minded that our greatness and legacy rest in the *example* that they provide for others, the examples we live that honor the long struggle for freedom and liberation that we are joining and its reverberations and echoes for generations after we leave. Too often we characterize legacy as something that has occurred a long time ago, solely as something that is left behind once we are no longer in the human realm. But the service that Chadwick Boseman provided for all of us was not just about being King T'Challa in our Wakanda. It was also about what it meant to literally *be* a king in the lives of Jackie Robinson, James Brown, Malcolm X, and beyond. The future that he portrayed and created was as much inside him—in his *spirit*—as it was behind or in front of him. And we also have the opportunity to live our legacy right now in our lives as teachers too.

Dr. Issa (re)minded me of the power of being and living legacy and the ways that seeing that spirit in action can help us to imagine and see the possibilities of living legacy. She and I were relaxing one day in my office, a place where we often met for lunch to check in with one another, give a needed hug, or to laugh out loud at the shenanigans of racism that typify our lives in the university as Black women scholars. In casual conversation about how this book about (re)membering was coming along, we started talking about the personal impacts of GSAE on Dr. Issa's own ability to imagine and live legacy even bigger and brighter than her already meteoric rise in the fields of education. Rather vulnerably, she shared a story that really touched me and that (re)minded me again to consider the notion of wholeness in the work of living and (re)claiming legacy. "You know, Dr. Dillard," she said. "I kept thinking while we were in Ghana. I know the Dr. Dillard who does this type of thing, this building, in the US. I know the US Dr. Dillard. But there in Ghana, I kept saying to myself: She is doing this in a *whole other country*! And it dawned on me: the curator of our experience needs to be *well*, to be whole to do that."

That last line points to the crux of the spirit of living legacy in everything we do, in everything we are being. It's the sort of king-being that Chadwick Boseman's spirit reverberated through, not only in his performance in *Black Panther* but in all of his characters. Beyoncé calls us to do a similar (re)claiming as Black women in her epic movie *Black Is King* and its soundtrack, *The Gift*. It's a call not only to be a king or a queen in role and responsibility but to embody "queen-being" as a verb, to *be* the queen spirit who teaches.

Black women have to be whole, full of trust and value in ourselves and our lives, to stand in the long traditions of our greatness as Black women, to stand in our queen-being. But Black women need models of that greatness up close and personal. Our sanctuary experiences in

Ghana gave us space to make bold choices about how our walk and talk in the world could *be* those examples of queen-being, of living and loving Black legacy, as bell hooks calls us to do in her book *Black Looks: Race and Representation*:

> *I choose to create in my daily life*
> *Spaces of reconciliation and forgiveness*
> *Where we let go of past hurt, fear and shame*
> *And hold each other close.*
> *It is only in the act* and *practice*
> *Of loving Blackness*
> *That we are able to reach and embrace the world*
> *Without destructive bitterness*
> *And ongoing collective rage.*[16]

Part of what we were able to do in Ghana was to both (re)claim the spirit of Black joy and that of Black rage in our stories. But like two sides to the coin, we also had to (re)cognize the places of ongoing rage that we carried as Black American women teachers that kept us from living legacy, from queen-being. The examples of Black history, Black herstory, Black excellence, and hospitality that was the context of Ghana showed us how to both (re)member that rage and to marshal it in ways that did not destroy us but instead *fueled* us, enlivened us. But make no mistake, we also understood then and understand now that the US is a context filled with white rage that is directed at us. It is woven into the very foundations and fabric of the country. We need only look at (and too often have experienced) the violence of racial and sexual injustice, police brutality, the inequities of the criminal (in)justice system and for-profit prison industrial complex. We know white rage through the lack of basic human rights for Black children and communities that shows up in unequal school funding, healthcare, and lack of economic opportunity. This is certainly something we have seen laid bare during the COVID-19 pandemic. Damaging outcomes on every measure have fallen disproportionately on

Black and Brown communities and schools, not just today but for millennia. But Black and Brown communities have always embodied the spirit of the phoenix and risen from these ashes despite incredible odds. We hold hope as our discipline. But the costs have been tremendous and our children and communities are continuing to pay those costs inside of our bodies, inside schools, and in society. In her book *White Rage: The Unspoken Truth of Our Racial Divide*, scholar Carol Anderson writes, "The truth is that enslaved Africans plotted and worked—hard—with some even fighting in the Union Army for their freedom and citizenship. After the Civil War, they took what little they had and built schools, worked the land to establish their economic independence and searched desperately to bring their families, separated by slavery, back together."[17] That took untold determination. Initiative. Resilience. Strength of spirit. Anderson's words were echoed in so many of our kitchen table conversations as Black women teachers both in the US and in Ghana. But what Anderson also says is that the trigger for white rage is Black advancement. Ambition—the kind we experienced in abundance in Ghana—is still, to a large extent, forbidden for Black people in the US, particularly for Black women: "It is not the mere presence of Black people that is the problem: Rather, it is Blackness with ambition, with drive, with purpose, with aspirations, and with demands for full and equal citizenship. It is Blackness that refuses to accept subjugation, to give up."[18]

So what has it meant to (re)claim and really lift up and rejoice in all that we were becoming as Black women teachers who were (re)membering, (re)claiming, and moving toward being and living legacy in those rare moments of freedom that were ours in Ghana? *It meant that we had to be the ones we were waiting for.* And we knew in our bones that there was something about consciously choosing to (re)claim Blackness on our terms, within the stories and lessons we had lived in Ghana, that would be much more difficult as we (re)turned to the context of white rage that is the US. But there was also something about walking through the centuries of brutality at the source of Black dislocation and pain that made our fight for freedom for ourselves and others even more urgent than the threat of white rage. We (re)claimed the forced kidnappings of our ancestors, the Middle Passage, and the trauma of brutal dislocations. We (re)claimed the centuries of forced labor and degradation on plantations and the great migration of Black folks determined to leave the oppressive context of Jim Crow. We (re)claimed the beauty of segregated schools and nightmares of integration and the rage that has (re)turned us to that same state in many schools today. We (re)claimed and honored Black folks and others in the streets, courtrooms, boardrooms and political forums who continue to show us how Black lives matter. And we (re)claimed our breath and our lives, our liberties and our pursuits of happiness in the names and spirits of all of those dead, until we join them in the realm of the ancestors. We (re)claimed Chadwick Boseman's Wakanda. We turned our whole minds, bodies, and spirits in the direction of (re)claiming the righteous lessons of struggle, triumph, and joy and taking our place as Black women teachers in that greatness. And with all of the work and struggle that it will require to live legacy with the joy and blessings it provides, our (re)claiming serves *us*. We become teachers who don't create many students: We are teachers who create many teachers.

## BE A QUEEN MOTHER AGAIN

Queen Bey says this:

> History *is* your future. One day, you will meet yourself back where you started but stronger. . . . Come home to yourself. Let Black be synonymous with Glory. . . . The elders are tired. . . . Don't disrespect the Crown by bowing your head.[19]

I am a queen mother, Nana Mansa II of Mpeasem, a small West African village in Ghana's coastal Central Region. In the ancient tradition of the various peoples of Ghana, a queen mother can literally be understood as a female king. She is chosen for this role by the elder head of the clan (family), the council of elders, and other prominent people of the village community. For the Western mind, we might understand her role as "one who [spiritually] owns the state as a mother owns a child."[20] A queen mother is considered a divine being, a founder of the state who is able to give life and maintain life in her state. And her specific moral responsibility is to serve as a wise guide and "mother" for the women of the village. In my case, as a queen mother of development, I am primarily responsible for mothering in a way that develops the village. And along with infrastructure projects like electricity and roads, I have chosen to develop Mpeasem through providing access and opportunity for education and economic opportunity for the women, children, and families of the village. Like the chief and others who are a part of the paramount system, I am called Nana and received, on the day of my enstoolment as queen mother, the chosen name of an ancestor and other symbolic gifts of gratitude and thanksgiving from the chief and the village community, including a beautifully carved wooden stool and a new piece of kente cloth to wear. Given that there are few diasporic Africans who have been called to this ancient and revered institution, one thing has been clear to me in learning to fulfill this honored role in Mpeasem: When I became a queen mother, I wasn't making history. History was making me.

Being a queen has lots of meanings in our Western contexts. But being a queen mother, as defined above, is really about mothering as service  to Black people. In my case it was about (re)cognizing that, in the rupture made in the transatlantic trade of Black people, I had much I needed to learn. So I started with our chief's mother, before she joined the ancestral realm. I asked her to tell me about Nana Mansa I, the queen mother after whom I was named. The chief's mother looked at me somberly and then told me my whole life in three short sentences. These three sentences cemented my purpose and helped me understand how and why I found myself, as a Black American woman in the village of Mpeasem. Helped by translation from Fante to English by one of our teachers, she said: "Nana Mansa was a very kind woman. She had many children, but they were taken away. You are the only one who has returned." In that moment, I realized that, as a Black woman teacher, my work of (re)claiming is also work of (re)claiming a central truth of my existence, beyond any doubt, echoed in the voices of all of the sister teachers gathered here: *There is* nothing *we can't do.*

So, as a queen mother who is also a teacher, I insist on being rooted in my truth and give myself permission to be a whole me. I stand steadfast like a tree, enduring in the strength and tenacity of my ancestors when I teach. I (re)member as I work and as I teach, I learn what I need to know. I am nothing without the worldwide Black community. I rule as a sharer, not a taker. When I have moments of doubt, I turn inward to my spirit and heart and quietly (re)turn to the God in myself whom I love fiercely. My freedom is tied to the freedom of my people in Mpeasem, in the US, and wherever Black people are. And I move toward freedom as a Black woman so that I can free others and live a legacy that would please the ancestors. As I say from my stool in Ghana, through my spirit as Nana Mansa II: "That is all. Let it be so. And so it is."

## YOU'LL MEET YOURSELF AT THE SHORE

The line that titles this section is from Beyoncé's movie *Black Is King.* Here is the line in its entirety: "*You'll meet yourself at the shore. The coast belongs to our ancestors. We orbit, make joy look easy.*" For the Black women teachers in GSAE, to (re)claim newfound cultural, spiritual, and historical knowledge, we had (1) to be both able *and* willing to (re)claim the legacy of Black African people, and (2) to take our place in and as living legacy in our work as educators. In the final interviews for this book, I asked the GSAE teachers to do a little freedom dreaming, to imagine Black women's futures as teachers in response to the following question: *What is possible when culture, race, spiritual knowledge, and pedagogies are marshaled together in the teaching and learning endeavor for the Black woman educator?*[21] To a person, every teacher did their own version of the blink, blink, pause I spoke of in chapter 2. But to this question, their response was unanimous: *"Everything is possible."* And one of the most amazing outcomes for me, as the leader of the GSAE, was to bear witness to the ways and means that these Black women teachers (re)claimed not only heritage knowledge and culture in the spirit of Africa but also the fierceness with which they leaned in to "[meeting] themselves at the shore," to "orbit[ing], mak[ing] joy look easy." Having traveled mind, body, and spirit to Ghana and back to the US, these experiences often shaped *everything* that they did from that point forward. To be clear: I am not saying that every Black woman who traveled to Ghana makes miraculous and total transformations in herself upon our (re)turn. But I am saying that if Black women left the US committed to the spiritual work of (re)membering, everything about them changed in bold and powerful ways. They (re)turned with a change in their spirits.

Throughout this book, I have shared my own stories of how being in conversation and relationship with Ghana has fundamentally changed my scholarly life, my pedagogies, the contexts of my practice, my body, mind, and spirit. I *carry* Ghana inside of me and the gift of her presence impacts everything outside of me. This was the spirit and the catalyst for developing the GSAE program that brought forward a kind of teacher professional development that centers Black women and people in ways that (re)member and heal not only Black women but everyone in our company. I want to briefly share just a few of the ways that the Black women in GSAE over the years have (re)claimed the rich, beautiful heritage that is Black women from the continent of Africa to the shores of the US, in the indomitable spirit of joy that Black women are, have been, and will be. These are testaments to what (re)membering has the power to do. I will highlight only a few of the many stories of Black women teachers in GSAE, examples of the powerful shifts in their lives and work toward education in the spirit of the work of (re)membering.

## TO BE A BLACK WOMAN LEADER

You may (re)call Olivia, one of only two non-education majors who participated in the GSAE over the seven years of this program. Despite all of her educational achievements, Olivia spent a good deal of time in our conversations reflecting on the real struggles she and her family went through growing up in the projects. The person Olivia had the greatest admiration for was her mother, who used every ounce of her determination to support Olivia's education. Olivia participated in the GSAE in her senior year at the university, obtained her bachelor's degree, and shifted from seeking work focused in her public relations major and instead started a career in teaching after her experience in GSAE. She says:

> It wasn't until I went to this school in New York and like watched the teaching happen. And I was like, I think I am supposed to be a teacher. . . . I think I am supposed to empower kids who look like me . . . that stream of connection. There's clearly something about Black kids, Black and Brown kids. . . . After the program, I was able to see how powerful education is and how important the village is.

Listening to that voice inside, Olivia realized quite quickly after the GSAE that her real work was as an educator, not a public relations person. In teaching at a charter school in Harlem, she was exposed to powerful Black women in leadership. And she began exploring deeply what it meant to be a Black woman leader in school contexts: "I thought leadership had a look, sound, a feel and be like this or that. And then I started to see women in leadership who were Black, who did not fit those molds but who are leaders nonetheless. And I started to realize, like, I can be all these things. I can a leader and I can be a competitive pole dancer. . . . I can be silly, I can be young, and I can still be a leader." Since beginning her teaching career, Olivia has served in a number of leadership positions within her charter school and is now the academic dean for the school. She has plans to begin a study abroad for her own students: "They need to be able to go to Ghana, or the Dominican Republic or Brazil. Anywhere in the diaspora, just so they can see people of power who look like them, and to understand the connection and the histories. They *need* to see that. . . . In Ghana, it was when like all these connections became real for me. . . . And I am living that spirit because of it."

## BUILDING A NATIONAL NETWORK

To be in Dr. Issa's presence is to be in the presence of greatness, to be in the presence of someone whose spirit and joy fill the room at the sheer mention of her name. I often tease her about how her students not only love her but have literally fallen in love with her each semester. Everything around Dr. Issa lets you know how much she loves Black culture and Black people. She adores us. But models of Black women were also a very important part of Dr. Issa's ability to (re)claim and live Black legacy on her terms as a queer Black woman.

Right before leaving for Ghana, Dr. Issa released a new book on abolitionist teaching and it immediately became a bestseller. While it hasn't yet hit the *New York Times* bestseller list (a goal for Dr. Issa), it has sold over one hundred thousand copies in just over a year. Even during the pandemic, Dr. Issa continued to be sought out for book talks and keynotes on Zoom and other social media platforms. I asked her if it was fair to say that her life and world changed as a result of her time in Ghana, to which she replied: "It's not that it [GSAE] was the only impact. But I learned to see my worth there. I could see what was possible in my life, in my home and in school. It was something about the way it was curated. You gave us gentle nudges to build, to not be silent anymore."

And silent she was not. Once Dr. Issa (re)turned to the US, she began the heavy lift of putting her plans in motion. While her book continues to sell widely, Dr. Issa started writing op-eds for national weekly education journals. She took the bold step of cofounding a national network for abolitionist teaching that is already breaking records for fundraising and visibility across the country. In the best traditions of Black abolition and the spirit of freedom, the organization offers professional development for Black and Brown children, families, and teachers; offers scholarships for Black women single mothers; and is embarking on funding a national cadre of education activists to support abolitionist teaching work in large city schools across the nation. Asked to serve on the board of directors for her newfound organization (and as the founder of my own nonprofit organization, Give.Build.Share, which funds our school building projects in Ghana), I know the long days and nights and the serious work that this (re)claiming and living legacy requires. But one thing I also know about Dr. Issa: she will move heaven and earth for Black people and will ride or die for Black women.

During one of her interviews, as Dr. Issa began to speak, her gestures felt a little different to me, like their own invitation into the world she is creating for Black people. Her arms gesture more openly, bent but always outstretched. Beginning this story, her gestures are almost wistful, as she speaks of being in the retreat center that my husband and I have built in Ghana. I come to learn that this was one of the most impactful catalysts for her own (re)claiming: "Just seeing y'all in your home. Now, I saw that first level where you lived as you built. You were roughin' it! And I only know the Coach-bag-havin' and luxury-hotel-stayin' Dr. Dillard. I had never seen the sacrifices, that side of Dr. Dillard. I kept saying to myself: 'This is what she does . . . in GHANA!' And I learned then that you have to sacrifice to build a vision."

### NO FRAGMENTATION, ONLY (RE)MEMBERING

So many stories of (re)claiming and living legacy abound in the Black women teachers' lives after Ghana. Some have developed their own study abroad programs centered on connecting students to the post-colonial realities of the US and Ghanaian higher education systems at other universities where they now work. Others are taking deep dives of self-study into African and Black studies and literature and preparing yearlong curriculums for upper elementary–aged children that center the contributions of Africans and African Americans. In addition to Dr. Issa, other professors have developed national education networks, started life coaching businesses, and finished book projects, all designed to serve the needs of Black people's bodies, minds, and spirits, as well as the educational needs of Black children—in Africa, in the US, and throughout the diaspora. Those who were doctoral students have changed their dissertation topics to more critically focus on Black stories, theories, and issues—and they have completed their PhDs. Another professor developed a database and archival space for documenting the trauma Black people have experienced from the continent of Africa to the diaspora both historically and in real time. And others have (re)vised their pedagogies and practices in ways that (re)member Ghana in their minds, bodies, and spirits and for their students.

And then there is Grace, the last doctoral student I will advise before I retire from the academy. I wanted to end this book with her story because it is indicative of how powerfully my students have shaped my *whole* life. Her spirit is also reminiscent of dozens of mostly doctoral students of color whom I have had the honor and privilege of working with over my academic career. Grace is the kind of Black woman student who is hungry to explore her own questions, most often about the place of culture, story, and Black womanhood in the work of teaching and learning. Her voice is the perfect ending for a book on (re)membering and the power of (re)claiming ourselves as Black women teachers, (re)claiming our spiritual lives and our stories.

For Grace, her commitment to vocation as a Black woman teacher focuses very specifically on the spiritual lives of Black and Brown children. As a practicing Christian, she (re)turned to the university to pursue a doctoral degree in order to explore the critical possibilities for Black education that centered spirituality, freedom, and liberation. Having experienced the often oppressive and limiting conditions for children of color in public education, as well as for Black teachers like herself, Grace sought new possibilities for teaching and learning based in the inherent brilliance and grace of Black people. And from the moment we met, I knew that our paths were divinely ordered and our work divinely purposed as well. She was in my life to help me (re)member.

Grace has traveled to the continent of Africa three times. Her first experience was on a Fulbright group trip to Tanzania, just months before her first study abroad to Ghana with the GSAE. The following year, she served as my graduate research assistant for GSAE as well as for this book project. For Grace, (re)claiming was centered on healing what she often described as our fragmentation as Black people and the freedom that is possible when we are able to move toward wholeness, especially as teachers. Her notion of fragmentation was intriguing, as it was a challenge and condition for which (re)membering could respond, especially in relation to the spirit. Here, she reflects on the detrimental outcomes of fragmentation for the Black student protagonist named Biko in Ayi Kwei Armah's novel *KMT in the House of Life*. This was one of the books we read in our GSAE study sessions. Grace explains:

> I think about Biko and his enthusiasm for coming to school, and how he just knew who he was. He knew his history. He was well read and nobody could shake it. And where did his murder happen? Where did that suppression of his spirit happen? It happened in schools. And they didn't touch that baby's body. It was the constant suppressing of his spirit and constant don't do this, don't do that. No, your people did not do this. It's the curriculum violence too. It's only teaching our kids one version of their history and it's the worst version. . . . I did a small study at a Christian school and when the teacher tried to advocate for Black History Month she was told, "Why should we put one race over the other?". . . I'm just like "My goodness." But over in Ghana, it was not like that. You could breathe in culture. You could breathe in our values. You could *feel* it. It was a transformative experience because I could feel it.

Grace has always been curious about the missing pieces of Black history and culture, beginning with her own family. With the deftness of a quilter, she had already pieced together several generations of her family's stories in the US and shared them often. That gathering felt like its own sort of (re)clamation to me. One powerful example rested in the sheer tenacity of her grandmother, a single parent of seven children and direct descendant of sharecroppers in Mississippi. She took her children one by one to Detroit in search of better life chances for the family. Interestingly, this same grandmother, while deeply spiritual, seemed always to be on a search for something more. Her grandmother's (re)search felt very connected to Grace's own (re)search and her motivation for (re)turning to doctoral study generally and the GSAE program more particularly:

> It was something she was not getting when she was not involved in any type of spirituality or religion, anything. So once she got [to Detroit] she found her answers in the Nation of Islam. . . . My Dad went to a Muslim school so he was constantly learning about our [Black] histories and there wasn't this curriculum violence. It was a celebratory curriculum where yes, we were enslaved, but we've been triumphant, and our history didn't begin there.

Given several conflicts that her father had both within and outside of the Nation of Islam, he was invited to a Pentecostal Christian church. It was there that he met Grace's mother, a woman of strict religious beliefs, and they eventually married. Grace continued: "But my Dad still had many remnants of the good part of the Nation with him. So we would learn Black history stuff. And my Dad would talk to us about stuff, and we would sit down as a family and have these conversations with my brothers about dealing with the police. They were just telling us about what it meant to be Black. . . . A lot of my friends did not have explicit conversations about that." Grace's thirst for answers (re)minds me so much of Biko, whom she'd referenced earlier. While Biko's explicit questioning and exposure of the contradictions and outright lies in curriculum as a Black student happened within the walls of the school, (re)membering her own family conversations led to more contradictions and questions for Grace, as a Black woman teacher and emerging scholar. These were questions that she was still working out in Ghana:

> I would ask [my parents] "How can we be Black and be Christian when that wasn't even our original identity? It wasn't our original spirituality. So how can we be comfortable doing that?" No answers. So I go to Ghana, and I start doing all this reading on slavery. And I read about

this idea of syncretism. And I think that's what showed up in schools in Ghana: there was no fragmentation of identities.

Clearly excited about her ideas, Grace breaks out in a smile as she gets more animated and shares the following litany of the challenges of being Black, being a woman, and being spiritual in the US:

> You know, you have to separate your womanhood from your Blackness. You can't bring your spiritualities into the academy. You can't . . . you can't. All these fragmentations that we're expected to do here in the US. But in Ghana, there was no fragmentation. Even when it came to a religion or spirituality, the fact that these babies could pray to a Christian God and also pray to Allah. They learn about Islam and Christianity and their traditional religions. . . . I got a lot of answers there for sure, that I was looking for. How can I be this *and* this? It doesn't operate if they're contradictory identities. In Ghana, it was like, a sense of freedom, a sense of liberation in that I don't have to fragment. I can just *be*. I can be whole. I can be Black and woman. I can be African and American. I can be Christian and still be pro-Black and love our people. I cannot appreciate the way Christianity came to us, but [I can] embody it in a way where I still honor my ancestors. I can still do that. I didn't know I could do that and still be a Christian. But I did that. In Ghana. In Ghana. So yeah, it expanded my mindset for sure.

I couldn't help but think about quilting as she talked, the ways that quilters bring together small pieces of cloth in various patterns and colors to create something altogether different, more expansive, and even more beautiful than any one piece of that cloth could be on its own. Grace was (re)claiming all the parts of herself, piecing herself back together again because, for Grace and for Black women generally, every part of our identities *matters*. Too often we have been forced to put little fragments of ourselves into little boxes in US contexts. We are asked, either implicitly or explicitly: Are you Black or are you a woman? Which is more important to you? Are you a member of this religious group, or that political party? Are you a man or a woman, gay or straight? Do you pledge allegiance only to the US and ignore or dismiss the continent of Africa as your "nation" too? Claiming and gathering all the pieces of who we are as Black women is a huge challenge and not for the faint of heart. For Grace, the piecing together that she was engaging—her (re)membering—was something that (re)membering requires in a teacher's life, an embodiment of her pseudonym, Grace:

> I think I have grace for my kids. (Re)membering requires grace for myself too. Knowing that I don't know everything. I'm not perfect. There are going to be days where I feel like I can take over the world. There's going to be days where, as a teacher, I felt like, "Man, it's me against the machine." But the grace to keep going. The grace to realize that I don't have to be perfect. The grace that my babies don't have to be perfect. . . . This has been the case for sure when I was a teacher where we would have a rough day or a student is acting up or has misbehavior. Instead of kicking them out, I tried to reconcile whatever was going on there. . . . I was definitely strict. I definitely had super high expectations for my students, but it was the grace within the classroom that made them feel like this is different. . . . It shows up as grace. It shows up in just the way I love my students, whether it's my baby's babies or even, moving forward, thinking about me as a professor.

Showing up fully. Showing up in grace. Showing up ready to love Black students. Showing up ready to love ourselves. Grace teaches that for Black women teachers, it is about showing up completely without the expectation to fragment, twist, subtract, or distort. Instead, as we (re)member, we grow bigger, especially as we (re)claim and live Black legacy as our work as teachers, in classrooms and beyond:

> It should be a place where you don't have to subtract your spirituality. You don't have to leave it at the door. . . . You are still not proselytizing your students. You can just *be*. Just period, full stop. You can just be. . . . I feel like when you're able to, as a Black woman, show up fully, you create a space for your students to do the same. . . . You are able to

*brae fie* [Twi for "come home"]. That has stuck with me for a year and I have used it so much. You can come home. . . . Do your work to go home. That *inner work*.

Grace (re)minds us that (re)claiming is always about doing that inner work, a home coming to the spirit of our work.

CHAPTER 7

# (RE)MEMBERING IS NOT OPTIONAL

*A Love Letter to Those Who Teach*

My Dear Teachers:

This is a love letter from my heart to yours. It is a love letter for who you are and what you do in this incredible work of teaching. I write this letter in hopes that it might both push and nurture your spiritual growth as a human and as a teacher. But I also write it as a (re)minder to you of something crucially important in this moment and always:

*(Re)membering is not optional.*

I start with words from the brilliant Haitian writer Edwidge Danticat, who issues a charge to all of us who write, a charge that also applies to all of us who teach:

> Create dangerously, for people who read dangerously, . . . knowing in part that no matter how trivial your words may seem, someday, somewhere, someone may risk his or her life to read them. . . . Somewhere, if not now...[as writers, teachers] we may also save someone's life.[1]

My hope is that you have read this book *dangerously*. That somewhere within these pages you have found inspiration to approach teaching, learning, and living in very different ways and maybe for very different purposes. Danticat shares how the work of reading, writing, and (re)membering (on which teaching relies) are always dangerous undertakings. She speaks of how the work of an intellectual is the work of an artist, of creating the world through one's words, one's art, one's *life*. I hope you feel the same way about teaching. Her call is one that incites us to look both forward and backward, to engage our cultural memories to produce new spaces in which we all might live more fully. I hope you have also heard it as a call to (re)cognize our roles as teachers and scholars as serious life-or-death endeavors. For each class of students we teach or each research study we undertake is imbued with the *possibility* of creating something new and different, even better than what already exists.

My prayer is that *The Spirit of Our Work: Black Women Teachers (Re)member* has been a dangerous text for you, one that causes you to sit with its words and to imagine their relevance in your life as a teacher. But I also pray that these words light a fire within to (re)member who *you* are and who we are, together. I believe that in order for teachers to teach all students well, they must know who Black people are in both the length and breadth of our complex histories, cultures, and spiritual traditions. Before we even begin to consider the culturally sustaining pedagogies, abolitionist teaching, and more equitable curriculum that we might develop to teach, we must have cultural and heritage knowledge enough to be *able* to marshal these frameworks and strategies in the spirit they were developed. (Re)membering Black thought traditions, stories, and peoples are prerequisites to helping our students engage in similar processes for themselves. But we must *know* in order to be able to *do*. We are calling you to (re)member that you have much to learn from Black people, a people who don't just happen to be in the US. It is through millennia of singing our Black national anthem, of "treading our path through the blood of the slaughtered" that Black people are still here in Africa and our diaspora.[2] If you want to know how to teach on behalf of the whole of Black humanity, *you must know and believe in it first.* You must, as the Black women in this book have shown you, turn the [slave] ships around and (re)member us, not just to heal yourselves but to also heal education.[3] You must see and know the power of the spirit of Black people as a model for healing the very spirit of education, education that serves to liberate and free everybody from the shackles of our woeful and often willful ignorance.

I have become a better human because I have learned decades of lessons from the voices of my students. For that and so much more, I thank you. And in the case of this book, I have learned *invaluable* lessons from the voices of the Black women teachers in the Ghana Study Abroad in Education program on which it is based. Lessons that inform my life as a teacher educator. Lessons about the kind of teacher education and professional development that honors and (re)members Black women and that supports us in our commitments to the academic, social, and spiritual lives of our Black students particularly, and all of our students more generally. Lessons about the necessity of teachers to be absolutely vigilant, especially in these troubling times, to caring and loving and nurturing our own spirits. Lessons about the power of relationship and love. In a recent dissertation proposal meeting of a Black woman graduate student alumna of GSAE, I learned yet another lesson. I asked Rita to share a bit more about the criteria she was using to select participants for her study. She talked through the criteria, and at the very end, shared a question that I must now share with you. She said she selects her participants based on a simple question: "*Who has more of the story to tell?*"

> And in this process of (re)membering,
> that person with more of the story to tell is you.

Every human being has heritage and cultural knowledge. We use it every day in every decision we make as teachers. And not all of it is something to be proud of. Some of these memories and ways of being are painful, and other parts are even joyful. They often scare us, making us afraid to explore our depths. *But how can we teach if we do not know what brought us to this place, the stories of our ancestors' movements and migrations, how we came to be who we are and the legacies that we embody?* To seek justice and equity in education is to lay these wounds and triumphs bare, the ones inside you and those of your ancestors. Because our healing is next to the wound as individuals, as collectives, and certainly in the systems of education where we work. And until we can (re)member and cry for the legacy of inequities and harm caused to Black people, including Black women, name that harm, and actively work to repair it, we will never be whole, regardless of the plethora of new models of practice we want to use in education. And as teachers, we will never be *well* enough to teach all of our students.

This book is an examination of Black women teachers and our (re)memberings. But these stories are also stories of the Black aunties, mothers, grandmothers, sisters, and Black women students whom we teach or teach with every day. They are the stories of your teacher colleagues who are Black women. They are the stories of that Black woman who served you at the bank or grocery store today. These are stories of the Black woman elected official you voted for (or didn't). These might even be the stories of a person who you call your best friend. But this call to (re)membering is for *all* teachers, not only Black women teachers. Because to teach any student well, we must see that Black people generally and Black students particularly also stand within long and powerful stories and legacies that the sisters in this book spoke about. Our students are also living Black legacies. And it is their *human* right to know intimately the Black and African heritages that have birthed them. It is their *human* right to know intimately their rich knowledge and cultural traditions, not just those from within the borders of their neighborhoods, states, or nations but also from across the world. And it is also the *human* right of non-Black students to understand these African and Black legacies too. For it was Europeans who enslaved and stole millions of African people from the continent of Africa to build systems of capitalism in countries in the Americas and Caribbean. And in the barbaric white supremacy that was the transatlantic trade, it was by design that Black folks *not* be allowed access to the languages of our homelands, our cultural ways of knowing, and the spiritual traditions that guide us. However, make no mistake; it was precisely because our history and stories were such powerful testaments to our collective spirit and humanity that these life-giving treasures were kept from us. But as elder Nana Peazant (re)minded us at the beginning of this book: *We still carry that spirit and humanity inside we.* For white teachers who may be like some of the teachers I had growing up in Seattle, your fear of allowing a young Black girl like me to read about Malcolm X or Angela Davis speaks volumes about the limited and racist narrative that *you* require to keep me where you need me to be. The liberatory alternative? Pick up the book yourself, open a window for me and so many like me, and watch us soar to the heights of Black legacy where we (re)write the hunter's story to fit *our* mouths as Black women. Then you and I will have two versions of the narrative of our being. We will move toward having an "us."

What I need everyone to understand is that when Black women have the time and space to (re)member, it is truly a new day, a day of celebration not just for us but for everyone. As the young Columbus-based organization Black Girl Miracle states in its motto about this moment in our history: "We're not taking over. *We're taking our place.*" I purposefully highlighted Black women's experiences of (re)membering in these pages not because we are the only people who (re)member: *It is because we are the people at the intersections who the world needs to know and learn from.* And I wanted to write a book that did not deviate from but instead mirrored the very intentions and purposes that the Ghana Study Abroad in Education (re)presented. I wanted to explicitly focus attention as a writer and scholar on Black women teachers' experiences. But if you listen carefully and *really* want to learn from the power and humanity of Black women, you will find lessons that you need to know to be the teachers that Black students deserve and that all students need.

**Black women offer you the invitation to (re)member.** That is the first lesson. And that is the invitation that you must also offer your students. But as their teacher, before you plan a lesson or develop any curriculum or syllabi, your inner life must be well. As the person responsible for your students' well-being and wholeness in mind, body, and spirit, you too must be whole. Not perfect, but having spent considerable time in reflection, careful study, and examination of your spirit, your knowledge of the children you teach, and the values embedded in the long traditions of *their* people. Like medical doctors, who take the Hippocratic oath to "first do no harm," as teachers who already have the gift of Black students in your care, you must take up even more urgently the invitational questions below, lest you unknowingly do harm to Black children in their educational experience. So before you teach Black students, you might start by asking yourself these questions:

1. Who am I? What are the racial, cultural, social, class, and other identities that I embody? Can I say them out loud in the company of those who do not embody the same identities?

2. When I think of my friends and colleagues, are there Black women or Black people in this group? Why or why not? Have I ever talked about our racial differences and really listened to what they were telling me?

3. If I am a white person, is there a knot in my gut as I talk about Blackness and Black people and how did it get there? How do I describe that knot to others and how does the act of doing so enable a *productive* dialogue with others, particularly across differences?

4. What is my life experience with Black women or Black people, not just in the US but across the globe? What additional experiences might I need to have in order to understand Black life more fully, and how do I responsibly and respectfully have those necessary experiences?

5. How have I prepared to approach the realities of Black women's lives in specific ways, with the attention that geographies, sexualities, economic class, languages, and other differences require?

6. What lessons am I learning about myself as I learn about versions of Black life from Africa to America and back again?

(Re)member: this is not an exhaustive list but simply offered as an invitation to begin to tap into your own spirit as a necessary first step to your teaching. It is also an invitation that is given to teachers of all racial, ethnic, and social identities. It is an invitation to you to do the courageous and important work of looking at yourself and what you know *before* you grab onto the brilliant curriculum frameworks in the Black tradition like Gholdy Muhammad's *Cultivating Genius: An Equity Framework for Culturally and Historically Responsive Literacy*; Gloria Ladson-Billings, *The Dreamkeepers: Successful Teachers of African American Children*; Django Paris and H. Samy Alim's *Culturally Sustaining Pedagogies: Teaching and Learning for Justice in a Changing World*; or Rich Milner's *Start Where You Are, But Don't Stay There: Understanding Diversity, Opportunity Gaps, and Teaching in Today's Classrooms*.

**Black women offer you the power of sanctuary.** I hope the words of this book have, if only for the length of its pages, been that sacred place for you, a starting place. While the stories here are a result of Black women's (re)membering of the roots of African American culture and traditions in the sanctuary that Ghana was for us, generations of our grandmothers and aunties have left us a plethora of texts that provide glimpses into various sanctuaries that Black women have created and experienced as we continue our long walk to freedom. Authors like Abena Busia, Alice Walker, Toni Morrison, Paule Marshall, Maya Angelou, nayyirah waheed, and Lucille Clifton have been sanctuary for me, providing models of how to breathe and resist oppression *and* to build on behalf of our freedom as Black women. They have been hush harbors in the harshness of a world that too often renders us invisible. But (re)member: in addition to being a refuge or quiet place for our minds, bodies, and spirits as Black people, hush harbors were also spaces where we *(re)membered who we were and whose we were.* Having temporarily escaped the confines of segregation and degradation, we found joy and purpose in (re)membered rituals of praise in song, dance, and prayer. It was our place to be affirmed in community with other Black people and to commune with the spirits of our ancestors. It was a space where our bruised and wounded souls could be healed and a world that embraced Black humanity could be created again. These spaces—whether through literature, gatherings, or in spaces of contemplation—are how we (re) member Black humanity when the hurt and hate are too much. *We* know that our Black lives matter. What we need in schools and educational spaces are modern-day hush harbors, spaces of (re)membering that enact community and collective kinship, places to organize, freedom dream, and resist.

If as a teacher you will join in the struggle for education and freedom that creates a sanctuary for Black students and communities, you need to know that the struggle you are joining did not start today. You need to know that the struggle for Black lives to matter began in the invasion of the continent of Africa and the subsequent plundering of her resources that continues today. And you will need to make a serious and ongoing commitment to critically study and unpack the length of that hurt, harm, and danger that you may have endured, both personally and professionally, and that in other cases you may have also caused or benefited from. As a teacher, you will need your own sanctuary to do this work, leaning on no one else to teach you what you do not know as a shortcut to the gift that critical learning and (re)membering can be for your spiritual and intellectual growth and development. In sanctuary, all the (re)membering processes are yours to grow through. That is the gift of sanctuary: it's a place where you can search again, vision again, think again, present yourself again, and, ultimately, claim and live legacy again. Who is a part of the sanctuary or sacred community you create will vary, but it may need to be made up of a racially or culturally homogeneous group at first: we all have a lot of healing work to do within and around those who share similar racial, cultural, and social identities. That is just fine. As we saw in chapter 2, (re)membering will partly arise from gathering the memories of our schooling and other segregated experiences in the US and beyond. The Black women teachers in the GSAE program had and continue to have multiple and different sacred communities within which we (re)membered, including the company of other Black women in church spaces, organizations, and the like. The key in sanctuary is to wrestle with the hurt, harm, and danger, as well as the joy, resilience, and strength of our ancestors, and to acknowledge and even revise our covenants with them. And when our teaching embodies spaces of sanctuary and freedom for our students that we ourselves have learned and experienced, as the Black women teachers in this book told us: *everything* is possible. Here are a few questions as you begin your work in sanctuary that might be helpful to your growth and examination of yourself as a teacher of the stories and accomplishments of Black people:

1. How do I hold differences in the stories I am reading or experiences I am having with Blackness sacredly with reverence, without judgment or denial?

2. Can I be comfortable in these experiences in a place where it is not always about me, not about what *I* know or feel, being empathetic enough to imagine a differing reality than my own?

3. Are humility, sacrifice, and selflessness at the center of my desire to "know" Black stories, Black culture, and Black people or am I collecting exotic stories to tell?

4. How does what I *thought* I knew about diverse Black people match what I am now hearing from engagements with diverse Black people?

5. Where are the places and people who could provide disconfirming stories to the ones I am experiencing? Have I sought out their stories, too?

6. How do I struggle within the tensions of the African continent and her diaspora and the relative and multiple meanings within the larger story of Black culture?

7. In what ways do the stories I'm hearing (or the texts I'm reading) map onto my experience and knowings? In what ways are they different? What does that help me to know?

8. What else do I need to know to imagine sharing my learning with my students? More importantly, what can they teach me?

**Black women offer up the need to live in the spirit of Black legacy.** What I found in this work with the GSAE is that different groups had different outcomes in their processes of (re)membering. For Black people, our work could be characterized as *(re)covery*, as being about *repairing* the spiritual, cultural, and material damages to ourselves and our communities through engagements with African heritage and culture. Our work as Black teachers was about standing in the brilliance and strength of the legacy of Black people unabashedly, with no apologies or permission needed, without the blink, blink, pause. For many of my white students, their ability to live Black legacy (in the spirit of being a co-conspirator that Bettina Love offers us) could be characterized as an *uncovering* of the history and culture of Black people that they did not know, in some cases could not imagine. This included the hard work of acknowledging legacies of inhumanity wrought by their ancestors. Their work was fundamentally about developing a new covenant with their ancestors and thus with humanity, one that (re)cognized both the harm perpetrated against Black life and the active abolition work needed to repair it, in honor of and in struggle with Black humanity. It needed to be active *work* toward justice, not just simple acknowledgment of or guilty feelings about injustice. For me, the story of the "how" of (re)claiming Black legacy and living is a story that white teachers might be better suited to tell. And I look forward to reading those stories and the hope that lies within them for true equity and justice. Living Black legacy requires that you be both able and willing to (re)claim the legacy of Black and African people and take your place in living this legacy in the work of being a teacher. But living Black legacy *necessarily* requires risk, sacrifice, and strength, as well as joy and an Ubuntu spirit to do the work. It requires abolition and freedom dreaming. It requires that we work with every breath to show up whole and without fragmentation, as Grace shared at the end of the last chapter.

One of my own attempts to live Black legacy as a Black teacher educator meant abolishing study abroad as a historically colonial project that does not love Black women and creating a program that gave us back a part of our lives. And this is something you will need to develop in order to *live* your own versions of Black legacy, regardless of the skin you are in. But a fundamental test for all of us will be this: as we create new spaces for Blackness in lessons or programs or lectures, will diverse groups of Black people (re)cognize our efforts to (re)claim Black legacy? In other words, will Black people be able to (re)cognize your efforts as being centered in Black *humanity*, not just today but for centuries? Here are a few more questions to consider as you begin your work in (re)claiming and living Black legacy:

1. What do experiences of Blackness *mean* to Black people and how do diverse Black people make meaning of their experiences?

2. Can I *hear* and *imagine* the deeper meanings of individual and collective Black people's experiences and empathize without trying to "save" them? In what ways do I become more "human" (and humane) in relation to and with Black life?

3. What do Black stories mean to me and what emotions and memories do they evoke?

4. What are the structures in place that have been and continue to be oppressive to Black people? How do I work diligently to tear them down and do my part to create sanctuary for those most harmed, as we rebuild structures of freedom for all?

5. When someone sees my teaching work, how will they know/ see/feel/experience that I approached this project with reverence for Black lives, cultures, and stories?

These are some of the gifts that the Black women teachers in this book have given us. But a gift is only a gift if the receiver accepts it. And gifts are very much like letters in that they are intimate and often something we desire, a (re)cognition that someone has (re)membered us. In her edited volume *Letters from Black America: Intimate Portraits of the African American Experience*, Pamela Newkirk speaks of the ways that the gift of letter writing "anchors us in the past with unparalleled intimacy and spontaneity, lighting the dark crevices of our private and public history."[4] She speaks further about why a book of intimate letters from African Americans also (re)presents the determination and resilience it took for Black people to learn to read and write during slavery and for hundreds of years following Emancipation: "A history of disparaging portrayals in popular culture has surely contributed to the reluctance by African Americans to expose their inner lives. This reticence poses a challenge for scholars seeking to depict the fullness of African American life and makes all the more precious the contributors to these pages."[5] So who has more of the story to tell? My dear colleague, *you* do. You have something to contribute to the greater story of (re)membering who we are *together*. Our legendary poet Lucille Clifton calls us to do just that when she speaks of whose memories we need to (re)member: *our own*.[6] (Re)membering who we have been and who we are is where we must begin in order to form more just and righteous spaces for education—and it is not optional for those of us who teach.

# AFTERWORD

This book is the response to the question: *What happens when education meets freedom and liberation through (re)membering and (re)turning?*

Our North Star, Dr. Cynthia Dillard, (re)minds Black women what happens when we (re)member. And something quite pure and magical happens—liberation, spiritual freedom, and educational progress.

When we (re)visit, (re)member, and (re)turn, we consequently have the blueprint to (re)form education. (Re)form has been a contentious word in education, captured in smallness through weak policies and legislation in the US because our so-called reforms have not transformed systems and structures to ensure that our children, namely Black children, reach their full potential. Rather, reform efforts have put fresh coats of paint on old, hindering structures in an attempt to make our educational system appear fresh and innovative. But Black children are still underserved by the oppressive walls of the system. In contrast, Dillard offers authentic (re)form that designs a blueprint for the walls of an educational schoolhouse where our children can breathe, live, and thrive freely.

In my own work to cultivate the genius and joy of Black students and teachers, I am (re)minded how the educational system in the United States is much like a *house*. And the walls, scaffolds, and structures of the house are weak, broken, and debilitated. The house is built from weak materials, steeped in whiteness—not created from the histories, cultures, or spiritual understandings of Black people.

The house is lacking Black liberation, Black identities, and Black genius, and lacks the ways we have educated our own. These walls of the house feel suffocating and stifling, producing inhumane conditions and curriculum for Black children and teachers. The blueprint was not designed for us; therefore, we need books like this to show us the way forward.

When the world has not loved us, honored us, or (re)cognized our brilliance, it becomes our obligation to (un)earth and to (re)member, as Dillard writes in "The Substance of Things Hoped For, the Evidence of Things Not Seen." When we (re)member, we resist—resist the oppressive walls and their flawed design. In this way, we must fight for ourselves and only then can we fight for and teach others. When we don't, we will accept the "house" as it is, and consequently real (re)form doesn't happen. But when the materials of the house are built upon Blackness, inside, we move toward self-empowerment, self-reliance, and self-determination. Dillard takes us home so we can experience these goals. If we don't (re)turn home, we will never know the possibility of who we are, who we are not, and who we are destined to be. Studying Ghana—the historical lives of ourselves and our students—positions us to better love and teach each other. Dillard provides the definition and conceptualization for this possibility and love of Blackness that we have all been waiting for.

The intentional use of the prefix *re-* in parentheses is not only captivating but purely brilliant as this rhetorical move centers the need to go "back," and to go back "again" to our histories, our roots, and our land. By visiting and experiencing Black women's teachings, we are going back again to a space and place that affirms who we are. Only then can we begin to enter and (re)form schools and classrooms in the US, to (re)build the house. When we (re)turn and go back, we (re)discover (perhaps again or maybe for the first time) our knowledge and our purpose. The use of the prefix *re-* also allows me to take some time with the root word and consider how it relates to history and the critical need to learn of the past to better navigate the present. In a world that moves so fast, we don't spend enough time resting a bit upon language, reflecting on its beauty and how we need to educate ourselves in order to educate others. To this end, Dillard's centering of Black women is key, as Black women teachers require our specificity in this moment. And Dillard loves us enough to pen such an important book that will become a part of the collection of abolitionist archives. Dillard and other Black women abolitionist theorists and educators provide us direction for advancing the state of education for Black children and other children as well, giving us the abolitionist tools to (re)build the house and (re)claim our authority to do so: sisters like Harriet Tubman, Anna Julia Cooper, Mary McLeod Bethune, and Clara Muhammad. We must center their scholarship if we are to truly (re)form.

Dillard offers five components in an endarkened feminist praxis framework to (re)build our "walls" from our historical understandings. These five "scaffolds" are our building tools to understand and to (re)construct and plan for education today:

**(Re)searching**: In schools, educators must seek and search for knowledge and truths about their students' histories and identities and connect this research directly to the multiple disciplines taught in and around schools.

Ask: *What knowledge do I carry and what knowledge must I seek about the cultural and racial histories and identities of my students? What is the history of mathematics, science, language arts, social studies, and how do my students' histories and identities connect to the discipline I am teaching? How do my students' identities and histories authentically show up in my curriculum, instruction, and leadership?*

**(Re)visioning**: In schools, educators must expand their notions of Black beauty and genius to dispel falsehood.

Ask: *What genius, beauty, and excellence can be found from Blackness in mathematics, science, language arts, social studies, health, and art? What misconceptions and falsehood need to be dispelled?*

**(Re)cognizing:** In schools, educators must learn and understand the genius and joy of Black people—including our accomplishments and successes. When we start the story with what oppressors have done to us, we have an incomplete, deficit, and false vision. We must teach children to know that people of color have brilliance and a history of genius.

Ask: *How are my children and their families brilliant? What is the genius of the African continent to the diaspora and how can this knowledge form my instructional and leadership practices?*

**(Re)presenting:** In schools, educators must authentically represent the lives, knowledges, and theories of Black women to shape and inform their curriculum, instruction, and leadership.

Ask: *Whose histories, identities, and liberation are represented or invisible in our learning standards, curriculum, assessment, teacher evaluation, and teacher education programs? How do we use Black women's theories and epistemologies in our practices?*

**(Re)claiming:** In schools, we must take our authority to plan and write curriculum, instruction, and leadership. For too long these areas have been indicative of whiteness. If we seek a solution, we must go back to the legacy of Black/African women for the solution.

Ask: *Which frameworks, methods, or approaches were used in schools and communities of Black women and how can they inform my work in schools and communities?*

Dr. Dillard creatively charges our minds and hearts through this very essential book. The five pursuits in the framework of (re)membering should be the new pre-planning tool for all educators who are responsible for teaching lesson plans or leading schools. When we follow this framework, we have the solution to decades of educational mediocrity. We have better preparation to educate students who deserve a liberatory education. When we allow our ancestors to guide us as Dillard details, we can truly welcome ourselves back home.

To download a worksheet of the framework, please go to beacon .org/Assets/PDFs/SpiritOfOurWorkworksheet.pdf.

Dr. Gholdy Muhammad

# ACKNOWLEDGMENTS

No one writes a book alone. Every word on these pages was enabled by "a laying on of hands," both literal and spiritual. For these hands and their gentle enduring touch, I am grateful.

For the *beautiful touch* of every participant in the Ghana Study Abroad in Education program (GSAE): thank you for your engagements and your stories. Please know that each and every one of you is a part of my (re)membering that is now this book. Some stories were voiced; other stories were an echo. I especially lift up and thank the Black women participants who are at the center of this book. I pray I have written a story that honors the collective spirit of our experiences and our lives as Black women who teach and who have begun the journey of (re)membering.

For the *organizational touch* of Carolyn Burroughs, who served as the extraordinary coordinator for GSAE for several years, keeping all the moving parts in order across two continents and dozens of participants. I could not have done the research for this book without you, Sis, and appreciate your careful attention, stewardship, and love of all things GSAE.

For the *collective touch* of now Drs. Kristen Duncan, Latoya Johnson, Stephanie P. Jones, and soon-to-be-Dr. Amber Neal, all who served as graduate research assistants at various points during the seven-year research project that led to this book. The collective brilliance and Black girl magic you brought to our data collection, analysis, and (re)presentation was one of the greatest joys of this work. As Black women researchers, we just *knew* and we trusted that knowing.

For the *life-changing touch* of Bettina Love: Having you in my life is one of the greatest gifts I have ever known, especially the early lunches in my office where we laughed and mused over the realities of being smart Black women in a world that often didn't know what to do with us! But as sisters, we *knew* that we were enough *together*. We *are* enough together. Thank you for walking this journey all the way back to Africa with me and for the gorgeous foreword for this book.

For the *brilliant touch* of Gholdy Muhammad: I am so grateful for your mind, for your spirit, and for your love. Thank you for the brilliant afterword too. It is our GPS for where we need to go next if we are to really weave Black women's spiritual knowings and curriculum *together*.

For the *mindful and reflective touch* of Jamila Lyisicott, who puzzled through those first few chapters with me as part of her writing retreat. Thank you for being my mirror, asking the questions that challenged my thinking and made this writing even better.

For the *critically affirming touch* of my editor, Rachael Marks, and the incredible people at Beacon Press who were such gentle and profound midwives for this book.

For the *gentle spiritual touch* of my father, Clyde Dillard, and elder sister, Octavia Dillard, who live in the world of the ancestors. I felt your presence and guidance as I wrote every page, especially when I struggled to find words to describe the work that ancestors like you do in our earthly lives as teachers. Thank you for sending those words to me.

For the *blessed touch* of my earthly family: my mother, Marion Dillard, siblings Celeste Dillard, Judith Dillard, Mitchell Dillard, and wonderful nieces and nephew, Taylor Dillard, Andreas Dillard, and Morgan Dillard. Thank you for your support and loving-kindness.

Finally, for the *unconditional loving touch* of my husband, Henry Oppong. I am grateful every day to be your wife and to live our lives on two sides of the water, together as Black people on purpose for a purpose. I love you fiercely and always.

# NOTES

INTRODUCTION

1. Phillips, *The Atlantic Sound*, 116.
2. Waheed, *Nejma*, 66.
3. Hull, *Soul Talk*.
4. Dash, *Daughters of the Dust*.
5. "Covenant," Merriam-Webster.com, updated July 26, 2017.
6. Yvonne Orji, *Momma, I Made It!*, HBO, 2020.
7. Dillard, "The Substance of Things Hoped For, the Evidence of Things Not Seen," 661–81.


CHAPTER 1: MY SPIRIT (RE)MEMBERS ME WHOLE

1. Armah, *Two Thousand Seasons*.
2. hooks, *Black Looks*; Collins, *A Different Kind of Public Education*; Love, *We Want to Do More Than Survive*.
3. Dillard, "The Substance of Things Hoped For, the Evidence of Things Not Seen," 661–81.
4. Foster, *Black Teachers on Teaching*; Irvine, *In Search of Wholeness*; Ladson-Billings, *Beyond the Big House*, *Crossing Over to Canaan*, and *The Dreamkeepers*; Milner, *Start Where You Are, But Don't Stay There*.
5. Foster, *Black Teachers on Teaching*; Clemons, "'I've Got to Do Something for My People,'" 141–54.
6. See Dillard, *On Spiritual Strivings*; Dillard and Okpalaoka, "The Sacred and Spiritual Nature of Endarkened Transnational Feminist Praxis in Qualitative Research"; Duncan, "'That's My Job'"; Ladson-Billings, *Beyond the Big House*; Milner, "The Promise of Black Teachers' Success with Black Students"; Palmer, *To Know as We Are Known*; Paris and Alim, *Culturally Sustaining Pedagogies*.
7. See Dillard, *On Spiritual Strivings*; Dillard, *Learning to (Re)member the Things We've Learned to Forget*; Hull, *Soul Talk*.
8. Hull, *Soul Talk*, 3.
9. hooks, *Talking Back*.
10. hooks, *Teaching to Transgress*.
11. Dillard, "The Substance of Things Hoped For, the Evidence of Things Not Seen," 661–81.
12. Dillard, "The Substance of Things Hoped For, the Evidence of Things Not Seen," 661–81.
13. Dillard, *Learning to (Re)member the Things We've Learned to Forget*.
14. Williams, "Spirit-Murdering the Messenger," 127.
15. Armah, *Two Thousand Seasons*, 76, emphasis mine.

16. Love, *We Want to Do More Than Survive.*
17. King, "Dysconscious Racism," 133–46.
18. Woodson, *The Mis-Education of the Negro*, xiii.
19. Feelings, *The Middle Passage*, 11.
20. Love, *We Want to Do More Than Survive*; Wynter, *Do Not Call Us Negros.*
21. Farber-Robinson, "Mrs. Lewis, a Tribute," 69.
22. Aaron, "Foreword," 1.
23. Bambara, *The Salt Eaters*, 3–10.
24. hooks and West, *Breaking Bread.*
25. Du Bois, *Dusk of Dawn*, 116.
26. McElroy, *A Long Way from St. Louie*, 2.
27. Dillard and Okpalaoka, "The Sacred and Spiritual Nature of Endarkened Transnational Feminist Praxis in Qualitative Research."
28. hooks, *Skin Again.*
29. James, *Spirit, Space & Survival*, 32, emphasis mine.
30. Oyêwùmí, "Conceptualizing Gender," 1–8.
31. King, "Who Dat Say (We) 'Too Depraved to Be Saved'?"
32. Kelley, *Freedom Dreams.*
33. Dillard, *On Spiritual Strivings.*
34. Dillard, "The Substance of Things Hoped For, the Evidence of Things Not Seen," 661–81.
35. Dillard, "The Substance of Things Hoped For, the Evidence of Things Not Seen," 661–81; Dillard, *On Spiritual Strivings.*
36. Carter, "Beyoncé Commencement Speech."
37. Hooks, *Spirit of the Yam*, 17.
38. Lorde, *Sister Outsider*, 38.
39. Hall, "Thinking the Diaspora," 1–18.
40. Hall, "Thinking the Diaspora," 3.
41. Hall, "Thinking the Diaspora," 4.
42. Hall, "Thinking the Diaspora," 14.
43. Oyêwùmí, "Conceptualizing Gender," 1–8.
44. Feelings, *I Saw Your Face.*
45. Shange, *For Colored Girls Who Have Considered Suicide/When the Rainbow Is Enuf.*

CHAPTER 2: "I WAS MISSING SOMETHING, SOMETHING SO IMPORTANT"

1. Toni Morrison, *Paradise*, p. 213, emphasis mine.
2. Dillard, *On Spiritual Strivings*, 16.
3. Collins, *Black Feminist Thought.*
4. Wright, "An Endarkened Feminist Epistemology?," 197–214.
5. Fanon, *Black Skin, White Masks*, 109.
6. Ani, *Yurugu*; Wynter, *Do Not Call Us Negros.*
7. Lyiscott, *Black Appetite. White Food*; Love, *We Want to Do More Than Survive*; Muhammad, *Cultivating Genius.*
8. Kendi, *Stamped from the Beginning*; McKinney de Royston et al., "'I'm a Teacher, I'm Gonna Always Protect You.'"

9.  Duncan, "'That's My Job.'"

10. Dee, "A Teacher Like Me," 158–65; Gershenson et al., "The Long-Run Impacts of Same-Race Teachers."

11. hooks, *Teaching to Transgress.*

12. Institute of International Education's *Open Doors* Report and the US Department of Education's National Center for Education Statistics, 2017–2018.

13. See Burgold and Rolfes, "Of Voyeuristic Safari Tours and Responsible Tourism with Educational Value," 161–74; Crossley, "Poor but Happy," 235–53; Dyson, "Slum Tourism," 254–74; Meschkank, "Investigations into Slum Tourism in Mumbai," 47–62.

14. Frenzel, "Slum Tourism in the Context of the Tourism Poverty (Relief) Debate," 122, emphasis mine.

15. Sharpe, *In the Wake*, 8.

16. Love, *We Want to Do More Than Survive*, 73.

17. King, "Who Dat Say (We) 'Too Depraved to Be Saved'?" 343–88.

18. hooks, *All About Love.*

19. Quashie, *The Sovereignty of Quiet*, 3.

20. Quashie, *The Sovereignty of Quiet*, 5.

21. Quashie, *The Sovereignty of Quiet*, 6.

22. waheed, *Nejma*, 157.

CHAPTER 3: THE EVIDENCE OF THINGS UNSEEN

1.  Busia, "What Is Your Nation?," 199.

2.  Onwuachi, *Notes from a Young Black Chef*, 73.

3.  Collins, *Intersectionality as Critical Social Theory*; Crenshaw, "Mapping the Margins," 1241–99.

4.  Oyêwùmí, "Conceptualizing Gender," 1–8.

5.  Greene, *Releasing the Imagination*, 4.

6.  Hurston, *Their Eyes Were Watching God.*

7.  Love, *We Want to Do More Than Survive.*

8.  Du Bois, *Dusk of Dawn.*

9.  Hull, *Soul Talk.*

10. See Ani, *Yurugu*; Armah, *KMT in the House of Life*; Hull, *Soul Talk*; Paris, *The Spirituality of African People*; Richards, *Let the Circle Be Unbroken*; Somé, *The Healing Wisdom of Africa*; Somé, *The Spirit of Intimacy.*

11. Richards, *Let the Circle Be Unbroken.*

12. Vanzant, *The Spirit of a Man*, xxiii.

13. Ephirim-Donkor, *African Spirituality.*

14. Shange, *For Colored Girls Who Have Considered Suicide/When the Rainbow Is Enuf*, 60.

15. Dillard, "The Substance of Things Hoped For, the Evidence of Things Not Seen," 661–81.

16. Greene, *The Dialectic of Freedom*, 21.

17. Greene, *Dialectic of Freedom*, 3, emphasis mine.

18. Du Bois, *The Souls of Black Folk*, 3.

19. Du Bois, *Dusk of Dawn*, 116, emphasis mine.

20. Du Bois, *The Souls of Black Folk*, 1.
21. Du Bois, *The Souls of Black Folk*, 3.
22. Delpit, *Other People's Children*.
23. Feelings, *I Saw Your Face*.
24. Feelings, *I Saw Your Face*, 1.
25. Somé, *The Spirit of Intimacy*, 33.
26. Somé, *The Spirit of Intimacy*, 29.
27. Somé, *The Spirit of Intimacy*, 30–31.
28. Collins, "Shifting the Center," 373.
29. Bethel, "'This Infinity of Conscious Pain.'"

·

CHAPTER 4: A CHANGE OF MIND AND HEART

1.  Gyasi, *Homegoing*, 42–43.
2.  Jackson, "'In the Morning, When I Rise,'" 54.
3.  Finney, *Head Off and Split*, xv.
4.  Dillard, "When the Ground Is Black, the Ground Is Fertile"; Dillard, *On Spiritual Strivings*.
5.  Hilliard, *The Maroon Within Us*, 69–70.
6.  Dillard, "When the Ground Is Black, the Ground Is Fertile," 287.
7.  See Busia, "What Is Your Nation?"; Dillard, "When the Ground Is Black, the Ground Is Fertile."
8.  Busia, "What Is Your Nation?," 197–98.
9.  Busia, "What Is Your Nation?," 199.
10. Brand, *A Map to the Door of No Return*, 5.
11. Brand, *A Map to the Door of No Return*, 17.
12. Baptist, *The Half Has Never Been Told*.
13. Bethel, "'This Infinity of Conscious Pain,'" 176–88.
14. Feelings, *The Middle Passage*, 6.
15. See Davis, *Are Prisons Obsolete?*; Morris, *Pushout*; Hill, *Nobody*.
16. Dillard, *Learning to (Re)member the Things We've Learned to Forget*.
17. Feelings, *The Middle Passage*, 2.
18. Dillard, *Learning to (Re)member the Things We've Learned to Forget*.
19. See Nadia Y. Kisukidi, quoted in Sarr, *Afrotopia*, 78–79.

CHAPTER 5: THE TRUTH WILL SET US FREE

1.  Lorde, "Showing Our True Colors," 409.
2.  Booth, *Communities of Memory*, 3, emphasis mine.
3.  Bargna, *African Art*, 25.
4.  hooks, *Yearning*, 104.
5.  Shaw, *Memories of the Slave Trade*, 2.
6.  Hall, "Thinking the Diaspora," 1–18.
7.  Durosomo, "The Dashiki."
8.  Durosomo, "The Dashiki."
9.  Somé, *The Spirit of Intimacy*.
10. Collier, "Why Telling Our Own Story Is So Powerful for Black Americans."
11. Sharpe, *In the Wake*, 8.

12. Collier, "Why Telling Our Own Story Is So Powerful for Black Americans."
13. Sharpe, *In the Wake*, 17.
14. Carter, "Beyoncé Commencement Speech."
15. Sharpe, *In the Wake*, 4, emphasis hers.

CHAPTER 6: THE INVITATION, SANCTUARY, AND LIVING LEGACY

1. Lorde, *Sister Outsider*, 132.
2. Jackson-Opoku, *The River Where Blood Is Born*, 55–56 (emphasis mine).
3. Carter, "Beyoncé Commencement Speech" (emphasis mine).
4. See Guy-Sheftall, *Words of Fire*.
5. Pohl, *Making Room*, 13.
6. Hooks, *All About Love*, 4–5 (emphasis mine).
7. Pohl, *Making Room*, 14.
8. Harvey, *Through the Storm, Through the Night*, 4.
9. Evans, *Hush Harbor*.
10. Harvey, *Through the Storm, Through the Night*.
11. Lester, *To Be a Slave*, 10.
12. Agosto and Karanxha, "Resistance Meets Spirituality in Academia"; Graham, "Womanist Preservations," 106–17; Kynard, "From Candy Girls to Cyber Sista-Cipher," 30–48.
13. Cameron, *Heart Steps*, 120.
14. Lorde, *Sister Outsider*, 41.
15. Trevor Noah, August 29, 2020, https://twitter.com/trevornoah/status/129977137 8745462784?lang=en.
16. hooks, *Black Looks*, ii.
17. Anderson, *White Rage*, 4.
18. Anderson, *White Rage*, 3–4.
19. Carter, Beyoncé Knowles, "Beyoncé Commencement Speech."
20. Jeffries, "The Image of Women in African Cave Art," 103–4.
21. Kelley, *Freedom Dreams*.

CHAPTER 7: (RE)MEMBERING IS NOT OPTIONAL

1. Danticat, *Create Dangerously*, 10.
2. Love, *We Want to Do More Than Survive*.
3. Love, *We Want to Do More Than Survive*.
4. Newkirk, *Letters from Black America*, xvii.
5. Newkirk, *Letters from Black America*, viii.
6. Young and Glaser, *The Collected Poems of Lucille Clifton*, 262.

# BIBLIOGRAPHY

Aaron, Cyrus (2020). Foreword. In Laurent B. Chevalier, *Enough*. New York: Kris Grave Projects.

Agosto, Vonzell, and Zorka Karanxha (2011). "Resistance Meets Spirituality in Academia: 'I Prayed on It!'" *Educational Leadership and Policy Studies Faculty Publications*. http://scholarcommons.usf.edu/els_facpub/7.

Alexander, Michelle (2012). *The New Jim Crow: Mass Incarceration in the Age of Colorblindness*. New York: New Press.

Anderson, Carol A. (2016). *White Rage: The Unspoken Truth of Our Racial Divide*. New York: Bloomsbury.

Angelou, Maya (1986). *All God's Children Need Traveling Shoes*. New York: Vintage.

Angelou, Maya (1990). *I Shall Not Be Moved*. New York: Bantam.

Ani, Marimba (1994). *Yurugu: An African-Centered Critique of European Cultural Thought and Behavior*. Trenton, NJ: Africa World Press.

Armah, Ayi Kwei (2002). *KMT in the House of Life: An Epistemic Novel*. Dar Es Salaam, Senegal: Per Ankh Publishing.

Armah, Ayi Kwei (2000). *Two Thousand Seasons*. Dar Es Salaam, Senegal: Per Ankh Publishing.

Baldwin, James (1956, repr. 2013). *Giovanni's Room*. New York: Vintage.

Baldwin, James (1971). "An Open Letter to My Sister, Miss Angela Davis (November 19, 1970)." *New York Review of Books,* January 7. Retrieved from https://www.nybooks.com/articles/1971/01/07/an-open-letter-to-my-sister-miss-angela-davis.

Bambara, Toni Cade (1980, repr. 1992). *The Salt Eaters*. New York: Random House.

Baptist, Edward E. (2014). *The Half Has Never Been Told: Slavery and the Making of American Capitalism*. New York: Basic Books.

Bargna, Ivan (2000). *African Art*. Milan: Jaca Books.

Battle, Michael (2009). *Ubuntu: I in You and You in Me*. New York: Seabury Books.

Bell, Derrick (1992). *Faces at the Bottom of the Well: The Permanence of Racism*. New York: Basic Books.

Bell-Scott, Patricia (1998). *Flat-Footed Truths: Telling Black Women's Lives*. New York: Henry Holt.

Bell-Scott, Patricia (1994). *Life Notes: Personal Writings by Contemporary Black Women*. New York: W. W. Norton.

Bethel, Lorraine (1982). "'This Infinity of Conscious Pain': Zora Neale Hurston and the Black Female Literary Tradition." In G. T. Hull, P. B. Scott, and B. Smith (eds.), *All the Women Are White, All the Blacks Are Men, but Some of Us Are Brave*, 176–88. New York: Feminist Press.

Booth, W. James (2006). *Communities of Memory: On Witness, Identity, and Justice*. Ithaca, NY: Cornell University Press.

Brand, Dionne (2001). *A Map to the Door of No Return: Notes to Belonging*. Toronto: Vintage.

Burgold, J., and M. Rolfes (2013). "Of Voyeuristic Safari Tours and Responsible Tourism with Educational Value: Observing Moral Communication in Slum and Township Tourism in Cape Town and Mumbai." *Die Erde* 144 (2): 161–74.

Busia, Abena (1989). "What Is Your Nation? Reconnecting Africa and Her Diaspora Through Paule Marshall's *Praisesong for the Widow*." In Cheryl Wall (ed.), *Changing Our Own Words: Essays on Criticism, Theory, and Writing by Black Women*. New Brunswick, NJ: Rutgers University Press.

Butler, Octavia E. (1998, repr. 2019). *Parable of the Talents*. New York: Grand Central Publishing.

Cameron, Julie (1997). *Heart Steps: Prayers and Declarations for a Creative Life*. New York: Tarcher Putnam.

Cannon, Katie G. (1998). *Katie's Canon: Womanism and the Soul of the Black Community*. New York: Continuum.

Carter, Beyoncé Knowles (2020). "Beyoncé Commencement Speech: Dear Class of 2020" [video]. YouTube. https://www.youtube.com/watch?v=vL 05XMjIJD8. Retrieved July 15, 2020.

Carter, Beyoncé Knowles (2020). *Black Is King* [film]. Disney Pictures.

Clarke, John Henrik (1930). *African People in World History*. Baltimore: Black Classic Press.

Clemons, Kristal Moore (2014). "'I've Got to Do Something for My People': Black Women Teachers of the 1964 Mississippi Freedom Schools." *Western Journal of Black Studies* 38 (3): 141–54.

Collier, Andrea King (2019). "Why Telling Our Story Is So Powerful for Black Americans." *Greater Good Magazine*, February 27. https://greatergood.berkeley.edu/article/item/why_telling_our_own_story_is_so_powerful_for_black_americans. Retrieved July 22, 2019.

Collins, Patricia Hill (1990). *Black Feminist Thought: Knowledge, Consciousness, and the Politics of Empowerment.* New York: Routledge.

Collins, Patricia Hill (2009). *A Different Kind of Public Education: Race, Schools, the Media, and Democratic Possibilities.* Boston: Beacon Press.

Collins, Patricia Hill (2019). *Intersectionality as Critical Social Theory.* Durham, NC: Duke University Press.

Collins, Patricia Hill (1994). "Shifting the Center: Race, Class, and Feminist Theorizing About Motherhood." In Donna Bassin (ed.), *Representations of Motherhood*, 371–89. New Haven, CT: Yale University Press, 1994.

Crenshaw, Kimberlé (1991). "Mapping the Margins: Intersectionality, Identity Politics, and Violence Against Women of Color." *Stanford Law Review* 43 (6): 1241–99. https:// doi.org/10.2307/1229039.

Crossley, Émilie (2012). "Poor but Happy: Volunteer Tourists' Encounters with Poverty." *Tourism Geographies* 14 (2): 235–53.

Danticat, Edwidge (2010). *Create Dangerously: The Immigrant Artist at Work.* Princeton, NJ: Princeton University Press.

Dash, Julie (1991). *Daughters of the Dust* [film]. Geechee Girls Productions.

Davis, Angela Y. (2003). *Are Prisons Obsolete?* New York: Seven Stories Press.

Dee, Thomas S. (2005). "A Teacher Like Me: Does Race, Ethnicity, or Gender Matter?" *American Economic Review* 95 (2): 158–65. doi:10.1257/000282805774670446.

Delpit, Lisa (1995). *Other People's Children: Cultural Conflict in the Classroom.* New York: New Press.

Dillard, Cynthia B. (2012). *Learning to (Re)member the Things We've Learned to Forget: Endarkened Feminisms, Spirituality, and the Sacred Nature of Research and Teaching.* New York: Peter Lang.

Dillard, Cynthia B. (2018). "Let Steadfastness Have Its Full Effect: (Re)membering (Re)Search and Endarkened Feminisms from Ananse to Asantewaa." *Qualitative Inquiry* 24 (9): 617–23.

Dillard, Cynthia B. (2006). *On Spiritual Strivings: Transforming an African American Woman's Academic Life.* Albany: State University of New York Press.

Dillard, Cynthia B. (unpublished manuscript). "Resting." In "Living Africa: A Book of Meditations."

Dillard, Cynthia B. (2000). "The Substance of Things Hoped For, the Evidence of Things Not Seen: Examining an Endarkened Feminist Epistemology in Educational Research and Leadership." *International Journal of Qualitative Studies in Education* 13: 661–81.

Dillard, Cynthia B. (2017). "To Stand Steadfast and Love Blackness in These Political Times: A Comparative Reflection from Ghana to the US and Back Again." *International Journal of Qualitative Studies in Education* 30 (10): 982–87.

Dillard, Cynthia B. (2008). "When the Ground Is Black, the Ground Is Fertile: Exploring Endarkened Feminist Epistemology and Healing Methodologies of the Spirit." In N. Denzin, Y. Lincoln, and L. T. Smith (eds.), *The Handbook of Critical and Indigenous Methodologies*. Thousand Oaks, CA: Sage.

Dillard, Cynthia B., and Chinwe L. Okpalaoka (2011). "The Sacred and Spiritual Nature of Endarkened Transnational Feminist Praxis in Qualitative Research." In N. Denzin and Y. Lincoln (eds.), *The Handbook of Qualitative Research*. 4th ed. Thousand Oaks, CA: Sage.

Donnor, Jamel K., and Adrienne Dixson (2013). *The Resegregation of Schools: Education and Race in the Twenty-First Century*. New York: Routledge.

Du Bois, W. E. B. (1940, repr. 1968). *Dusk of Dawn*. New York: Library of America.

Du Bois, W. E. B. (1903, repr. 1989). *The Souls of Black Folk*. New York: Bantam.

Duncan, Kristen E. (2020). "'That's My Job': Black Teachers' Perspectives on Helping Black Students Navigate White Supremacy." *Race Ethnicity and Education*. doi: 10.1080/13613324.2020.1798377.

Durosomo, Damola (May 28, 2017). "The Dashiki: The History of a Radical Garment." www.okayafrica.com.

Dyson, Peter (2012). "Slum Tourism: Representing and Interpreting Reality in Dharavi, Mumbai." *Tourism Geographies* 14 (2): 254–74.

Easton-Brooks, Donald, Derrick Robinson, and Sheneka M. Williams (2018). "Schools in Transition: Creating a Diverse School Community." *Teacher's College Record* 120 (13).

Ephirim-Donkor, Anthony (1997). *African Spirituality: On Becoming Ancestors*. Trenton, NJ: Africa World Press.

Evans, Freddi Williams (2008). *Hush Harbor: Praying in Secret*. Minneapolis: Carolrhoda Books.

Fanon, Frantz (1967). *Black Skin, White Masks*. London: Pluto Books.

Farber-Robinson, Anita (2003). "Mrs. Lewis, a Tribute." In Gloria Wade-Gayles (ed.), *In Praise of Our Teachers: A Multicultural Tribute to Those Who Inspired Us*. Boston: Beacon Press.

Feelings, Tom (2005). *I Saw Your Face*. New York: Dial Books.

Feelings, Tom (1995). *The Middle Passage*. New York: Dial Books.

Finney, Nikki (2011). Acknowledgments. *Head Off and Split: Poems*. Evanston, IL: Northwestern University Press, xv.

Foster, Michele (1997). *Black Teachers on Teaching*. New York: New Press.

Freire, Paulo (1970). *Pedagogy of the Oppressed*. New York: Continuum.

Frenzel, Fabian (2013). "Slum Tourism in the Context of the Tourism Poverty (Relief) Debate." *Die Erde* 144 (2): 117–28.

Gershenson, S., C. Hart, J. Hyman, L. Constance, and N. Papageorge (2018). "The Long-Run Impacts of Same-Race Teachers." NBER Working Paper no. 25254.

Graham, Angelina (2016). "Womanist Preservations: An Analysis of Black Women's Spiritual Coping." *International Journal of Transpersonal Studies* 35 (1): 106–17.

Greene, Maxine (1988). *The Dialectic of Freedom*. New York: Teachers College Press, 1–23.

Greene, Maxine (1995). *Releasing the Imagination: Essays on Education, the Arts, and Social Change*. San Francisco: Jossey-Bass.

Grossman, James R. (1991). *Land of Hope: Chicago, Black Southerners, and the Great Migration*. Chicago: University of Chicago Press, 16.

Guy-Sheftall, Beverly (1995). *Words of Fire: An Anthology of African-American Feminist Thought*. New York: New Press.

Gyasi, Yaa (2016). *Homegoing*. New York: Random House.

Hall, Stuart (1999). "Thinking the Diaspora: Home-Thoughts from Abroad." *Small Axe* 6: 1–18.

Harvey, Paul (2011). *Through the Storm, Through the Night: A History of African American Christianity*. New York: Rowman and Littlefield.

Hill, Mark Lamont (2016). *Nobody: Casualties of America's War on the Vulnerable, from Ferguson to Flint and Beyond*. New York: Atria.

Hilliard, Asa G. (1995). *The Maroon Within Us: Selected Essays on African American Community Socialization*. Baltimore: Black Classic Press.

Hilliard, Asa G. (2012). *The Teachings of Ptahhotep: The Oldest Book in the World*. Grand Forks, ND: Blackwood Press.

hooks, bell (2000). *All About Love: New Visions*. New York: William Morrow.

hooks, bell (2009). *Belonging: A Culture of Place*. New York: Routledge.

hooks, bell (1992). *Black Looks: Race and Representation*. Boston: South End Press.

hooks, bell (1999). *Remembered Rapture: The Writer at Work*. New York: Henry Holt.

hooks, bell (1993). *Sisters of the Yam: Black Women and Recovery*. Cambridge, MA: South End Press.

hooks, bell (2017). *Skin Again*. New York: Little, Brown.

hooks, bell (1989). *Talking Back: Thinking Feminist, Thinking Black*. Boston: South End Press.

hooks, bell (1994). *Teaching to Transgress: Education as the Practice of Freedom*. New York: Routledge.

hooks, bell (1990). *Yearning: Race, Gender, and Cultural Politics*. Boston: South End Press.

hooks, bell, and Cornel West (1991). *Breaking Bread: Insurgent Black Intellectual Life*. Boston: South End Press.

Hull, Akasha (2001). *Soul Talk: The New Spirituality of African American Women*. Rochester, VT: Inner Traditions.

Hurston, Zora Neale (1937, repr. 1978). *Their Eyes Were Watching God*. Urbana: University of Illinois Press.

Institute of International Education. *Open Doors* Report and the US Department of Education's National Center for Education Statistics, 2017–2018. Retrieved from https://www.nafsa.org/policy-and-advocacy/policy-resources/trends-us-study-abroad.

Irvine, J. J. (2002). *In Search of Wholeness: African American Teachers and Their Culturally Specific Classroom Practice*. New York: Palgrave.

Jackson, Fleda Mask (1995). "'In the Morning, When I Rise': My Hands in Spiritual Soil." In Gloria Wade-Gayles (ed.), *My Soul Is a Witness: African-American Women's Spirituality*. Boston: Beacon Press, 54.

Jackson-Opoku, Sandra (1997). *The River Where Blood Is Born*. New York: One World.

James, Joy (1993). *Spirit, Space & Survival: African American Women in (White) Academe*. New York: Routledge.

Jeffries, Rosalind (1997). "The Image of Women in African Cave Art." *Journal of African Civilization* 6 (1): 103–4.

Keating, AnaLouise, ed. (2015). *Light in the Dark/Luz en lo oscuro: Rewriting Identity, Spirituality, Reality*. Durham, NC: Duke University Press.

Kelley, Robin D. G. (2002). *Freedom Dreams: The Black Radical Imagination*. Boston: Beacon Press.

Kendi, Ibram X. (2016). *Stamped from the Beginning: The Definitive History of Racist Ideas in America*. New York: Nation Books.

King, Joyce E. (2011). "Who Dat Say (We) 'Too Depraved to Be Saved'?: Re-Membering Katrina/Haiti (and Beyond): Critical Studyin' for Human Freedom." *Harvard Educational Review* 18 (2): 343–88.

King, Joyce E. (2009). "Dysconscious Racism: Ideology, Identity, and the Miseducation of Teachers." *Journal of Negro Education* 60 (2): 2, 133–46.

King, Martin Luther, Jr. (2001). "The Birth of a New Nation." In Clayborne

Carson and Kris Shepard (eds.), *A Call to Conscience: The Landmark Speeches of Dr. Martin Luther King, Jr.* New York: Warner Books.

Kynard, Carmen (2010). "From Candy Girls to Cyber Sista-Cipher: Narrating Black Females' Color Consciousness and Counterstories in and out of School." *Harvard Educational Review* 80 (1): 30–48.

Ladson-Billings, Gloria (2005). *Beyond the Big House: African American Educators on Teacher Education.* New York: Teachers College Press.

Ladson-Billings, Gloria (2001). *Crossing Over to Canaan: The Journey of New Teachers in Diverse Classrooms.* San Francisco: Jossey-Bass.

Ladson-Billings, Gloria (1994). *The Dreamkeepers: Successful Teachers of African American Children.* San Francisco: Jossey-Bass.

Ladson-Billings, Gloria, and William F. Tate IV (1995). "Toward a Critical Race Theory of Education." *Teachers College Record* 97 (1): 47–68.

Lester, John (1968). *To Be a Slave.* New York: Puffin.

Lorde, Audre (1994). "Showing Our True Colors." In Patricia Bell-Scott (ed.), *Life Notes: Personal Writings by Contemporary Black Women.* New York: W. W. Norton.

Lorde, Audre (1980). *Sister Outsider.* Freedom, CA: Crossing Press.

Love, Bettina L. (2019). *We Want to Do More Than Survive: Abolitionist Teaching and the Pursuit of Educational Freedom.* Boston: Beacon Press.

Lyiscott, Jamila (2019). *Black Appetite. White Food: Issues of Race, Voice, and Justice Within and Beyond the Classroom.* New York: Routledge.

Marshall, Paule (1983). *Praisesong for the Widow.* New York: Plume.

McDonald, Brian (2017). *Invisible Ink: A Practical Guide to Building Stories That Resonate.* Omaha: Concierge Marketing.

McElroy, Colleen J. (1997). *A Long Way from St. Louie: Travel Memoirs.* Minneapolis: Coffee House Press.

McKinney de Royston, Maxine, Tia C. Madkins, Jarvis R. Givens, and Na'ilah Suad Nasir (2020). "'I'm a Teacher, I'm Gonna Always Protect You': Understanding Black Educators' Protection of Black Children." *American Educational Research Journal*, pp. 1–39.

Meschkank, Julia (2010). "Investigations into Slum Tourism in Mumbai: Poverty Tourism and the Tensions Between Different Constructions of Reality." *GeoJournal* 76 (1): 47–62.

Milner, H. Richard, IV (2006). "The Promise of Black Teachers' Success with Black Students." *Educational Foundations* 20 (3): 89–104.

Milner, H. Richard, IV (2010). *Start Where You Are, But Don't Stay There: Understanding Diversity, Opportunity Gaps, and Teaching in Today's Classrooms.* Cambridge, MA: Harvard Education Press.

Milner, H. Richard, IV, H. B. Cunningham, L. Delale-O'Connor, and E. G. Kestenberg (2018). *"These Kids Are Out of Control": Why We Must Reimagine "Classroom Management" for Equity*. Thousand Oaks, CA: Corwin/SAGE.

Morris, Monique W. (2018). *Pushout: The Criminalization of Black Girls in Schools*. New York: New Press.

Morrison, Toni (1987). *Beloved*. New York: Alfred A. Knopf.

Morrison, Toni (1997). *Paradise*. New York: Vintage.

Morrison, Toni (2019). *The Source of Self-Regard: Selected Essays, Speeches, and Meditations*. New York: Knopf.

Muhammad, Gholdy (2020). *Cultivating Genius: An Equity Framework for Culturally and Historically Responsive Literacy*. New York: Scholastic.

Newkirk, Pamela, ed. (2009). *Letters from Black America: Intimate Portraits of the African American Experience*. Boston: Beacon Press.

Onwuachi, Kwame (2019). *Notes from a Young Black Chef*. New York: Alfred A. Knopf.

Oyêwùmí, Oyèrónké (2004). "Conceptualizing Gender: Eurocentric Foundations of Feminist Concepts and the Challenge of African Epistemologies." In *African Gender Scholarship; Concept, Methodologies and Paradigms*. Dakar, Senegal: CODESRIA, 1–8.

Palmer, Parker (1983). *To Know as We Are Known: Education as a Spiritual Journey*. San Francisco: Harper.

Paris, Django, and H. Samy Alim (2017). *Culturally Sustaining Pedagogies: Teaching and Learning for Justice in a Changing World*. New York: Teachers College Press.

Paris, Peter J. (1995). *The Spirituality of African People: Toward a Common Moral Discourse*. Minneapolis: Augsburg Fortress Press.

Phillips, Caryl (2001). *The Atlantic Sound*. New York: Vintage.

Pohl, Christine D. (1999). *Making Room: Recovering Hospitality as a Christian Tradition*. Grand Rapids, MI: William B. Eerdmans.

Quashie, Kevin (2012). *The Sovereignty of Quiet: Beyond Resistance in Black Culture*. New Brunswick, NJ: Rutgers University Press.

Richards, Dona (1980). *Let the Circle Be Unbroken: The Implications of African Spirituality in the Diaspora*. Lawrenceville, NJ: Red Sea Press.

Sarr, Felwine (2019). *Afrotopia*. Minneapolis: University of Minnesota Press.

Shange, Ntozake (1975). *For Colored Girls Who Have Considered Suicide/When the Rainbow Is Enuf*. New York: Collier Books.

Sharpe, Christine (2016). *In the Wake: On Blackness and Being*. Durham, NC: Duke University Press.

Shaw, Rosalind (2002). *Memories of the Slave Trade: Ritual and the Historical Imagination in Sierra Leone*. Chicago: University of Chicago Press.

Smith, Lillian (1994). *Killers of the Dream.* New York: W. W. Norton.

Somé, Malidoma (1998). *The Healing Wisdom of Africa: Finding Life Purpose Through Nature, Ritual, and Community.* New York: Tarcher/Putnam.

Somé, Sobonfu (1997). *The Spirit of Intimacy: Ancient African Teachings in the Way of Relationships.* New York: William Morrow.

Tatum, Beverly Daniel (1997). *"Why Are All the Black Kids Sitting Together in the Cafeteria?" and Other Conversations About Race.* New York: Basic Books.

Vanzant, Iyanla (1996). *The Spirit of a Man.* New York: Harper Collins.

Ventura, Michael (1988). "A Report from El Dorado." In Rick Simonson and Scott Walker (eds.), *Multicultural Literacy: Opening the American Mind.* Minneapolis: Graywolf Press.

Wade-Gayles, Gloria, ed. (2003). *In Praise of Our Teachers: A Multicultural Tribute to Those Who Inspired Us.* Boston: Beacon Press.

Wade-Gayles, Gloria, ed. (1995). *My Soul Is a Witness: African American Women's Spirituality.* Boston: Beacon Press.

waheed, nayyirah (2014). *Nejma.* CreateSpace Independent Publishing Platform.

Walker, Alice (2006). *We Are the Ones We've Been Waiting For: Light in a Time of Darkness.* New York: New Press.

Williams, Patricia (1987). "Spirit-Murdering the Messenger: The Discourse of Fingerpointing as the Law's Response to Racism." *University of Miami Law Review* 42: 127.

Woodson, Carter G. (1933, repr. 1990). *The Mis-Education of the Negro.* Trenton, NJ: Africa World Press.

Wright, Handel K. (2003). "An Endarkened Feminist Epistemology? Identity, Difference and the Politics of Representation in Educational Research." *International Journal of Qualitative Research* 16: 197–214.

Wynter, Sylvia (1990). *Do Not Call Us Negros: How "Multicultural" Textbooks Perpetuate Racism.* San Francisco: Aspire.

Young, Kevin, and Michael S. Glaser, eds. (2012). *The Collected Poems of Lucille Clifton, 1965–2010.* Rochester, NY: BOA Editions.

# INDEX

Aaron, Cyrus, 8
abolitionist education, 167–68, 176, 184, 189. *See also* education
adinkra cloth, 50, 80, 125, 153–54. *See also* African aesthetics; textiles
African aesthetics, 19, 116–22, 158. *See also* art
African art, 91, 121, 190
African cosmology, 37, 62, 115. *See also* spirituality
African diaspora: aesthetics of, 18–19, 116–22, 158; (re)turning and (re)membering, 17–20, 28–29, 52, 96. *See also under* Black identity; Ghana; transatlantic trade of African people
"African Homeland" (song), 69
African identity, 12–14, 96–97, 116–17, 178–79. *See also* Black identity
African Methodist Episcopal (AME), 63
*Afrotopia* (Sarr), 109
Akan languages and traditions, xv, 79, 136, 137, 153
Akuaaba, 145, 147
Alim, H. Samy, 181
*All About Love* (hooks), 140
Allah, 79
*All God's Children Need Traveling Shoes* (Angelou), 88
ambition, 10, 47, 161
American identity, 12
ancestors: covenant with, xv–xvi, xvii, 14; letter to, 97–98; (re)membering

our, 63, 92–96, 135–36, 172; solidarity with, 157; spirituality and, xvii; visiting slave dungeons and, 101–2; of white students, 184. *See also* temporality
Anderson, Carol, 161
Angelou, Maya, 12, 86, 88, 109, 181
anger, 104–5. *See also* emotional labor; rage
Anzaldúa, Gloria, 113–14
Armah, Ayi Kwei, 1, 4–6, 170
art, 91, 121, 138, 176, 190. *See also* African aesthetics
Ashante kente weaving. *See* kente cloth

Baldwin, James, 45, 47
Bambara, Toni Cade, 8, 9, 10
Baptist Church, 63, 66
bead traditions, 116
beginnings, 1, 8, 35–36, 48, 50, 90, 104–5, 131. *See also* home coming; origin stories; (re)turning
Bethune, Mary McLeod, 189
Beyoncé, 15, 19, 138, 159, 162
Black children: educational support for, 3–4, 86, 122, 168; families and mothering support for, 10–11, 56, 74–78, 123; sharing stories and (re)membering for, 98–99, 178; spiritual support for, 78–84. *See also* Black identity; education
Black feminisms, 10–16, 19, 138–40, 189–91
Black Girl Miracle (organization), 179